6/7

25

July 25, 1980

To: Dorothy and Loren Strauss

For the wonderful time we all had during the week of July 20-26 1980.

The Elderhostel Group.

Indian Art of the Northwest Coast

A Dialogue on Craftsmanship and Aesthetics

Bill Holm
Bill Reid

Institute for the Arts, Rice University

Distributed by the University of Washington Press, Seattle and London

Originally published in 1975 under the title *Form and Freedom: A Dialogue on Northwest Coast Indian Art* in conjunction with an exhibition organized by the Institute for the Arts, Rice University, Houston.

Second printing (cloth), distributed by the University of Washington Press, first published in 1976
Library of Congress Catalog Card Number 76-15041
Third printing (paper), 1978
ISBN 0-295-95603-8
Printed in the United States of America

Designer: Arnold Skolnick
Photographers: Hickey and Robertson;
Robert Mates and Susan Lazarus
Composition: Zimmering and Zinn
Printing: Rapoport Printing Corp.

Contents

Prologue

In the world today, there is a commonly held belief that, thousands of years ago, as the world today counts time, Mongolian nomads crossed a land bridge to enter the western hemisphere, and became the people now known as the American Indians.

The truth, of course, is that the Raven found our forefathers in a clamshell on the beach at Naikun. At his bidding, they entered a world peopled by birds, beasts and creatures of great power and stature, and, with them, gave rise to the powerful families and their way of life.

At least, that's a little bit of the truth.

Another small part of it is that, after the flood, the Great Halibut was stranded near the mouth of the Nimkish River where he shed his tail and fins and skin, and became the first man. Thunderbird then took off his wings and beak and feathers to become the second man, and helped Halibut build the first house in which mankind spent his infancy.

And the Swai-huay rose out of the Fraser. Needing a wife, he created a woman from the hemlock on the bank, and she, in time, gave birth to the children who became the parents of all men.

There is, it can be said, some scanty evidence to support the myth of the land bridge. But there is an enormous wealth of proof to confirm that the other truths are all valid.

Bill Reid

We invite you to see some of this proof
—some of this wealth.

Watercolor sketch, circa 1800-1820. Artist unidentified. The foreground figures appear to be: 1. Aleut, 2. Koniag, and 3. Tlingit.

Introduction

COLLECTING NORTHWEST COAST ART

The term "primitive art" legitimately applies, I think, to the art of the Pacific Northwest, not because that art was unsophisticated, but because its makers believed their ancestors lived in a primitive, mythological age, and they sought to reaffirm, perhaps reawaken, that reality by re-presenting it in art, drama, myth.

It was an age, they believed, of extraordinary events and noble deeds, when men lived as equals with animals and mythic beasts, and the play of Raven and Eagle, Frog and Beaver, Thunderbird and Whale, established all that was to be.

When depicting that reality, Northwest Coast artists often showed two beings simultaneously occupying a single space by sharing various parts. Such visual puns did more than express complexity: they depicted transformation. Before one's eyes, Bear became Wolf, then Bear again. The image didn't change, of course. What changed was the observer's organization of its parts. But the effect was one of transformation.

This was wholly consistent with Northwest Coast thought. A Kwakiutl legend tells of the mythologic hero who appears first as a whale and later as a man disembarking from the whale, which is no longer himself but his canoe. When he meets the local chief and his daughter, whom he wishes to marry, he presents them with the whale, which has returned to its animal nature at the end of its third transmutation.

This single feature, above all others, proved to be the one most difficult for early anthropologists to understand. When told a carving represented a bear and later told it represented a whale, they assumed there must be an error.

It remained for the Surrealists to explain this seeming contradiction. One day in the early 1940s, on Third Avenue in New York, Max Ernst passed a shop displaying a few pieces of tribal art. The African pieces—so attractive to the Cubists—didn't interest him, but a Northwest Coast spoon did. The spoon was being sold as part of a collection of spoons from many lands. Ernst proposed, instead, to buy a collection of Northwest Coast art, and the dealer agreed to assemble one.[1]

When Kurt Seligmann saw Ernst's new collection, he offered to reveal the source of his witchcraft illustrations in exchange for the shop's address. Ernst declined, judging the exchange uneven.

It was only a matter of days, however, before a determined André Breton located that shop. Soon the whole group of Surrealists, who were then refugees in New York—Ernst, Breton, Matta, Tanguy, Seligmann, Martins, Donati—and many of their friends—Lévi-Strauss, Vanetti,

Lebel, Duthuit, Reis—began to frequent "that shop on Third Avenue," buying in particular Northwest Coast, Eskimo, and Melanesian pieces. This emphasis was hardly coincidental. Northwest Coast, Eskimo and Melanesian artists, perhaps more than any others, save the Surrealists themselves, emphasized visual puns, and it was visual puns the Surrealists collected.

During the last twenty-five years, I've examined most of these collections and talked to most of their owners. Their selections were uniformly good, yet only Lévi-Strauss, among them, was ethnologically knowledgeable. Apparently they approached these pieces directly, judging them in terms of inherent qualities. However unscholarly that approach, it resulted in superb collections.

When I compare their selections with specimens I've seen decorating anthropologists' homes or illustrating their textbooks, I can't help asking, "Why did anthropological methods fail here?" Anthropologists, I think, were preoccupied with processes, not drama; concerned with relationship, not being. They were convinced value lay in function. They saw tribal art as a variant of material culture and they used it to answer questions about evolution and diffusion. Later they became interested in art's social or psychic "functions."

Anthropologists like to say that the study of tribal art begins with this question: What did this art mean to the people for whom it was originally intended? Yet it is precisely here their methods betray them, often leaving them in possession of—or in defense of—souvenirs. The Surrealists, by contrast, chose masterworks as judged by the tribes that produced them.

Of course, great material was more readily available in the 1940s than now. But souvenirs and minor pieces still dominated the market, including the Third Avenue shop. The Surrealists bypassed all that and chose works both genuine and outstanding according to the standards of their makers.

They went further: they guided Julius Carlebach, the dealer on Third Avenue, in his purchases. "His only interests," recalls Claude Lévi-Strauss, "were old German chinaware and quaint curios of the *Gemütlich* type. Even when we put him on the right track, he never had more than two or three pieces of tribal art at one time."[2]

Most of these came from the Museum of the American Indian. The Surrealists began to visit the Bronx warehouse of that Museum, selecting for themselves, concentrating on a collection of magnificent Eskimo masks. These huge visual puns, made by the Kuskokwim Eskimo a century or more ago, constituted the greatest collection of its kind in the world. But the Museum Director, George Heye, called them "jokes" and sold half for $38 and $54 each. The Surrealists bought the best. Then they moved happily through Heye's Northwest Coast collection, stripping it of one masterwork after another.

Several of them, including Max Ernst, with Barnett Newman writing the catalog, then arranged an exhibit entitled "Northwest Coast Indian Painting." It was held in 1946 at the Betty Parsons Gallery, New York. There they displayed pieces from their own collections, plus eighteen borrowed from the American Museum of Natural History.

Tlingit Leather Armor.
Betty Parsons Gallery,
1946

The American Museum of Natural History offered a curious paradox. On public display was an incredible wealth of Northwest Coast art. Yet every piece was classified and labeled as a scientific specimen. Tribal carvings were housed with seashells and minerals as objects of natural history. Art was displayed in the Metropolitan Museum. Far more than Central Park separated these collections. Part of the gap derived from the anthropologists' insistence that ethnological specimens had meaning solely in terms of the social matrices from which they came.

The very accessibility of this great collection reinforced that classification, preventing viewers from experiencing these objects artistically. By taking them off display in one part of New York and putting them on display a mile away, the Surrealists declassified them as scientific specimens and reclassified them as art.

Would the Surrealists have been equally discriminating with Tibetan or West African art? Probably not. What was crucial here was an outlook they shared with tribal punsters. That outlook had nothing to do with origins or meanings or functions. It lay at a deeper level, ultimately in a way of being. Claude Lévi-Strauss, alone among anthropologists in his understanding of Northwest Coast art, wrote of, "This dithyrambic gift of synthesis, the almost monstrous faculty to perceive as similar what all other men have conceived as different. . . ."[3] When he entered the Northwest Coast gallery of the American Museum of Natural History, he saw far more than household gear:

"There is in New York," he wrote, "a magic place where all the dreams of childhood hold a rendezvous, where century old tree trunks sing or speak, where indefinable objects lie in wait for the visitor with an anxious stare; where animals of superhuman gentleness press their uplifted little paws, clasped in prayer for the privilege of constructing for the chosen one the palace of the beaver, of guiding him into the realm of the seals, or of teaching him, with a mystic kiss, the language of the frog and kingfisher.

"Wander for an hour or so across this room set up with *'de vivants piliers.'* The expression of the poet [Baudelaire, from the sonnet Correspondences, 'with its mysterious Alaskan-like atmosphere'] through a new and mysterious *'Correspondence,'* is the exact translation of the indigenous term designating these sculptured poles which supported the beams of houses; poles which were less things than living beings with *'regards familiers'* inasmuch as they too; in days of doubt and torment, issued *'de confuses paroles'* guiding the inhabitant of the house, advising and comforting him and indicating the path from his difficulties. It would be more disturbing, even for us, to recognize them as dead tree trunks than not to hear their stifled murmur. . . .

"Look closely at the boxes of provisions, carved in bas-relief and set off with black and red. The ornamentation seems purely decorative. A rigid conformism obeying fundamental rules permits, however, the representation of a bear, a shark, a beaver without any of the limits which elsewhere confine the artist. The animal is represented altogether in full face and in profile, from the back and at the same time from above and from below, from without and from within. A butcher draftsman, by an extraordinary mixture of convention and realism has skinned and boned, even removed the entrails, to construct a new being coincident by all points of its anatomy with the parallelepiped or rectangular surface and the object created is at once a box and an animal—many animals, and a man. The box speaks, it actually guards the treasures entrusted to it in the corner of a house where all proclaim that it is, itself, the inner part of some more enormous animal which one enters by a door which is a gaping jawbone and wherein rustles, in a hundred friendly and tragic aspects, a forest of human and nonhuman symbols."[4]

Anthropologists helped Lévi-Strauss place these pieces in historical perspective; Baudelaire and the Surrealists helped him appreciate them as art: "These objects—beings transformed into things, human animals, living boxes—seem as remote as possible from our own conception of art since the time of the Greeks. Yet even here one would err to suppose that a single possibility of the aesthetic life had escaped the prophets and virtuosos of the Northwest Coast. Several of those masks and statues are thoughtful portraits which prove a concern to attain not only physical resemblance but the most subtle spiritual essence of the soul. The sculptor of Alaska and British Columbia is not only the sorcerer who confers upon the supernatural a visible form but also the inspired creator, the interpreter who translates into eternal *chefs d'oeuvre* the fugitive emotions of man."[5]

Finally, Lévi-Strauss gives a résumé of a Tlingit legend recorded by Swanton, entitled "The Image that Came to Life." It tells "the story of a young chief desperately in love with his wife who

dies of an illness in spite of the care of the best shamans. The inconsolable prince went from carver to carver begging them to carve a portrait of his wife, but no one could attain a perfect likeness. Finally he met one who said to him: 'I have seen your wife a great deal walking along with you. I have never studied her face with the idea that you might want someone to carve it, but I am going to try if you will allow me.' The carver began the work, finished the statue and when the young chief got inside his house he saw his dead wife sitting there, just as she used to look. Filled with a melancholy joy he asked the carver the price of this work. But the carver, sorry to see this chief mourning for his wife, said: 'It is because I felt badly for you that I made it; so don't pay me too much for it.' But the chief paid him very well, both in slaves and in goods. The chief had the feeling that his wife had come back to him and treated the image just like her, dressing it in his wife's clothes. One day he had the impression that the statue began to move and from that moment examined it attentively every day, for he thought that at some time it would come to life. But, although the image daily grew more like a human being and was unquestionably living, it could neither move nor speak. Some time later the image gave forth a sound from its chest, like that of crackling wood, and the man knew that it was ill. When he had it removed from its accustomed place he found a small red-cedar tree growing there on the top of the flooring. He left it until it grew to be very large, and it is because of this that cedars on the Queen Charlotte Islands are so good. When people there find a good tree they say, 'This looks like the baby of the chief's wife.' The image, however, never became really alive and the nostalgic conclusion of the story is imprinted with respect for the autonomy of the work of art, for its absolute independence in face of every sort of reality: 'Every day the image of the young woman grew more like a human being, and when they heard the story, people from far and near came in to look at it, and at the young cedar tree growing here, at which they were much astonished. The woman moved around very little and never was able to talk, but her husband dreamed what she wanted to tell him. It was through his dreams that he knew she was talking to him.''[6]

I've quoted at great length from this little known but fascinating article because it records so eloquently Lévi-Strauss's response to Northwest Coast art as *art.*

Early traders on the Coast saw these pieces as curios. They collected randomly, with untrained eyes, yet what they gathered leave us spellbound. Almost without exception, pieces collected in the late 18th and early 19th centuries are of high quality. Clearly, the artistic level that prevailed at this time was extraordinarily high.

Most of the fine, old pieces in this exhibition were picked up by sailors between 1778 and 1830 and taken back to England or Boston to become the delight of antiquarians and the wonder of schoolboys. Many were much too fragile even for ordinary handling. The spindle whorl, #13, is as fragile as a biscuit; the "cockle" rattle, #82, lacks the natural strength of an eggshell. Yet each crossed half the world in a crowded ship and survived nearly two centuries of private ownership. Obviously everyone who touched them cared.

By 1820, the demand for curios had created a souvenir industry. Great quantities were turned

out. The Northwest Coast people had known luxury during the height of the sea-otter trade and were reluctant to give it up. Curios were a poor substitute for sea-otter pelts, but there was little else to trade.

One mask in this exhibition, #88, was probably made for this market. It belongs to a distinct genre of almost identical masks made between 1820 and 1870. Some are so similar as to be almost interchangeable. I've seen about two dozen and heard of others. Perhaps as many as thirty could be easily located. Most seem to be the work of three carvers. All have prominent, stationary labrets. Sailors wanted curios, especially human likeness showing lip distortion. About 1826, a Boston captain wrote on the back of one (now at Harvard): "A correct likeness of Jenna Cass, a high chief woman of the Northwest Coast signed J. Goodwin, Esq." In 1850, P. T. Barnum illustrated one in a catalog to his American Museum, describing it as "an exact representation of the human face, as far as shape and features are regarded."

I find most of them very dull. Compared to #94 and #96, two dance masks with movable labrets, both made for native use and showing much wear, these souvenir masks are lifeless. All are well executed, but technique cannot conceal that meaningless quality everywhere characteristic of art without belief.

In the catalog for the "Far North" show, 1973, three such masks are identified as shamans' masks and their painted designs interpreted as totemic clan emblems.[7] But shamans' masks are quite different in form and generally much weathered, having been exposed on graves, whereas souvenir masks are often in mint condition, having seen no use. I suspect that the designs on the souvenir masks are largely meaningless. Certainly they differ from traditional face and mask designs. A totemic emblem was a privilege, personal or family—not suitable for export. Souvenir masks were addressed to alien audiences. I'm reminded of a Dufy composition incorporating a musical score which can't be played; or an actor, playing a physicist, who doesn't put real formulae on the blackboard—unless he performs at M.I.T.

The first serious collector on the Northwest Coast was Captain James Cook who gathered ethnographic materials as part of his general fact-finding endeavors. Two specimens in this exhibition, #12 and #87, were collected by him from the Nootka in 1778.[8] Captain James Magee, commanding the *Margaret* out of Boston, collected from the Nootka in 1792 and gave this collection to the Massachusetts Historical Society.[9] It can now be seen at Harvard. Commander Alejandro Malaspina, leader of a Spanish exploratory expedition, collected at various points along the coast in 1792.[10] The specimens are now in Madrid. Captain Urey Lisiansky of the *Neva,* leader of a Russian expedition, collected at Sitka in 1804.[11] The specimens are now in Leningrad.

This tradition was continued by the American government's Wilkes Expedition, 1838–41, which collected throughout the Pacific, including Northwest Coast material acquired from a Hudson's Bay Company trader. George Foster Emmons (1811–1887), a member of that expedition, must have been particularly interested in ethnography, for his home in Princeton

was said to have been decorated with Polynesian and Northwest Coast objects, and a number of early museum acquisitions bear his name.

His son, Lt. George Thornton Emmons, USN (1852–1945), became *the* name in Northwest Coast collecting. Beginning very early, at Sitka, he collected in great quantity, including the contents of shamans' graves. The Tlingit themselves shunned these graves, believing that only the deceased shamans had possessed the power to control these sacred objects. Yet I find no record that Emmons's collecting disturbed the Tlingit, and it's certain he enjoyed a lifelong friendship with them.

He dedicated over sixty years to placing on record the meaning of life to these northern seafarers. Neither he nor his Canadian counterpart, Charles F. Newcombe, a Victoria physician, ever profited financially from the tens of thousands of documented specimens they shipped to museums. They refused to sell to collectors and dealers. They trusted only museums and that trust was largely kept, the one major exception being the Museum of the American Indian which, for over thirty years, has regularly sold and traded masterworks. At least eighteen pieces in this exhibition bear that museum's catalog numbers or once did. Of these, most were collected by Emmons.[12]

Emmons was one of a handful of men, who, around the turn of the century, committed their lives to preserving, in every available medium, what remained of Indian culture. What couldn't be kept alive, they wanted to preserve in books, museums, photographs, even recordings and films. They did this under the umbrella of "science," though their personal motives were far more humanistic.

I had the good fortune to know a number of these men, several quite well. Ali were so remarkable, I've often wondered what shaped them. Most, I noticed, had strong fathers. Emmons's father, after serving on the Wilkes Expedition, led a detachment from the Willamette Valley to California; distinguished himself in the Civil War; raised the flag at Sitka in 1867; and rose to the rank of Admiral, commanding the Hydrographic Office and later the Philadelphia Navy Yard—facts not lost on the Tlingit, who accepted G. T. Emmons as the son of a noble warrior.

And all of these men—at least, those I knew—expressed affectionate memories of mothers whose aesthetic, even mystic interests and affiliations, were sharply at variance with the world of applied power in post–Civil War America.

Those two temperaments joined in these men, the first in arduous exploration and disciplined scholarship, the second in mystic and aesthetic modes of thought. These latter were initially treated as subjects of study, but later openly acknowledged as personal persuasions. Consider Dr. John R. Swanton, author of precise, accurate studies of Northwest Coast mythology. When he retired from the Smithsonian, he circulated a letter to friends stating that, as a public servant, he hadn't thought it suitable to express private convictions, but now felt free to record his longstanding belief in extrasensory perception.

Emmons, I'm sure, would have understood. He lived, by choice, between two worlds, at home in both but happiest in-between, like a man attracted to a beach or tidal pool where contrasting elements meet and interact. Impeccable in dress and speech, conservative in politics, courtly in manner, he was a frequent guest at the White House where he pleaded the Indian cause with his friend Theodore Roosevelt. Yet his closest friend, between 1882 and 1888, was Shartrich, the famed Tlingit chief who, in the winter of 1852, led a war party over the Chilkat Pass, 300 miles into the interior to capture and burn the Hudson's Bay Company post at Ft. Selkirk.[13]

In his later years, Emmons spoke of the Tlingit as "we." It was no affectation. After retiring from naval service and leaving his home in Sitka, he returned at every opportunity to the Northwest Coast, making long trips by open boat to remote villages, always collecting art. He delighted in deciphering its designs. Franz Boas is credited with this achievement, but letters between them reveal that Emmons taught Boas.[14] Deciphering this art seems simple today. We even correct Emmons here and there. But it lay outside our grandparents' understanding. Artists of their generation simply couldn't interpret this art, much less accurately illustrate it. Despite all the years she devoted to painting pictures of totem poles, Emily Carr never understood their iconography. Eighteenth- and 19th-century illustrators, though experiencing little difficulty with strange flora and fauna, were almost uniformly inept at portraying alien art.

Emmons consulted native artists. He personally prepared illustrations for his Chilkat blanket monograph,[15] as well as for Boas's *Primitive Art.*[16] These are among the first accurate representations of Northwest Coast design.

Of all the collectors on the Northwest Coast, Emmons was by far the most active and successful. His first shipment to the American Museum of Natural History numbered 2775 specimens. This was quickly followed by 1351 more. I estimate the number of catalogued Northwest Coast specimens in museums today at 115,000 to 125,000. Emmons was responsible for a significant portion of these, and a very high proportion of the finest. The remainder were largely assembled by—my notes list fifty—missionaries, traders, teachers, geologists, naval men, geographers, illustrators, and anthropologists.

Anthropologists were particularly active in gathering material for the World Columbian Exposition, Chicago, in 1893, as well as for museum displays and study purposes. They often commissioned specimens from living artists, thus inadvertently creating a new type of specimen, the "anthropological specimen." This was consciously more traditional in form, but in craftsmanship came out of the souvenir industry. Distinctions between objects made for native use, for tourists, and for anthropologists became muddied.

Today nearly all surviving Northwest Coast material culture is in public hands. I can think of no other area in the world where this applies, at least to this degree. Emmons, Newcombe, and a few others deserve full thanks. Little escaped their efforts. A few pieces, especially in England, have been in private hands since they left the Coast long ago. Others remain in Indian hands, often out of sight. But nearly all great Northwest Coast pieces, privately owned—and there are

only a few—once bore museum numbers. They left museums through sale, trade, gift, fraud, theft. At least eleven museums once owned pieces in this exhibition. Most came out at a time when curators traded freely, sometimes not even recording transactions. They felt free to do so because, until about 1955, this material had no more market value than seashells or beetles. Much of it wasn't even recognized as Indian by the general public, to whom "Indian" meant what Frederic Remington painted.

When I tell collectors that I once hesitated to pay $3.00 for a fine mask, since this was double the highest price I had previously paid, they express envy and regret at not having enjoyed such opportunities. But everyone enjoyed such opportunities. The point is, few cared.

Anthropologists were less interested in specimens than in information about specimens. I knew one who regularly exchanged specimens with an illustrator for illustrations of these specimens. He needed the illustrations for publications.

Certain museum directors loved to swap, sell, give. When setting up new exhibits, even temporary exhibits, they traded and borrowed. Often loans were never recalled.

One result of all this subtracting and adding was that documentation often got separated from specimens. The one beneficial result was that specimens often became accessible. The great Tlingit collection assembled between 1867 and 1868 by Lt. Edward Fast, USA,[17] and shortly thereafter deposited at Harvard, remained almost unknown until recently, save for pieces that "got out" and became known through exhibitions and catalogs.

Mask #89, collected in 1878 by George Dawson and published by him in a sketch no larger than a postage stamp,[18] lay in storage for nearly a century—never exhibited, never loaned, never studied. This is still true of many Northwest Coast masterworks and, until very recently, was true of nearly all.

Between 1910 and 1940, that is between the time the great collections were assembled and the time artists discovered Northwest Coast art, only Emmons, Newcombe and a handful of others maintained a deep interest in this subject. Marius Barbeau continued to collect for Ottawa. Frederick Douglas collected for Denver and Erna Gunther for Seattle. In Mexico, Miquel Covarrubias, Wolfgang Paalen, and their fellow artists collected and published privately.[19] All were interested in art. Only a few had museum appointments and even they were regarded by professional anthropologists as working "outside" anthropology. Anthropologists had lost interest in material culture and had never been interested in art.

Emmons, though he lived to be 93, never lost his love for this art. He had retained the right to trade pieces in and out of most of the collections he assembled, and did so with 7% of the collection he assembled for the American Museum of Natural History. He frequently visited these scattered collections, adding new information to their catalogs.

One other collector requires mention. Louis Shotridge (1886–1937), grandson of the Tlingit noble, Shartrich, was born in Klukwan, famed Tlingit citadel of tradition and art. When he was

19, he met Dr. George Gordon, Director of the University Museum, Philadelphia, who was passing through Haines, collecting. Gordon bought a fine, old dagger from Shotridge and asked for more. More followed, to become, over the years, a small collection unparalleled in quality.[20]

If "Colonel" Gordon had collected railroads, he might have linked oceans. Instead, he collected ancient art. He wasn't loved by scholars, but he could recognize great art and he wanted the best from Egypt, China, Greece, Mexico—and Klukwan.

At what point Gordon devised the plan to have Shotridge infiltrate his own culture to obtain its treasures, the record doesn't show. In the beginning, he simply asked Shotridge to buy for him. Then he put him on staff. It was common practice then for a museum to employ an Indian as general helper and occasional lecturer—in Indian dress—to school children.

Shotridge was handsome, intelligent, friendly. He was married to a Tlingit girl of like virtues. Sitka, where he attended school, offered no opportunities. Haines, where he was living, was a military town left over from the Gold Rush. His father, a strikingly proud, handsome man in photographs, was an alcoholic. So were several uncles. Home was mud, boredom, alcohol. Gordon offered an escape.

Coudahwot and Yehlh-Gouhu (father of Louis Shotridge), chiefs of Con-nuh-ta-di, Klukwan. Photograph: Winter and Pond

During the two years it took to finalize this employment, he toured the U.S. with Indian shows. Indian shows and mission schooling were perfect preparation for a "museum Indian." Shotridge proved a great success, popular with school children, a favorite of the press, the hunting companion of Theodore Roosevelt and John Wanamaker.

He was equally popular as an anthropology student. He studied under Franz Boas, working mornings for him as a linguistic informant. At Columbia University he had regular contact with leading ethnologists. At the University Museum, Frank Speck and Edward Sapir, two giants in the field, were his colleagues, contemporaries and friends. He lived for a time at Speck's home.

In 1915 Gordon sent Shotridge to Klukwan. His first report begins: "Upon my arrival in Chilkat . . . I proceeded in the usual way of obtaining information from the natives, which is to hire an informant."[21]

Louis Shotridge at the University Museum.

Two photographs from this period are especially interesting. One shows a trim house set apart from the squalor of Haines. The second shows the interior of the house: immaculate, spare, with fashionable wicker furniture, including a coffee table complete with fresh pad of paper and sharpened pencil. Crossed tennis rackets lean against the table. Shotridge's caption reads: "University Museum Expedition, Field Headquarters."

Shotridge had large purchasing funds. He had a still camera and a movie camera. The Museum had made, to his specifications, a typewriter with phonetic typeface for recording Tlingit texts. John Wanamaker gave him a powerboat, the *Penn,* large enough for him to live aboard with his family while on collecting trips. Photographs show him in tweeds, always with a camera slung from his shoulder. He appears on horseback, driving a dogsled, piloting the *Penn,* always apart, in dress and manner, from his kinsmen. They called him arrogant. They still revile his name.

"I obtained [the Kaguanton Shark Helmet] . . . from the last of the house group. . . . When I carried the object out of its place no one interfered, but if only one of the true warriors of that clan had been alive the removal of it would never have been possible. I took it in the presence of aged women, the only survivors in the house where the old object was kept, and they could do nothing more than weep when the once highly esteemed object was being taken away. . . ."[22]

He spent most of the next twenty years collecting on the Coast. He knew where pieces were and how to recognize the best. He offered large sums. But, even when accepted, these offers were resented, partly, I think, because Shotridge was Tlingit, but had "gone out."

"I am now the only right heir who is in a position to dispose of any or all of the objects if I chose to do so, but it is not going to be an easy thing to take away the Bear Emblem. . . . My plan is to take the old pieces one at a time."[23]

Unlike Emmons, he didn't limit offers to pieces no longer in use or no longer valued. Offers he made in Klukwan greatly exceeded the sums he paid elsewhere for comparable pieces, yet were generally rejected. In the end, he tried to steal the Rain Screen and houseposts from the Whale House in Klukwan.

These particular pieces, by general consensus, were the Tlingit's greatest surviving treasures.[24] Shotridge had promised them to Gordon as early as 1906, laying claim to them on the grounds his father had been the Master of the Whale House. But Tlingit descent is matrilineal. Shotridge had no claim. He didn't even have the right to enter the Whale House, except by invitation.

First he offered $3500. There probably wasn't $100 cash in all Klukwan at that time. He spoke eloquently, at great length, in the Whale House. He said Gordon was an honorable man, that he

Interior of the Whale House, showing the rain screen in the background and two of the four house posts. Photograph: Winter and Pond

Detail,
Whale House,
Klukwan

would protect these treasures, that they belonged to the world and would forever reflect the glory of the Whale House. The answer was an unequivocal no.[25]

Finally, with the Museum's knowledge, he laid plans to steal them while the men were away fishing. "We plan to take this collection," he wrote to Gordon, "regardless of all the objections of the community,"[26] and Gordon replied, "I am glad you have found a way to overcome the serious difficulties in obtaining full possession."[27] But a "gun went off," narrowly missing him. This traditional Tlingit custom, midway between execution and assassination, was no mere warning. Shotridge sponsored a feast to reestablish peace.

The Depression worsened and the Museum let him go. He received no pension, merely a letter of regret. He was left without means or purpose in a hostile community. His bank was in difficulty and he couldn't withdraw his savings. He couldn't collect money he had lent others. His food bill had been turned over to a collection agency. Another child was due. He mailed twelve pieces of beadwork to the Museum, suggesting the staff might want to buy them if the Museum didn't. They averaged less than $3.00 each. Only one was purchased. Another was lost.[28]

Finally he got a job as inspector in the Salmon Canneries, actually a river guard. Nothing better illustrates his status than this despised job. But he had buried one wife. His second wife was ill. He had five children. He was ill. The last known photograph of him shows him beside a small, torn tent pitched in snow. He holds a blackened coffee-pot over a wood fire. His face looks like mask #90, sometimes called the "Dying Warrior."

The circumstances of his death are still discussed. At Klukwan, some say he was killed for taking treasures. At Sitka, some say he was killed for ordering a fisherman off the river. The official report states that he "fell from scaffolding," breaking his neck.[29] But there was no scaffolding where his body was found. He lay beside a little cabin he had built. Even if his death was an accident, that doesn't explain why he lay unattended, for days, until a teacher took him to a hospital. I accept the Sitka version. But, however he died, he died an "outlaw," unprotected by community codes.

An interesting story, but how relevant? If we judge Shotridge by his visible role, the bitterness at Klukwan can be understood, the Museum forgiven, the man forgotten. But I think he was larger

than these events. Speck must have thought so, too, because he kept a portrait of Shotridge on the wall of his summer home.

When Shotridge was young, he had no interest in traditional Tlingit life. Even after he returned, his sympathies were elsewhere. But he was well trained, and when he documented a piece, he did a first-rate job. He found that the old speeches, associated with major pieces, were still remembered in all their detail and eloquence: proposals in council to commission a work of art; speeches made in reply; payments made for a work; speeches made when it was worn or displayed; the capture of a piece by enemies; their treatment of it; ransoming the work; etc., etc. He recorded, as well, detailed accounts of the mythic creatures depicted in these works, and detailed myths about the works themselves. Always with attention to detail!

I know of no other record, in all the literature of anthropology, that carries the reader so far into alien modes of thought associated with art. Reading these lengthy reports, one soon realizes that the physical object was only part of a complex pattern, and at times could become almost irrelevant. Consider three minor incidents relating to the Whale House screen and posts: At a time when there was hunger in Klukwan, the owners rejected $3500, but then left the screen exposed outside, where it weathered badly. More recently, I stopped two roughhousing children from damaging this screen during a feast in the Whale House. No one else seemed concerned, though shortly afterwards they rejected an offer of $750,000 and ordered the dealer who made it to leave. One member of the Whale House, speaking in council, urged that the screen and post be sold: "What is it we Chilkat respect? Power and money. We hire artists. A Tsimshian made the Rain Screen for us. We bought it for prestige and power. We should sell it for the same reasons."

Art, like so much else in Tlingit life, was often used for power. It was even used as a weapon. Shotridge's efforts to acquire pieces still in use were interpreted as a bid for power and fought by the Tlingit at every turn. Gradually he lost interest. He spent long periods in areas where there was nothing to collect, seeking out recluses, blind elders living alone in otherwise abandoned camps, far up remote tributaries. He lived with them, listening. I find no evidence that Gordon encouraged him in this, yet it was these trips that proved ethnologically most fruitful and, I believe, helped turn Shotridge, in the end, into a tribal elder himself.

Much of the art he obtained was the very best. My impression is that very little great art ever leaves a tribe. Its owners burn it or let it rot before they let strangers see it or take it. I suspect we have little idea what lies hidden in some of the most prosaic villages. In New Guinea I once saw a Sepik village burn, in twenty minutes. After carrying infants and elders to safety, men tore walls and roofs open to take out hidden treasures. These were put on rafts, then quickly covered, but for a moment I glimpsed absolutely magnificent pieces. In Borneo and New Guinea I've entered abandoned settlements and seen the very finest treasures under rotting rafters. The elders who had remained behind to guard them had all died.

I think this was equally true on the Northwest Coast. Aside from the efforts of Emmons, Newcombe, and Shotridge, only chance permitted us to see truly great pieces. Many were lost in house fires. Others were deliberately destroyed. I don't think even the early explorers got the best, save for rare presentation pieces. Most of what passes for Northwest Coast art is mere merchandise, made for commoners, and souvenirs, made for us. The fact that even this material is generally good, both in design and execution, encourages us to look no further.

In failing to look further, we sell this art short. There were masterpieces of the highest order on the Northwest Coast. The people on the Coast knew them, guarded them, needed them. The few now in our museums usually lie buried in storage or lost in bad lighting. But, seen on their own terms, they can be recognized. They stand out.

Dominique de Menil expressed the desire to exhibit such masterworks. The plan was to search everywhere and select the best. This proved unfeasible. Someday it may be done, in book if not in gallery, but I think it will be achieved only as the culmination of a lifetime effort by a single person, perhaps Bill Holm.

We next considered exhibiting the Shotridge collection. Shotridge himself once displayed it[30] with the crest objects of one clan facing the crest objects of the opposite clan; with the right piece in the right place displayed the right way, its label reflecting the eloquence of its owner and the truth of its legacy. The visitor, he wrote, should be made aware, at all times, what each piece was, why it was there, and how it related to every other piece. It was an exhibition in which everything related to everything else and nothing was spiritually meaningless.

In comparison to the exhibition of masterpieces we had first considered, the Shotridge exhibition seemed fairly simple. Most of the collection was still in the University Museum and the Museum enthusiastically endorsed our proposal. Some pieces had been taken by George Heye when he moved his collection out of the University Museum to his own museum in New York. But nearly all could be located. We invited the Klukwan house groups to participate, both personally and by exhibiting pieces, including the Whale House screen and posts. This invitation met a divided reception in Klukwan and plans for a Shotridge exhibition were abandoned.

Finally, Mrs. de Menil decided to display those Northwest Coast pieces that she and her husband, Jean, had assembled as part of a teaching collection on loan to Rice University. To these were added pieces owned by her children. It's a modest collection, varied in quality, locale and date. As such it's ideal for general study and has been treated as such in both this exhibition and catalog.

Since the emphasis of the exhibition is on art, we asked two artists to discuss the collection. Most catalogs are written by curators addressing themselves to curatorial problems. We wanted to hear what one artist talking to another artist had to say about these pieces.

Detail, housepost,
Whale House, Klukwan

Bill Holm and Bill Reid both said they were always happy to look at Northwest Coast pieces. Each is an active artist in this field.

In his *Northwest Coast Indian Art,* the definitive work on this subject, Bill Holm writes: "Some of the most skillful artists of the southern Kwakiutl are among the best dancers and song composers. . . . The constant flow of movement, broken at rhythmic intervals by rather sudden, but not necessarily jerky, changes of motion-direction, characterizes both the dance and art of the Northwest Coast. . . . I, myself, have derived a certain physical satisfaction from the muscle activity involved in producing the characteristic line movement of this art, and there can be little doubt that this was true also for the Indian artist."[31]

Bill Holm has studied Northwest Coast cultures for most of his adult life and regularly participated, as a dancer-singer-carver, in Kwakiutl dances and ceremonies. He tells me he finds this participation inseparable from his understanding and enjoyment of their art.

I don't regard as coincidental the fact that all recent contributions to our understanding of Northwest Coast art come from men who are themselves carvers.

Bent-corner bowl, "crouching man," yew wood with red cedar bottom. Made by Bill Holm, 1967

Bill Reid's carvings rival the finest ever produced by his Haida forebears. His mother came from Skidegate, his grandmother from Tanu, the now-vanished village that was once the crowning gem of West Coast art.

I've followed his career for many years and come to believe that, in some strange way, the essence of Haida art, once the lifeblood of an entire people, now survives within him, at a depth, and with an intensity, unrelated to any "revival," but deriving from primary sources and leading to daring innovations. Witness his carving of the Raven discovering mankind in a clamshell: flawless technique combines with courage and freedom. It's pure Haida, but like no other Haida carving. It's monumental, yet only a few inches high. It's newly carved by a man we know, yet belongs to the distant past and to another reality. Its intricacy, its compressed power, its tense relationship between man and Raven, all these express—in Bill's own words—the precariousness of a society so highly structured, so highly developed, "All its parts had to fit together perfectly to function as it did."

Reid, 1970

Bill left that society to explore other realities. But he returned, first in study, then in love and identity. There's much I don't understand in all this, but then, there's always mystery in how great art came to be, no less so when the artist is a friend.

Conversations between Bill Reid and Bill Holm provided the text for this catalog. They spent three days together, examining the pieces, turning them in hand, talking about them. Transcripts of those conversations were left essentially unedited. The pauses are gone, of course, and modifiers have been shifted to precede nouns and verbs, thus introducing a certain positiveness absent in the original. But all the other uncertainties, contradictions, explorations, occasional discoveries and frequent differences remain.

Bill Holm said he was embarrassed to read how he sounded. He's a superb writer, very concise. He missed that conciseness. But the dialog has a life of its own, unrelated to conciseness. A reader feels he's listening in on a conversation—which he is—and may be encouraged to join in this ongoing exploration.

Edmund Carpenter

Dialogue

REID: Well, I don't know what we do.

HOLM: No. I think we have to pick something and start in.

REID: Go by category?

HOLM: That's fine with me. What's a good category to start with?

REID: Happen to have a pipe here.

HOLM: All right, go ahead. Well, one thing I'm wondering—do we want to limit the kind of thing we talk about?

REID: I think we should talk about the things we're interested in, as opposed to what we imagine the general public would be interested in.

HOLM: I think that's the best thing.

I

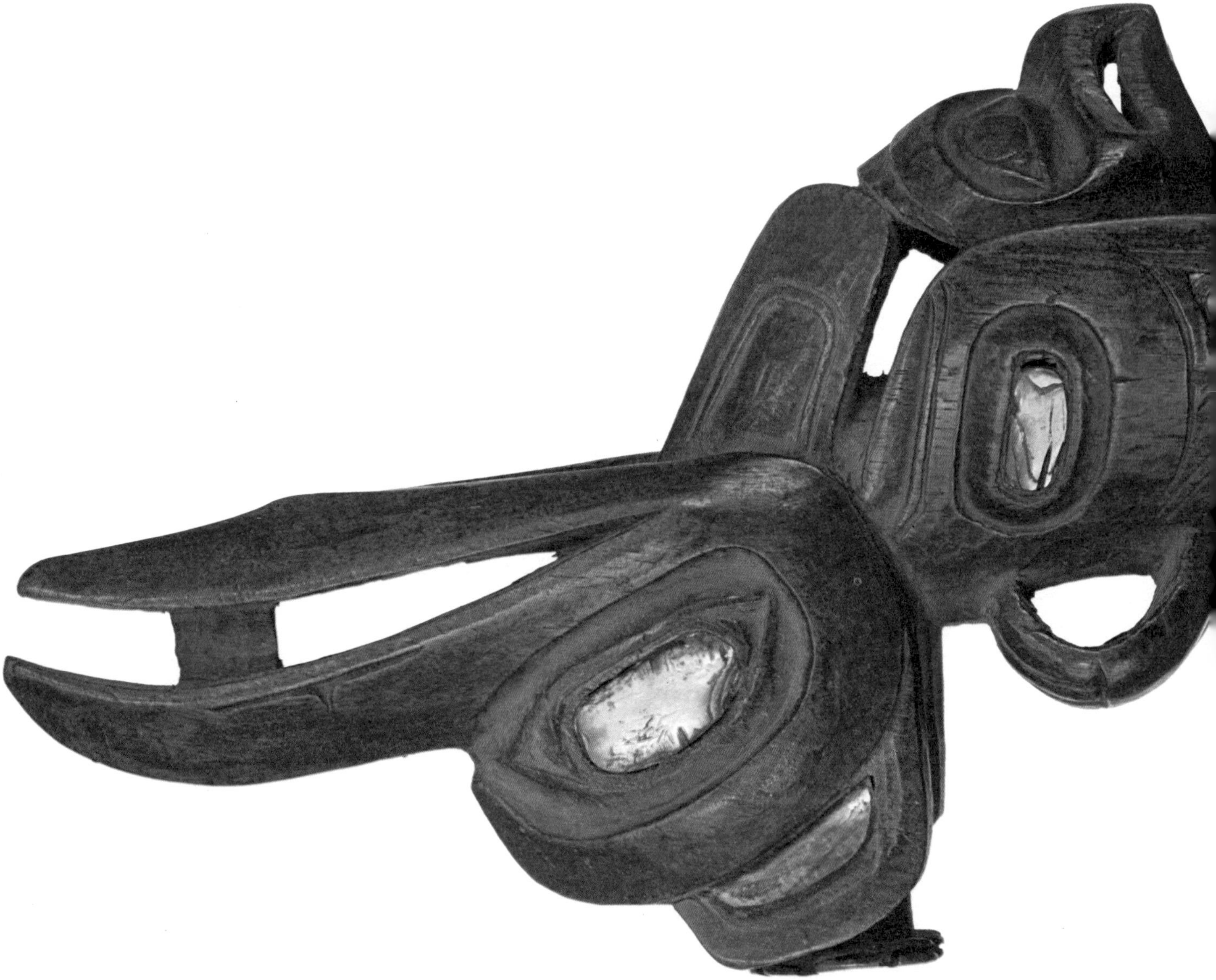

REID: Aside from being an intriguing piece, I don't think its overall form reads as a great unity. What really interests me is that it has all these things going on. It was made as a virtuoso piece. The fact is, it was a hell of a hard thing to build this little figure inside the other. That has nothing to do with aesthetic appreciation or anything else, just that so much care was spent in doing that particular thing, which wasn't really necessary, but had this relationship between the person who made it, what he was doing, and the owner's joy at possessing a virtuoso carving.

HOLM: I agree. I don't see this as quite the unified composition some others are, but it has all these different things going and each part works out really well. They do go together, though they break into different units.

What strikes me and really excites me about such pieces is their impact. That gets me first. Then, surely because of my interest in the structure of this art, I see the great organization, not only in the whole, but in every detail of every part. This one shows it. They all do. Here we have this composition of the whole silhouette and the parts that make up the bird, and the other figures joined with it: this thunderbird-like face which dovetails with the main figure, and the little bird, or whatever he is, on the breast. Also, the way all the details are put together—for instance, this two-dimensional business on the wings. Every little part follows the "Northern style" of Northwest Coast art. It just works out.

Another thing that gets me is the rich surface, the color, the inlay.

REID: Suppose we try to project ourselves into this carving. Both of us have carved and know how carving works: you have an idea and you make a form.

In Northwest Coast art, perhaps more than in any other art, there's an impulse to push things as far as possible. Here the carver probably first outlined the bird's wings and the figure projecting from its belly. You can just see him cutting deeper, finally almost separating the two figures altogether. He must have spent hours getting inside, eliminating all nonessentials, leaving nothing but the whole power and impact of the essential unit and the disparate parts that make up its whole.

HOLM: There was a functional aspect of all this carving, too. The carver took weight away. That was part of it. There was no real purpose in hollowing out this little head on the breast, although it's nice to be able to see these shapes through it. Hollowing the main head was basically just relieving weight, but done as part of the design. I see this widely in rattles, backs of headdresses, and so on.

There're so many things we could say about each piece, but let's leave this one for a time.

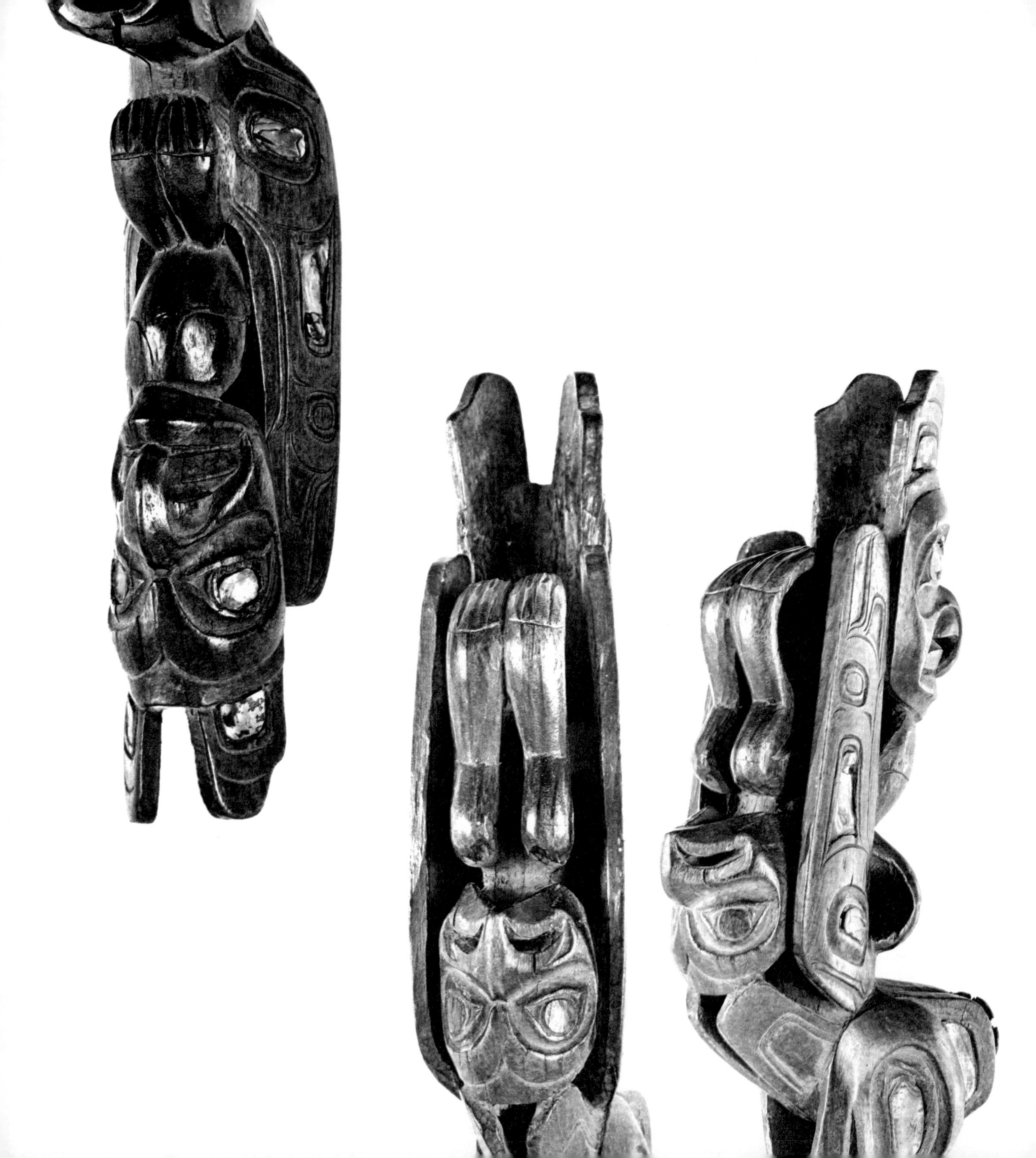

2

HOLM: The same thing happens to me when I see this next pipe. First, I see this great little bird with an almost human face, its beak jutting out, curving back, combining with another figure.

Then I see this great organization over the whole thing, the detail of the wings, the way the little figure on the breast is compressed into his face.

What about some of the other information, aside from just the artist approach? What about the pieces themselves, what they are, what they represent, their period? Do you want to get into that? It's part of it.

REID: I'm sure it is, but I'm also sure that's your field almost exclusively. I'm not an historian, not a scholar. History will never be my primary interest.

HOLM: I'm interested. It's something I like to think about when I look at these things. They have historical meaning to me. I get an impression of that.

Both these pipes, I think, are pretty darn old. They have that feeling. They resemble—in detail and structure—well-documented argillite pieces from the early 19th century, at least from the first half of the 19th century. Probably the same people who made these pipes made argillite carvings.

The first pipe, #1, looks very Haida to me, probably because it resembles, in structure, argillite pipes that came from the Haida. This pipe seems less Haida, more Tlingit. What first suggests that to me is this little man, although there are plenty of little men in Haida carvings. But something about the modeling of the face resembles well-known Tlingit carvings.

Then, as you go up into the main face, it's more difficult to pin down, but even that has characteristics more Tlingit than Haida: a little more roundness and softness, chunkier, more compressed, less crisp.

If this were a known Haida piece, one we could be positive was made by a Haida, I wouldn't argue it, because it's not clearly one or the other. But, that's my feeling and my main reason for thinking these two pipes aren't from the same hand. They're from the same period, the same general region, the same basic art tradition, but different. The first looks like the work of a Haida slate carver; this one doesn't.

What's your impression of this little guy?

REID: A feeling of tremendous power. It's no more than 5-by-4 inches—a small thing, formed of playful elements. Yet it adds up to a monumental piece.

This is what makes Northwest Coast art: this tremendous, compressed power, tension, monumentality, in all the good pieces, no matter what the scale.

The fact is, this is a pipe, not an important ceremonial or religious object, yet it has its own intrinsic importance, its own being.

I'm looking at it now from the belly side—this little man is all tensed up like a coiled spring. Somehow, through this; the whole intricacy and precariousness (perhaps that's not the right word, but it comes to me all the time), the *precariousness* of the society is expressed. It was a society that had been highly structured over a long period and had developed to a point where all its parts had to fit together perfectly to function as it did. This comes out in the works of the great carvers.

HOLM: It had to be that way for these things to happen this way.

I was soaking up this little face which combines with the tail feathers of the raven. It's a very structured, organized patterning of the face planes, closely related to flat design. One thing that often happens, so beautifully in these pieces, is the way various planes relate to one another, all in an organized way. In this case, the recessed eye socket comes merging on into this powerful beak, then curves on around to the lip. That plane—as it comes out of the eye socket and bends around the beak—produces a nose that, to me, is just a wild thing. It's so strong and works so perfectly in closing that nostril and then comes right into the broad, flat, direct lips.

Those kinds of things, to me, have great power and meaning. All the little details go together to make a total mask. You can see this face, with that same kind of plane relationship, in a big totem pole. It's part of that scale picture you were talking about.

REID: That's really what it's all about. That's why so much contemporary revival doesn't work. You have to push a carving to the ultimate, beyond what seems immediately logical. You work it down to a certain level, where you think it ought to be, only to find that the real object you are looking for is still further underneath. And you keep pushing and pushing until you finally arrive at that point where it all comes together, where one area relates perfectly to another. And that point, somehow or other, determines itself. It's this crazy mystique of the object inside the wood, which of course is madness, yet it's never been explained in a better way.

HOLM: If you don't understand that or can't feel that, you can never reach that point. You have to feel the piece in there. I don't like to compare these masterpieces with contemporary attempts but, just from a very practical view, unless you visualize that piece and know what's in there, you can spend an awful lot of time working from the surface down, trying to get there. The artist has to see that form in there.

REID: Words are inadequate in these discussions, but the word that comes to my mind (when talking to others about this and thinking about it in terms of what I do myself) is courage: the courage to take it beyond the point your mind tells you is logical.

In the first pipe, #1, that's what the carver did. He had it safe at one point when he was working on it, and then he threw safety away and came up with something which—technically, aesthetically and in every way—is a masterpiece, in spite of an overall form which, though it works, isn't quite satisfactory.

HOLM: I've seen a photograph of #1. It works better in actuality than in a photograph. It seems to have more unity, whereas in a photograph its silhouette has a broken feeling.

You spoke of the courage it takes to carry this art beyond its logical conclusion. What constantly amazes me about these pieces is the *balance* between the courage to go beyond logic and, at the same time, to hang in there with tradition. Sure, anybody could go beyond it—there're lots of wild things one could do. What we've got here is something that fits in that notch so clearly there's nothing else you can say. The detail of this wing follows a set of clear rules: it doesn't violate one. Yet it's unique, all part of this courageous act on the artist's part.

3

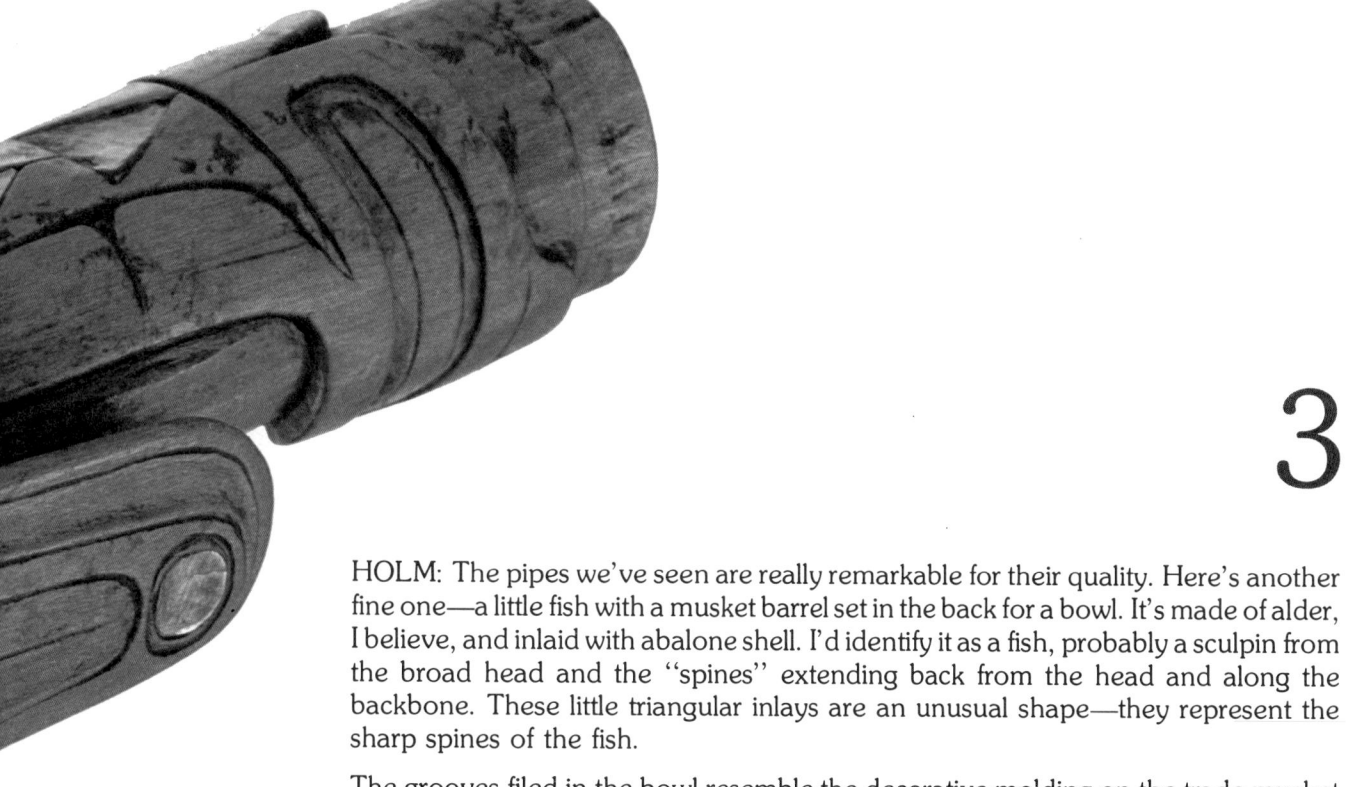

HOLM: The pipes we've seen are really remarkable for their quality. Here's another fine one—a little fish with a musket barrel set in the back for a bowl. It's made of alder, I believe, and inlaid with abalone shell. I'd identify it as a fish, probably a sculpin from the broad head and the "spines" extending back from the head and along the backbone. These little triangular inlays are an unusual shape—they represent the sharp spines of the fish.

The grooves filed in the bowl resemble the decorative molding on the trade musket barrels used in many of these pipe bowls. The artist not only incorporated this exotic material in his pipe, but also borrowed a decorative element from it. Some pipes using gun-barrel bowls have evenly spaced grooves filed around them to simulate the effect of basketry cylinders on crest hats.

REID: A beautiful feeling of strength and simplicity, yet decoratively very rich. And beautifully made. Northwest Coast carvers set eyes in carvings in ways that really show imagination, as well as knowledge of anatomy. These eyes are particularly fine.

REID: Another pipe. In this case the carver wasn't interested in saving weight—this is a chunky piece of wood in the form of a raven. It has a huge tobacco container made of copper, hand-formed probably. Its condition isn't particularly good—wear or dry rot or something has removed some of the detail, but enough remains. It was never a fine, detailed carving like #1 and #2. Here we have just plain, raw, concentrated power. It would be a strong man who smoked that pipe.

It adheres strictly to conventional form, with variations which distinguish the artist. Beautifully tapered eyebrows or eye sockets. Heavy-lidded, very humanoid eyes. Powerful, blunt beak. Short, stubby wings, patterned in simple, straightforward Northwest Coast flat design. I don't understand what he was trying to do with the body of the bird except . . .

HOLM: . . . I think that's just the backbone. He's carrying through his chunky, bold style here to an extreme degree.

REID: There's a rather crudely carved face which is part of the tail. He obviously wasn't all that concerned about detail, although two little faces, projecting from either side of the beak, are nicely done. But the overall effect isn't one of exquisite purity of technique. Just concentrated power.

HOLM: To go back to the question of these carvings as objects in time, I wonder if we aren't awfully conservative in dating them. This pipe must be post-contact, of course, if tobacco was post-contact, and the copper looks like sheet copper, not copper hammered out of nuggets. But I think this pipe is very early. I just can't imagine it acquiring that surface in a short time. Even if you've had pieces around for years and handled them a lot, they still don't have surfaces like this. This surface accumulated over a long period. I think this piece goes way back.

Its style is very different from #1 and #2, yet the same tradition is so strong, in each, we find the same shapes, same details, and same progression of shapes from primary formlines on down through various details. Yet the whole is so different that no one, not even someone totally unfamiliar with Northwest Coast art, could imagine these as carved by the same person. All are simply products of a very strong tradition.

This pipe differs from #1 and #2, not only in detail and lack of refinement, but in overall shape—this big, wide, massive thing with bold forms coming out. Yet, take it apart, detail by detail, and it shares the same basic structure and concept as the others.

4

It's going to be fun when we start looking at that Salish spindle whorl, #13, and see where it fits in with this thing. Because, it fits there; it has a place in the whole scheme. I think we're going to talk about a lot of things on a single piece, and some of those comments and feelings and ideas can splash over onto others.

5

HOLM: Fairly massive pipe of wood. Bowl made from the gun barrel of a typical muzzle-loading musket of the time. The barrel section is thinner on one side than on the other—scary, but that's the way they were. It's set into the top—has a little flange of what appears to be copper around the base. The carving is a bird's head: massive beak, turned-down mouth, little tongue showing, little nostrils carved in—the whole very bold. Has a heavy encrustation, a combination of paint, dirt, grease, and so on—a rich, intriguing surface. The carving is fairly rough. Some feather-like forms, very Northwest Coast in feeling, go back from the head. A pretty exciting thing—very simple, fairly crude workmanship.

REID: I don't find it exciting, though it has a certain strength. I just don't see it as a pleasant form. The workmanship is crude . . . I don't know that there's any point in talking about it much . . .

HOLM: I don't see it as a masterpiece at all, but it's a big cut above many pieces that could be put in the same class. We shouldn't necessarily compare it with another pipe, but with pipes as a whole. This does more for me than a lot of pipes do, but I'm not trying to push it into the masterpiece class at all.

6

HOLM: Reclining bird's head with copper-lined, copper-rimmed bowl in the mouth. The bird's windpipe is clearly shown. Simple formline decoration on the neck, with very deeply carved, ovoid eye sockets. Beak detail. Brownish wood. Northwest Coast or adjacent Tahltan style. A strong, direct thing. Better workmanship and more adherence to classic Northwest Coast arrangement than #5, but it doesn't do for me what #5 did. So we may have another difference of opinion.

REID: This does considerably more for me than #5. I like these big, round bulgy eyes when they occur in Northwest Coast art. I think they're strong elements. It's not a masterpiece, but it could have been a good thing. In places the carver showed enough skill to have done a better job. He just didn't bother. It's one of those pieces about which there's nothing much to say. It's adequate. You wouldn't be ashamed to smoke it in the presence of your peers.

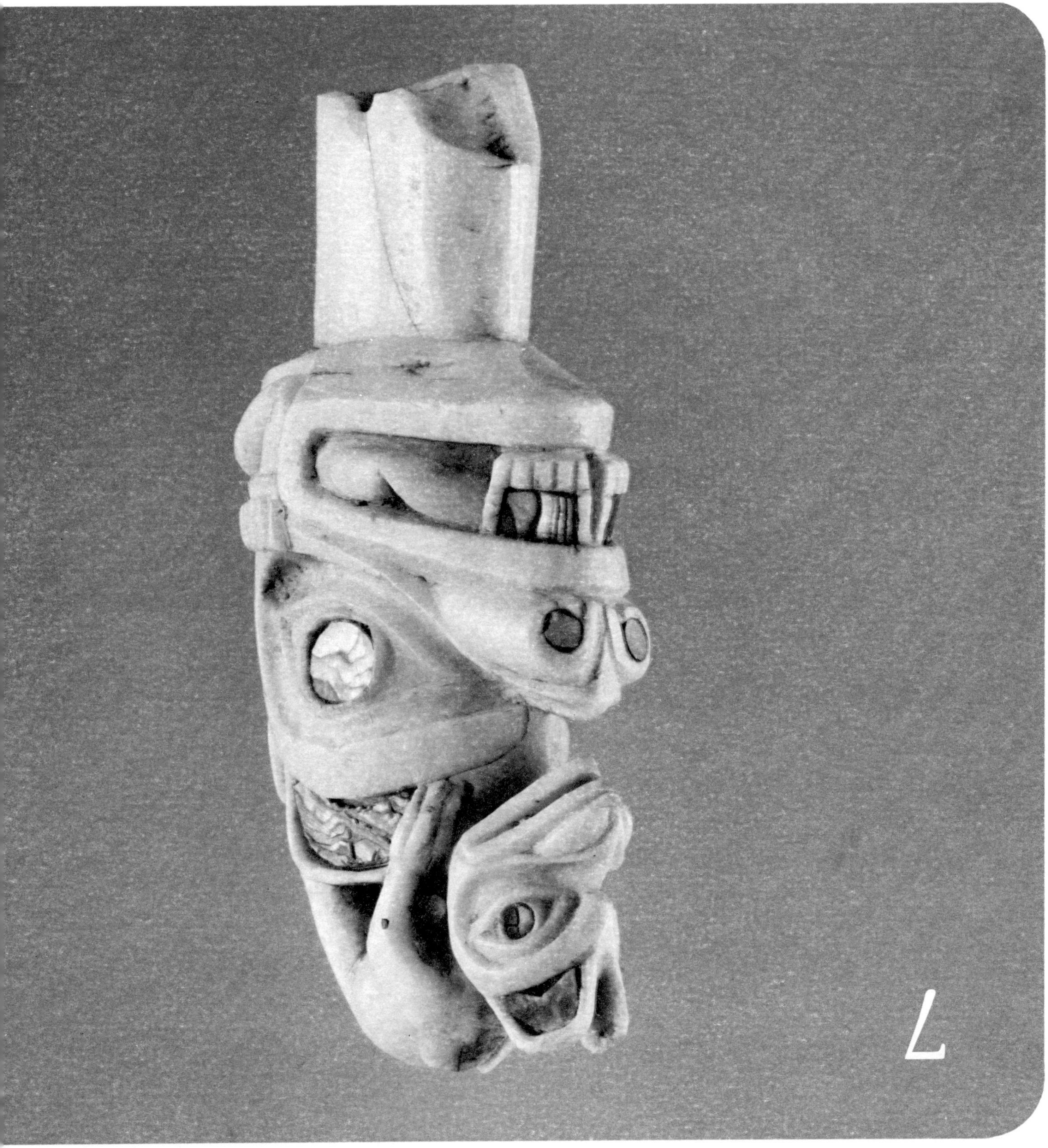

L

HOLM: Dagger hilt of walrus ivory or sperm-whale tooth, in the form of an animal's head with a smaller, bear-like animal on top of it, between the ears.

Then we have one of those strange things that happen—a human figure extends right through the head, its legs and knees sticking out each side of the main figure's mouth. The arms and the head of this little human extend out the back of the main head, a pretty illogical thing, yet something Northwest Coast artists seem to have no trouble with at all. It happens all the time. One creature interlocks with another in a completely illogical way. I don't know how to explain that—maybe it has something to do with that fearlessness we were talking about, the ability of the artist to go right ahead with his imagination.

Certainly some of these carvings have specific meanings related to particular traditions or stories, or particular crest figures or decorations. But I think a lot of this strangeness is just exuberance and fearlessness.

This is a pretty strong thing, a little too bold for me in some ways. But it sure illustrates the richness possible in some of these materials. The abalone inlay sets the color off beautifully.

REID: This, for me, really has it all together. One of the great joys I've gotten out of the Northwest Coast is the feeling I have that these people looked at the world in a very different way than we do. They weren't bound by the silly feeling that it's impossible for two figures to occupy the same space at the same time. So we have this human figure, plus a bear's head or whatever, coexisting in space and time.

The little arched figure of the bear cub, or whatever he is, on the top, didn't have to be that way. But he is that way. Incredible tension has been built into that form by arching him that way.

And there's fun going on. The little abalone inlay in the soles of the feet makes no logic except to add interest.

HOLM: The feet in the mouth double for teeth. The abalone serves as soles for the feet of one figure and as teeth for the other figure.

REID: I like complexity. I like the whole way the artist just went crazy with imagination. In detail, it's marvelous. A human face which is also part of a bear's head! Of all the pieces we've looked at so far, I'd like to own this one.

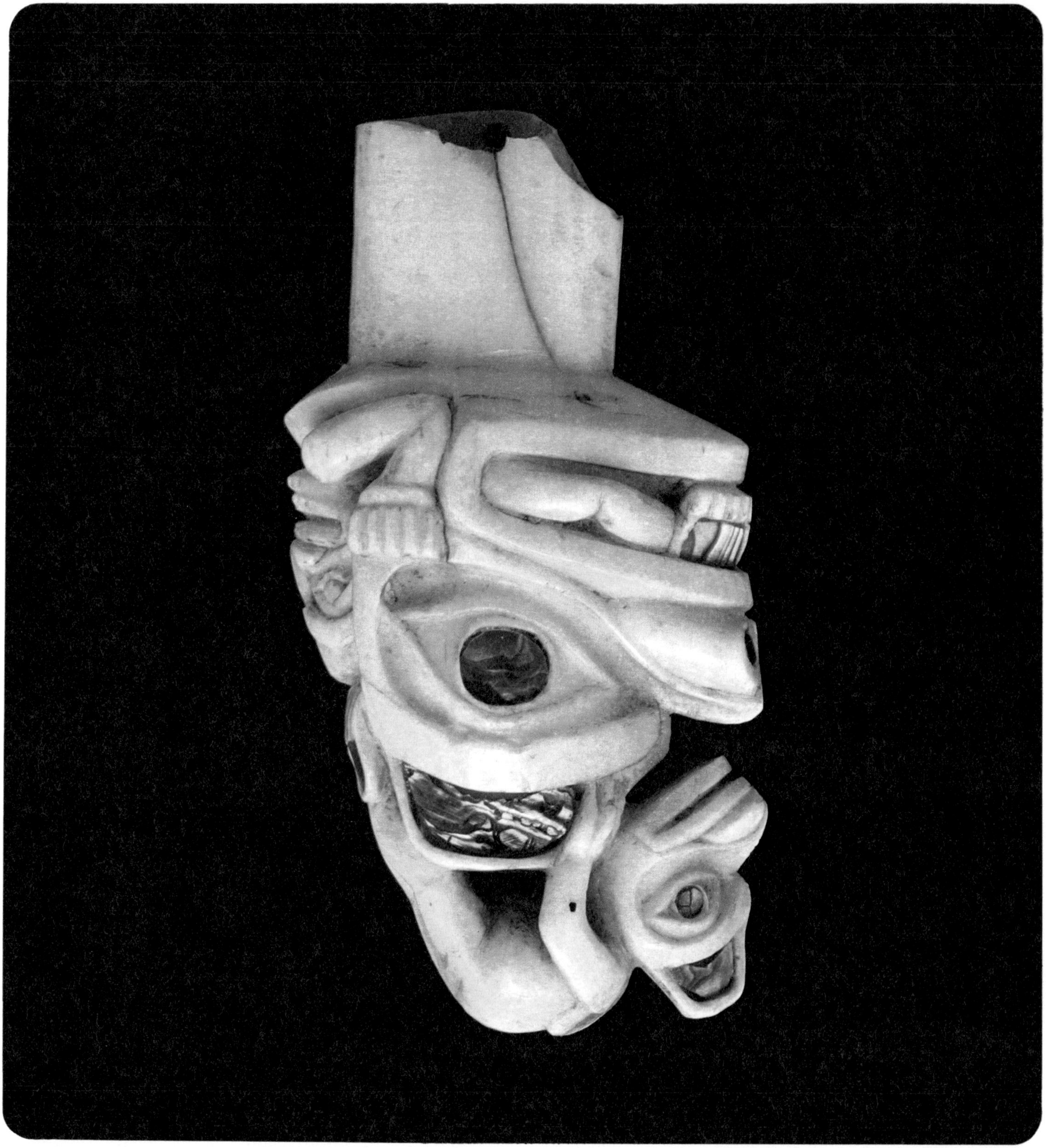

8

HOLM: A very highly finished, one-piece steel or iron dagger, beautifully made on the concave back side, with a series of flutes running down the convex front of the blade, and a shallowly sculptured upper section in the form of an animal's head.

Of the one-piece daggers I've seen, this is one of the better made. It has fine copper work on it. Two pieces of copper cover the broad bases of each of the two blades. The main one is nicely engraved on both sides with perfectly stylized formline patterns. The grip was once bound with what appears to be split spruce root—most of it is gone.

Daggers of similar form go far back in other parts of the world. I don't think this was an original Northwest Coast concept, although there may have been very similar daggers here in ancient times, perhaps made of native copper. I feel this dagger form was imported from Asia. The blade's shape, the fluting, the gradual taper with sudden taper at the point—all these go back to ancient times in Asia Minor and other parts of the world.

Beautifully made, elegant as can be. A little bit of abalone inlay touches off the eyes, which are altogether Northwest Coast eyes. I think it's early 19th century, from the North, exactly where I don't know.

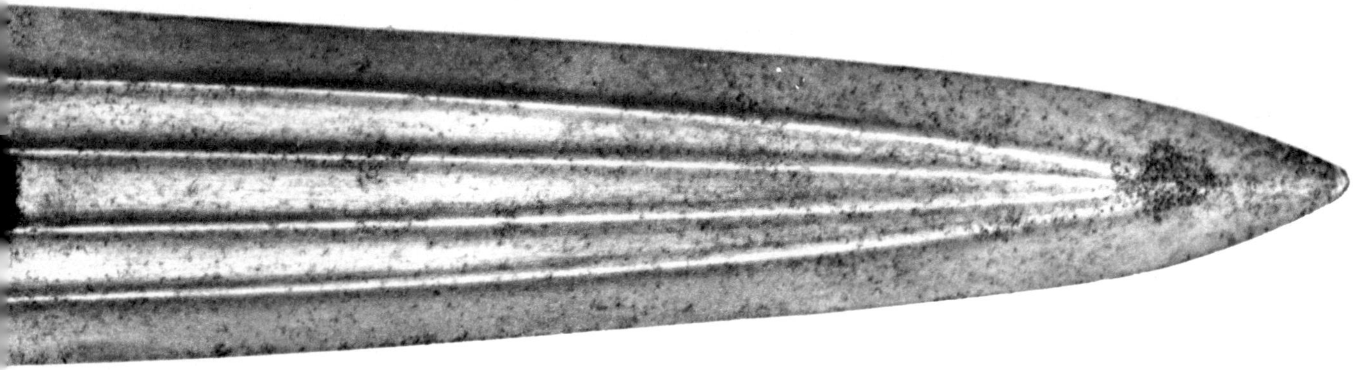

REID: The upper blade or pommel or whatever has been badly worn. It's hard to tell how excellent the workmanship was originally, but it seems to have been nicely made. Anybody who could execute the rest of it in such style obviously wouldn't fall down on the other part.

The copper engraving is beautifully done, perhaps even better on the backside than the front. Certainly it loses nothing by the patina and oxidized coloration accumulated through the years. It's nice—a good thing—a fine piece of weaponry.

REID: Tlingit dagger, beaver hilt, fluted blade, abalone inlay. He made settings for the abalone and riveted them in some way. I guess he sweated them in. If you heat steel up enough, it will weld—forge. The holes go all the way through, so the abalone shows through the back.

HOLM: Why was the abalone brought flush with the surface, or is that just a thin layer of metal?

REID: A thin layer of metal. I don't have the foggiest notion how they made these things. Until you make one . . .

HOLM: . . . one of these days I'm going to find out. I've got a forge and I've been collecting blacksmith tools with this in mind. Of course, all I'll know when I've made one is how I made it. That's not going to tell me how this one was made.

9

I'd doubt it was Indian work, except for the fact that no 19th-century European copyist, that I know of, could have made this dagger and come off with the shapes right, the way they are.

REID: Russian literature says the Tlingits became very good metalworkers.

HOLM: John Dunn said that the Haida in the 1830s made 18-inch, beautifully fluted daggers out of flat files, as highly finished as if turned out by a first-rate maker's hands in London.[32] I'm sure they did. It wouldn't be too hard to carve this metal with the same technique used in engraving silver.

REID: If you heated it up, you could forge . . .

HOLM: . . . forge most of it, then finish it with the engraving tool. Forging is a pretty fancy thing to do. The fluting was harder than the engraving because of its length and regularity. You can work out the little details of the hilt, but to make that blade so regular and straight would be most difficult. Of course, there's a lot of grinding on it afterwards, after the forging, just to finish the surface. That would make it more regular. Some have a very elaborate business where the fluting converges and ends up in a single division of planes. That seems to me a tough thing to do.

There's an interesting dagger still in Indian hands in Chilkat country. It has ridges on both sides of the blade, which is more complicated. A round pommel, with petal-like decorations on the edge has a face on each side. The eyes, I think, are drilled right through. The mouth is drilled through in a series of holes, as I remember it. The eyebrows and other features of the modeled face are applied. I think they're just pieces of iron riveted on both sides and modeled.

That dagger, according to family tradition, is supposed to have been made in prehistoric times by a woman who hammered it out of a meteor on a stone anvil. That's the family tradition. The dagger is big. Its blade is very wide, with two widely spaced ridges on each side. It tapers rapidly, then parallels off with a little point at the end. I suppose it could have been made from a meteor, but most were made from files.

They were generally used in war. Most have a loop like this, wrapped around the hand or thumb and twisted around the wrist, so it could be held without dropping.

They often show evidence of what, in forging, blacksmiths call "cold shut." When iron layers aren't properly welded, the metal is folded over and shaped. Most iron daggers, that I've seen, show evidence of that on their backs or flattened surfaces. Might be a clue as to how they were made.

John Witthoft argues that prehistoric copper daggers, cut with stone saws, were the prototype for these steel daggers.[33] The idea of cutting a dagger blade out of a big copper nugget sounds likely. Copper is soft. In the old days this would have been a more likely way to do it than trying to hammer out an odd-shaped nugget with available tools, especially since that was the way they cut jade and other stones for adze blades. It would be a natural extension of that technique.

But these steel daggers weren't made that way. They were hammered out of bars or files. Some still have the remains of file teeth.

Actually, a lot of daggers were made by Europeans—there's plenty of evidence for that. Old journals tell of ships' armorers making swords and daggers. Japanese were imported to make steel adze blades, daggers, spearpoints. John Jewett at Nootka was a skilled armorer who made harpoon points and all sorts of things.

But I believe these daggers were made by Indians—just how, I don't know. What convinces me more than anything else are the details on daggers like this one. All the copies I've seen by craftsmen in the old days, who didn't understand the structure of this art, missed the boat. This one doesn't. So, even though it seems incredible—well, not completely incredible—but even though it's hard to attribute such advanced ironworking to people with limited experience and tools, I think they are of Indian manufacture.

The leather cap is for the beaver. Double daggers often have that. There should also be a plug inside the bottom of the sheath, with a little hole in it for the dagger point. Fine, twisted sinew was wrapped tightly around that part of the sheath, holding the plug in place. I've seen some with metal ends, others with the sheath sewn closed and cloth wadded in the bottom.

Most of these daggers have concave backs and most are thin in cross section, except where the ribs of the fluting come. The ribs strengthen the dagger without adding weight. And the flutes are so elegant! I think the idea of the channel being a blood gutter is an old wives' tale. It's functional only in making the blade light, strong and elegant.

10

HOLM: Dagger with iron or steel blade, sheep-horn pommel, its handle wrapped with what looks like rawhide, a bit of human hair attached, and abalone inlay in the eyes of the creature represented on the handle. Looks very Tlingit.

A natural curve in the horn handle has been left so the animal head curves around it. The head is thin, really flat-to-relief carving, but works well. It's old.

REID: It's nicely done. The artist worked with material at hand. I doubt if he considered it more than a utilitarian weapon. It doesn't come across to me as anything great. It's a nice piece—worth having; it makes a good "part" of a collection.

11

HOLM: Very fine dagger. Wooden pommel in the form of a bear's head, its eyes inlaid with abalone. Handle wrapped with hide. Ivory guard. The sheath is a beautiful example of one of my favorite kinds of beadwork—the Tahltan style—one of the most elegant beadwork styles in North America. The sheath beautifully combines trade cloth, beads, and trade copper. That's fairly typical.

I've a feeling the blade is a piece of a sword. I know quite a few with this partially double edge or false edge. They appear to be made from old naval cutlasses or sword bayonets. Some may have been made out of iron stock in imitation of these forms. So, I don't know for sure what this may be.

If it isn't Tlingit, it's probably Tahltan. Some daggers Emmons illustrates in his monograph on the Tahltan Indians were really Tlingit daggers or daggers used by the Tahltan but made by other Northwest Coast tribes.[34] It's hard to say what this dagger is. The carving is on the borderline of the normal Tlingit style. It could be from their neighbors up the river. It's an elegant piece.

The pommel is walnut, probably a piece of gunstock. A perfect example in Emmons's work on Tahltan pipes has enough gunstock left to be positively identified.[35] I know of one gunstock cut halfway off, ready to make something out of it. Several of them have remains of the butt-plate tang recess. One or two have the butt plate still on. Plenty of pipes are made of walnut of a size that could have come out of a musket stock. Lots of pipe bowls are from musket barrels. The chances of a piece of walnut no thicker than a musket stock being anything but a musket stock are pretty thin. There were plenty of muskets around, and they wore out. The Tlingit and Tahltan had them over a long period. I doubt that they threw walnut away.

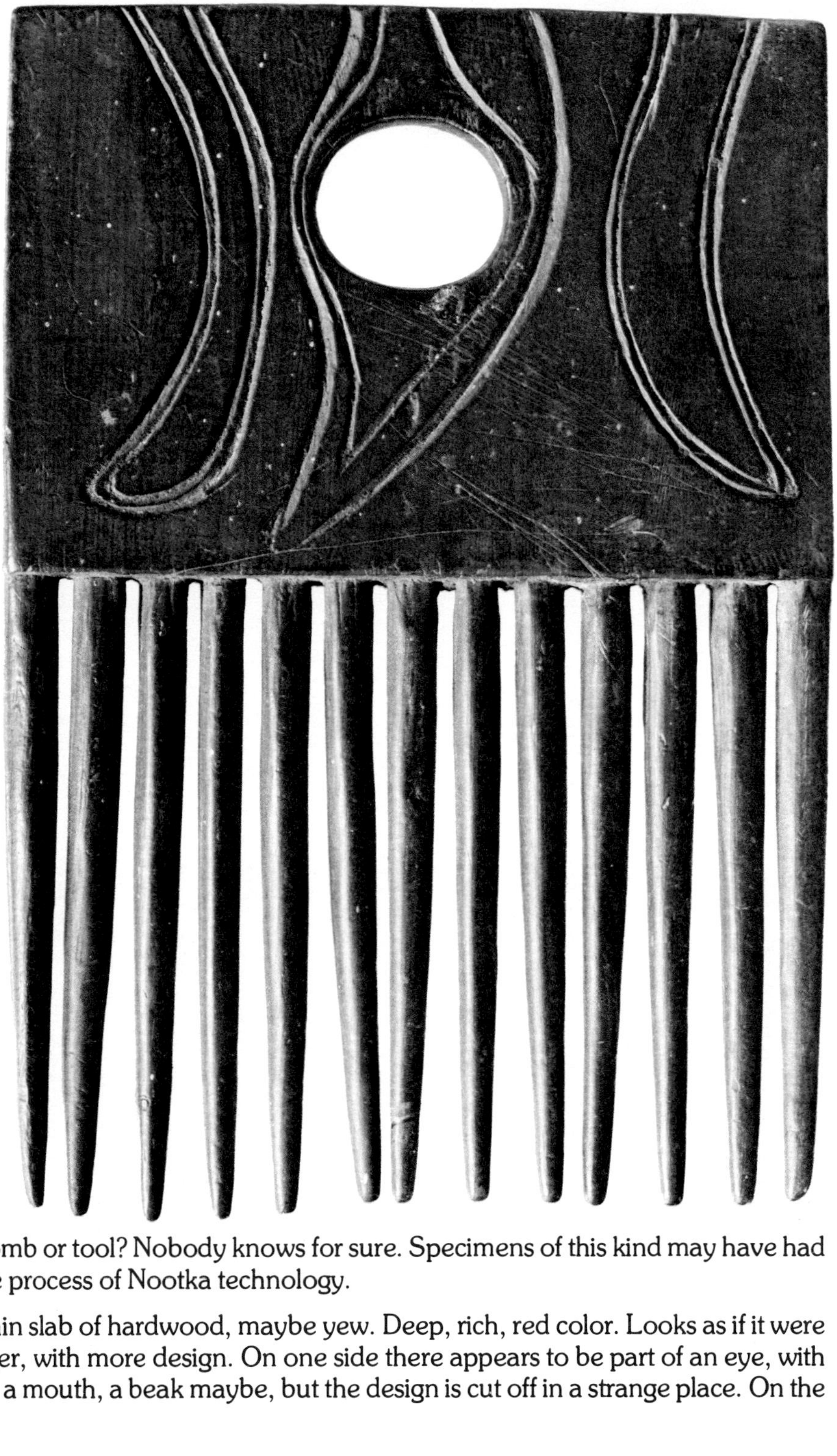

12

HOLM: Hair comb or tool? Nobody knows for sure. Specimens of this kind may have had to do with some process of Nootka technology.

It's made of a thin slab of hardwood, maybe yew. Deep, rich, red color. Looks as if it were once much larger, with more design. On one side there appears to be part of an eye, with something else, a mouth, a beak maybe, but the design is cut off in a strange place. On the

opposite side it has what appear to be two stick-like arms coming down and ending in fingers, as if representing a human torso. The whole top is missing, cut off cleanly a long time ago. I don't know how to explain that, but what remains is strong. The hole through the middle is the iris of the eye on one side. I don't know whether it's a huge navel or stomach or torso on the other side. The hole combines these two designs.

REID: My subjective view about this Salish spindle whorl is that, as artists, the Salish were nuts. They didn't seem to be able to do anything except make blankets, apparently funny-looking houseposts, great Shwaikhwey masks and spindle whorls.

Of all the great spindle whorls I've seen, this is the best. I suppose it's a female flanked by two birds. I assume these are joint marks on the wings, made of human faces—a Northern characteristic, except that it certainly isn't any Northern form. There's a creature looking vaguely fish-like. Or it may just be viscera in the abdomen of the woman and may have some significance there. Perhaps it's the fetus—I hesitate to guess. A beautiful thing. Makes you wonder why the Salish didn't do more things like that.

HOLM: They did do quite a few things like this, although numerically far fewer than Northern artists. I think this has something to do with their whole way of life.

Some interesting things are happening here. All three mouths are pierced right through. There're also two little holes in the ears, but I'm not sure they're original. Maybe they were made to hang the spindle whorl up.

13

You mentioned faces in the birds' wings. I don't read these as wings. I think each is the body of a bird. You spoke of this as a Northern characteristic, but we might see it another way. I see Georgia Strait Salish art as related to other southern coastal arts—Nootka art, things from the Columbia River, etc. I see them all as a development, an extension, of a widespread, basic art expression which ultimately lay behind both this art and Northern art. This art may actually be closer—this is really conjecture, there're lots of missing links—but this may be closer to that earlier, widespread tradition.

The interesting thing to me, after having studied how the Northern formline system works on two-dimensional art, is to become suddenly aware that these things also have basic formline-like characteristics. Some show this more clearly than others. Not superficial similarities and not watered-down Northern characteristics—which is the way a lot of people have seen this, as being a backwoods imitation of Northern formline work—not that at all, but the same basic concept of representation and the same use of line and form widely used in the Northwest.

When you begin to read the patterns on the pommels of Nootka whalebone clubs or Shwaikhwey masks or this spindle whorl in terms of the doughnut-hole relationship—where you ignore holes and concentrate on spaces between holes, which is the basis of Northern formline art—then you find they all work like formline designs.

In pieces from the Columbia River and in certain Nootka things, we see little rows of triangles interlocking with other rows of triangles. If we can quit looking at the triangles and look at the spaces between, we find neat little wavy lines and zigzags. With

Shwaikhwey masks, if—instead of seeing bunches of little, long triangles below the central face, along the sides and at the top—we look at the spaces between the triangles, suddenly the whole bird hops right out at us with tail feathers, wing feathers, and feet, all connected to the central nose.

The same thing is happening here. Because the long triangles are larger in scale, compared to the positive forms between them, they're more difficult to see. But actually all these crescent and T-shaped things seem to be reliefs, slots between feathers. They read clearly that way. There's no problem on this piece, compared with some others. This really isn't far from the Northern system—just another direction that must have been taken. This little foot of the bird—you could carry that out and have a nice little formline foot. This leg with the relief and this conjectural thing in the abdomen of the human figure—I'm not sure I see it as female—are almost straight formline seen that way.

Another thing going on, not found in the North, is the repetition of both a series of little reliefs and a series of parallel lines. So we end up with a more geometric handling of the whole space, but also the kind of naturalism seen in some of the Northern things. A higher percentage of Salish figures have naturalistic proportions—straightforward representation, rather than the stylization more noticeable in the North.

This is a great combination of this very patterned, very geometrical handling of the birds and the naturalistic figure. And we have this thing which repeats the bird forms and whatever this central motif is meant to be—to me it's really successful. I share your feeling that this is certainly among the greatest known spindle whorls. There're some nice ones and the nice ones look like this. But they can't be seen in the same way as Northern pieces. They're different. I think it's wrong to compare Salish pieces with Northern pieces, except to see how they're related.

Round faces like this and bodies in unlikely places are typical of the Salish. I think they're part of the same tradition of extraneous faces we've been seeing all day. I don't know how to explain it.

Another thing the Salish often did, and this artist did beautifully, was to incorporate the spindle hole into the design so well that the guy is holding the shaft—which is just neat! Or the woman, if it's a woman.

REID: I suppose you're right. The bird wings are these thin things on the sides here, while this would be the tail.

HOLM: And here are the feet coming in from the body. Some of these Salish spindle whorls have great punning going on—parts coming together to form extra faces, which aren't really parts of a face at all—just arranged in such a way they make a face. I'm sure this artist had that in mind. This also occurs in Salish horn rattles. The one in the "Far North" show was full of great punning.[36]

Very often one creature merges with another in a very surprising way—you don't see it here, at least I haven't seen it—but you get some suggestion of it. This whole body, with arms coming out here, can be read that way and maybe that's an example. It often can't be justified when you look closely. You first say, "Oh, that's a double face!" and then, when you look closely, you see it really isn't, but the impression is that way.

That's what we have here with the bird's feet coming into the lower part of the body. It also can be read as arms coming out of an extra little figure. You can say the claws are in the wrong place for that to happen, but they also look like little shoulders. I don't know whether to make anything out of that, but it happens so often in the carving of this region, I think it's part of the play going on there.

REID: I'd like to know what that's all about—in the center, in the womb—in the womb of the man.

HOLM: If it is. Unfortunately, that carver wasn't too anatomy-minded. He didn't give us many clues. Some Salish figures are pretty specific. Gender is generally clear.

REID: This one is interesting because there's no head—just features.

HOLM: That's what happens. These two parts overlap and merge. That's one of the exciting things about it—it's illogical, like some of the other things we've been looking at. You think you see something—then you don't.

REID: And these are mythical birds, you think?

HOLM: I don't know. Probably. Some have features like birds in nature, but I think they're mythical. One problem with Salish art is that so much symbolism is personal, concerned with individual guardian spirits and private experiences with supernatural powers, unrelated to tribal mythology. This makes it almost impossible to read or decipher design meanings. But someone really familiar with the mythology of the Georgia Strait people could come up with some pretty good guesses. But they would only be that—just educated guesses.

I liked this spindle whorl real well when I first saw it. I like it better now—after I've had a chance to look at it and really think it through.

The concave side is where the wool goes—when it's on the spindle. In the old days, the spinner held the spindle in both hands and faced the carving. Nowadays, Salish spinners use a shorter spindle held with one hand and don't face the spindle. Some modern spindles have simple, geometric stars, but I've never seen one with elaborate decoration.

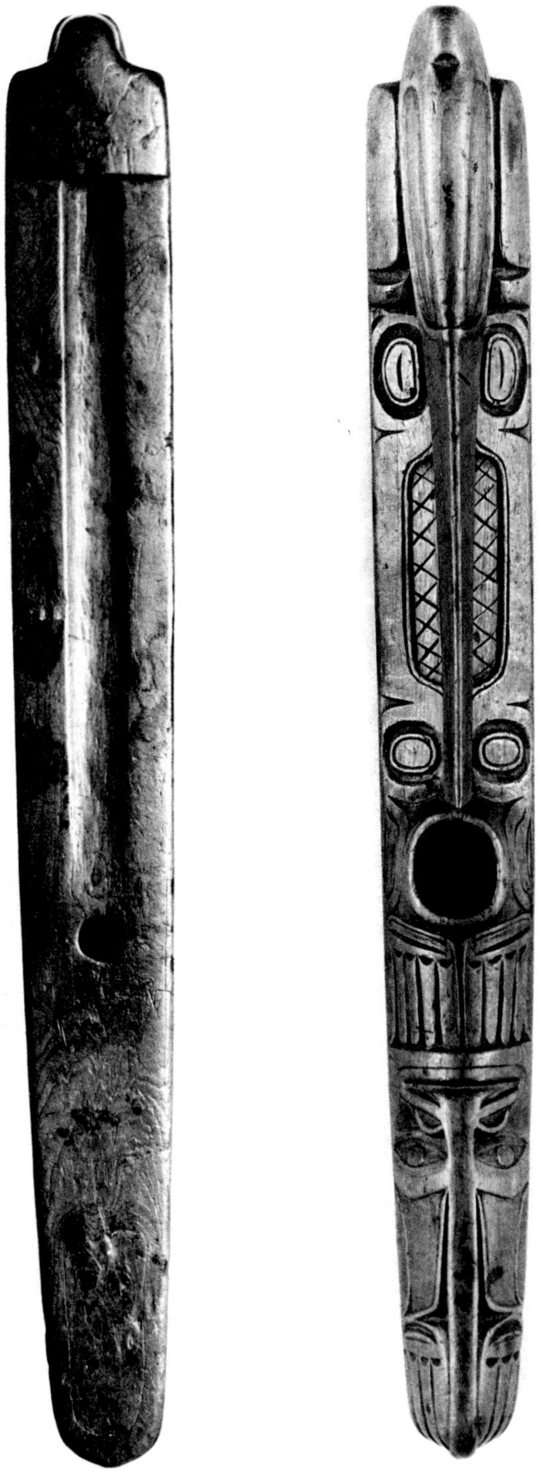

14

REID: I don't know a damn thing about spear-throwers—where this one comes from or anything else. What gets through to me on this one is the incredible imagination of its creator.

Working strictly within convention, he's done some remarkable things. For instance, under the chin of a face—which is the focus of the upper portion—he's carved hands different from anyone else's concept of hands. Yet they work perfectly, not only as hands, but as a fringe enhancing the face. I won't attempt to explain the various other parts; they may or may not belong to a bird's head. This is a functional object which, through the genius of the artist, far transcends its function. It retains its function, but becomes something else. Parts of it are fun. The fingerhold is a mouth with eyes. It's a satisfactory thing on many levels. Its function of throwing a spear is just a beginning. From then on it's a possession to provide hours, days, a lifetime of amusement and satisfaction.

HOLM: It must have provided hours of satisfaction because it's really well worn. The whole surface is polished and rounded with handling. It wouldn't be that way if it had stayed in the sea hunter's tackle box all of the time.

This little fellow with the face and strange hands is fun. Instead of coming out and down, as you might expect, his tongue turns up and runs the whole length of his head and reaches his hind legs, which sprout out of his head, or maybe they are the feet of this long bird that starts at the other end. We could see it in many ways.

My guess is that it comes from the westernmost Tlingit. Maybe even outside the true Tlingit area, as far as Prince William Sound, getting over to the Chugach country where Aleut and Northwest Coast traditions overlap. Spear-throwers aren't common on the true Northwest Coast. I know of only three or four. All have strange things in them which, to me, suggest the fringes of the basic culture area. The sculpture of the little man's head is Tlingit, yet several strange things suggest pieces from that borderline area where basic Northwest Coast patterns and sculpture persist, but odd innovations occur. I'm sure it's Tlingit or, if not Tlingit, from the adjacent Eskimo area.

Its color is incredible. You don't get that in a short time.

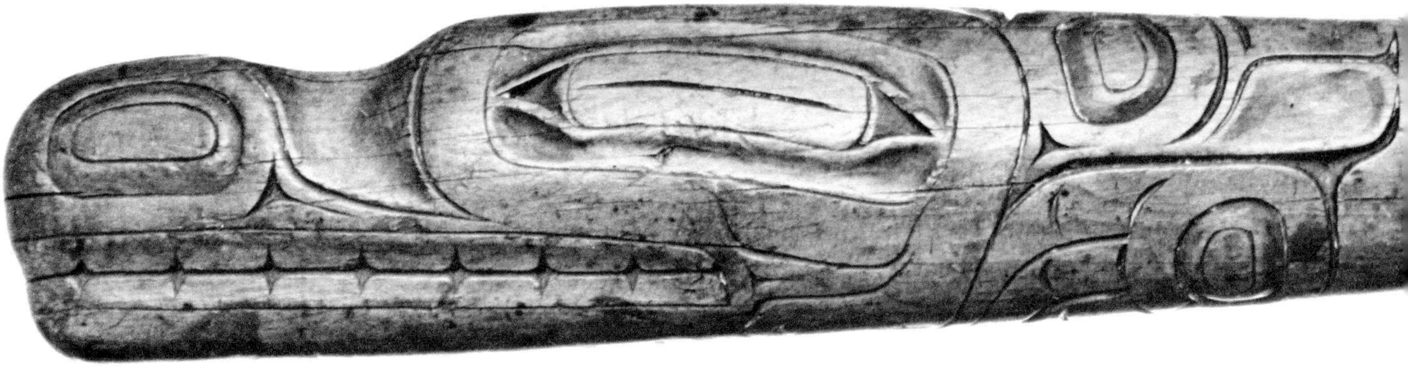

15

REID: What kind of beast do you think this is?

HOLM: I don't know. It looks like some kind of quadruped. Might be a sea lion. That would be my first choice. That would be as good a choice as I could make. All the parts are there.

REID: In any case, it's a fish or seal club. You could interpret this as a spout hole and make the creature into a sea monster with whale characteristics.

HOLM: You could do that, but I would not.

REID: In any case, that's not the important thing. This club conforms to all our criteria of what makes the Northern style of Northwest Coast art what it is. It has heavy formlines and squared-off, flattened ovoids here and there. As a whole, it works throughout. You could spend a lot of time looking at it. It has things going on. Might be visual puns. This could be a bird's head between the eye forms. These are obviously vertebrae. Whether an analysis of the anatomy adds much to the appreciation of the piece is doubtful, but, as seal clubs go, this is one of the better examples.

HOLM: I agree with everything you said. It's meant to do a job. It's a functional object. It has the weight and balance needed for a seal club. The animal design worked into that space and overlaid on that shape is organized exactly like a design on a box or some other flat-painting object. Yet it looks like it was meant to be here and gives the club a remarkable sculptural quality. It's certainly a successful adaptation of that kind of design to another specific and peculiarly shaped object.

REID: To devote such care to an object designed for brutal but necessary tasks, perhaps shows some respect for the animal whose death it's required to bring about.

HOLM: That's acceptable to me. You'd do it, I'd do it—we'd embellish any tool we made, first for satisfaction in doing so, then to enjoy a beautiful instrument, handle it, have it beside us. I'd rather have this beside me in a canoe than a lump of wood.

And there must have been this other feeling—respect shown to the creature you are using it on.

HOLM: Model of an archaic-type Northern canoe which apparently doesn't exist today except in models, and dishes, and memories, and in drawings by Europeans who first came to this coast. Sometimes they misrepresented these canoes in one way or another, but we have a good idea as to their form.

This is a fine model—quite large—with a long, flat fin at each end. The fin that looks like the stern is the bow, and the one that looks like the bow is the stern. The gunwales are peculiar—they go along at a normal level and then turn up sharply, just at the beginning of that fin. That's 100% characteristic of this type of canoe. It has the little groove along the gunwales on the inside, just like some of the bowls and ladles here.

66

It has a fine shape as a whole, though that shape is much distorted from an actual canoe. The proportion of the fin length to the total length is exaggerated, and the proportions of this model aren't true of the full-sized canoe. The model is shorter and wider. But this is characteristic of models.

The end paintings are very nice, with red primary formlines and a perfect adherence to rules. Some dark green paint in the tertiary areas. Fine craftsmanship in the painting, nice layout—an altogether successful expression. The design is so abstract, pushed so far, I don't think it's possible to identify the creatures represented. But the design successfully fills the space and is well done. The lines are very regular. The spacing of parts is carefully planned. Even the inner ovoids in the eyes and joints have little tertiary lines running around them; these are nonconcentric—there's greater space at the bottom than at the top, which is characteristic of the better examples. A little geometric painting on the inside bottom is obscure—a circle with straight lines—and mysterious to me, but that kind of thing happens on the sides of boxes and a few other odd places in this art.

REID: These canoes must have been remarkably unfunctional in a cross wind . . .

HOLM: . . . I think so. Several people, including myself, want to make one someday—not a very big one—just to find out what they can do. They don't seem very practical. They went out of use in the last century. None exist as far as I know.

REID: But, as ceremonial boats, they would have been fine . . .

HOLM: . . . except the drawings show whole flotillas of them—little ones, big ones—it's just a crazy thing. I can't imagine anybody who used canoes making one of these by choice. I'd like to try one out to see what it's like. They're dandy to paint on.

16

REID: Of the painted objects here, this is one of the best. I'm particularly impressed—perhaps because I'm not skillful at it—by the beautiful, thin, even, outlining lines, which have all the appearance of being made by a man taking a brush and making a great, sweeping curve. But the curve is such a shape that it would be impossible to do that. It would have to be done carefully, detail by detail, and yet it gives the impression of effortless ease.

HOLM: The spacing illustrates that very well—consistent throughout. The little outlining ovoids are spaced close on one side and far apart on the opposite side. That's part of the whole nonconcentric aspect of this art. It's amazing they could do it. I'm always overwhelmed by those lines in fine paintings. It's a beautiful thing.

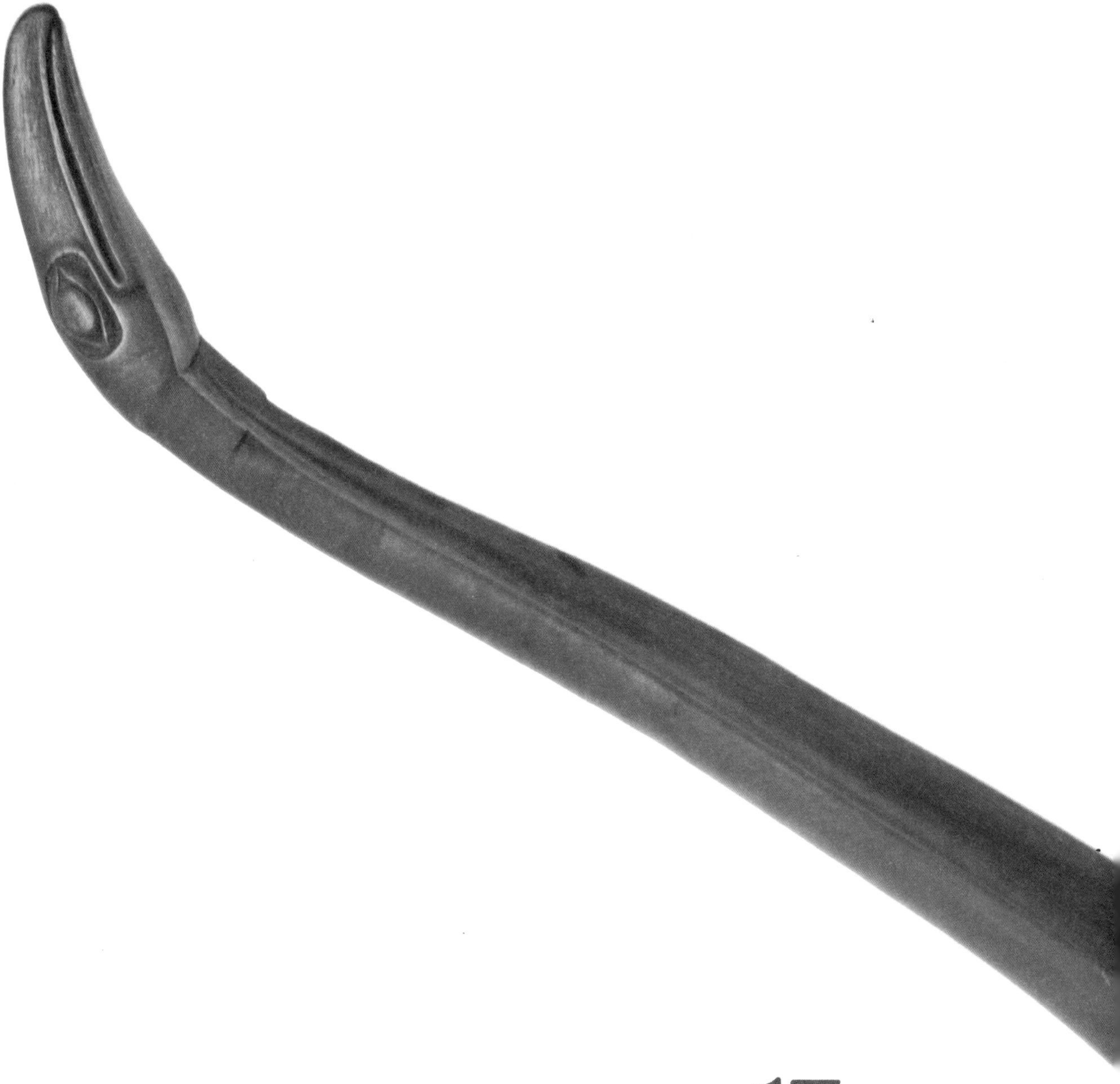

17

REID: Spoon similar to #18 in form and in the fact that the handle terminates in a bird's head, but without carving on the back of the handle. Everything we said about the construction of #18 applies to this one, especially as to beauty of form, which is perhaps even more apparent here, being unadorned. It doesn't have a lip or rim as does #19. It's simply a big ladle.

HOLM: The lip is there, but it's worn and pretty smooth. It's not as sharply defined as with #19.

REID: It's almost impossible to see now.

HOLM: Over on this side you can see it a little better.

REID: And it's quite apparent on the handle. I don't think one can overemphasize how beautiful this material is when it gets this transparent quality—elegant, deep, honey color. When spoons are made as well as this and have this nice symmetrical form, they're just beautiful objects.

HOLM: The carving on the bird's head isn't as well handled as on #18. But, all in all, the combination of material, color, and surface, works well.

Sheep horn has a fiber that other materials don't have in quite the same way. As you get to the handle, you get a fibrous effect—little bars—characteristic of sheep horn, adding to the richness of it. These show on #18 very well.

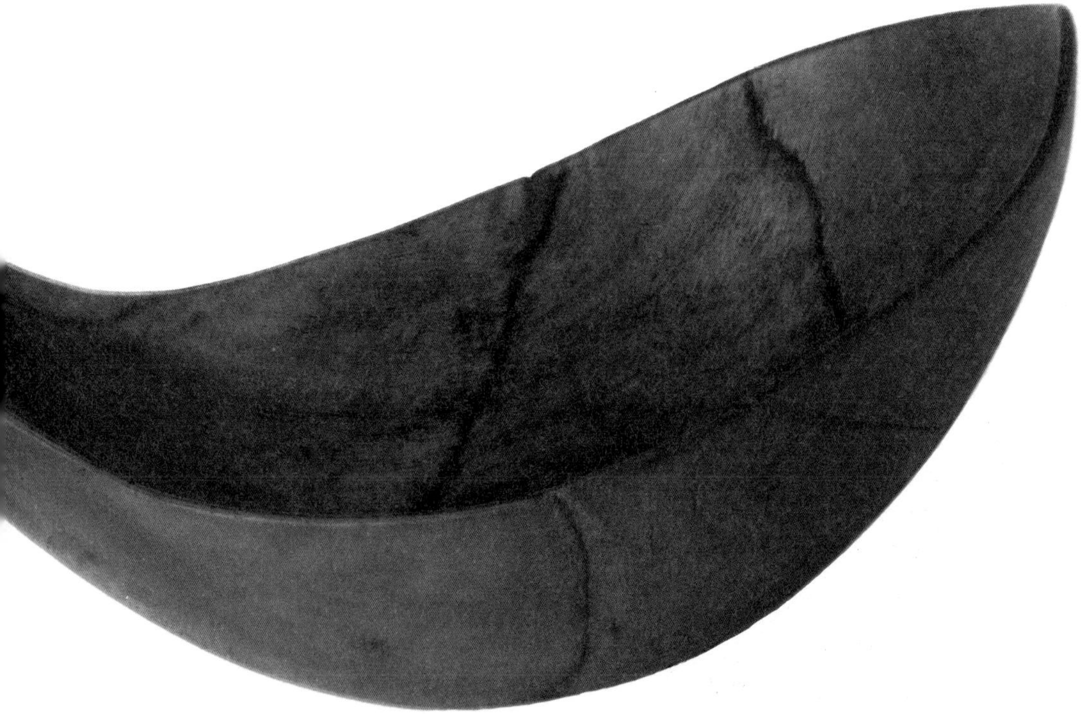

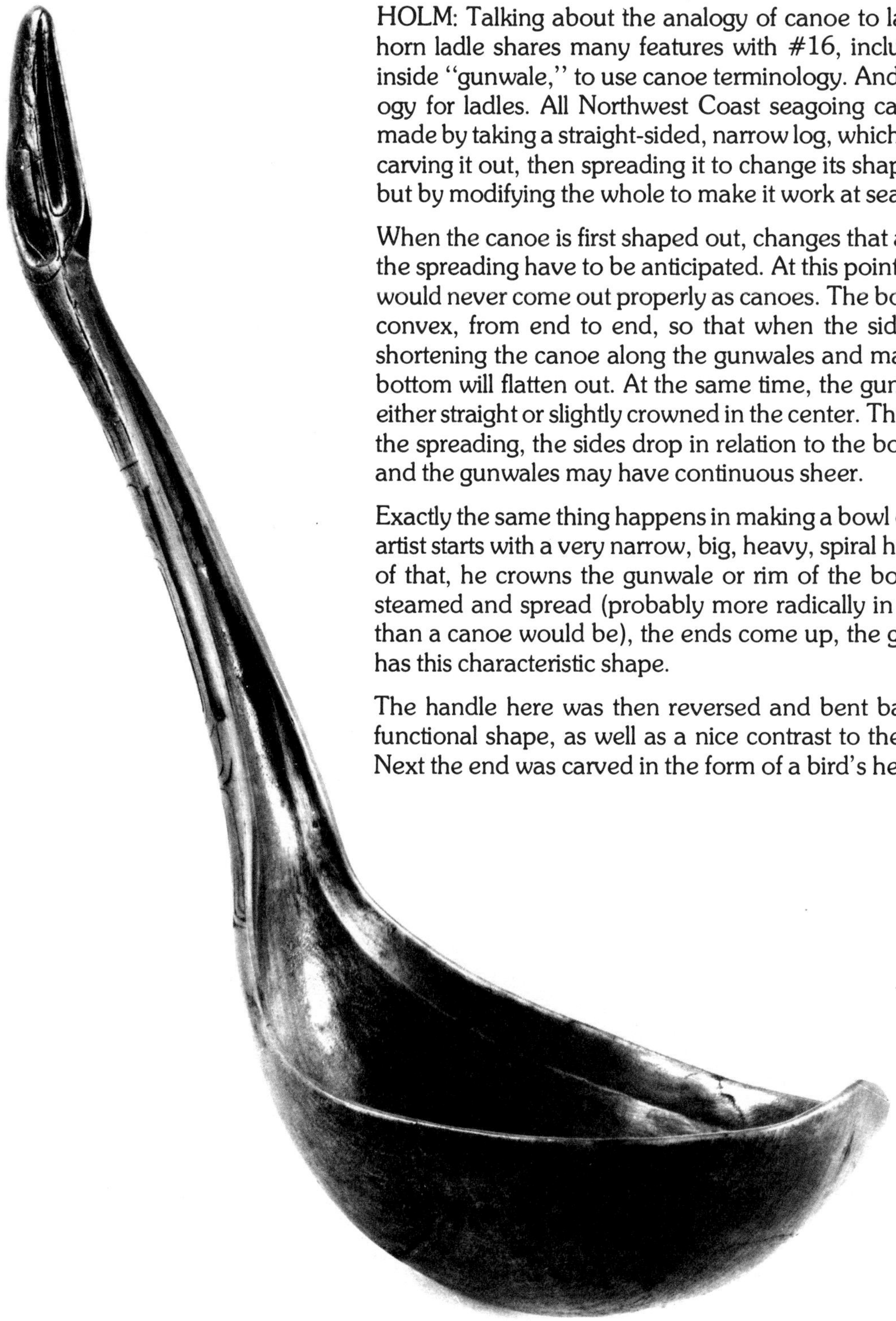

HOLM: Talking about the analogy of canoe to ladle construction, this sheephorn ladle shares many features with #16, including this little rim under the inside "gunwale," to use canoe terminology. And that's a reasonable terminology for ladles. All Northwest Coast seagoing canoes, to my knowledge, are made by taking a straight-sided, narrow log, which isn't a very seaworthy shape, carving it out, then spreading it to change its shape, not merely by widening it, but by modifying the whole to make it work at sea.

When the canoe is first shaped out, changes that are going to take place during the spreading have to be anticipated. At this point certain shapes look as if they would never come out properly as canoes. The bottom has to be carved slightly convex, from end to end, so that when the sides are spread (consequently shortening the canoe along the gunwales and making the ends come up), the bottom will flatten out. At the same time, the gunwales themselves have to be either straight or slightly crowned in the center. Thus, when the ends come up in the spreading, the sides drop in relation to the bottom. This crown is removed and the gunwales may have continuous sheer.

Exactly the same thing happens in making a bowl or ladle from sheep horn. The artist starts with a very narrow, big, heavy, spiral horn. In chopping the ladle out of that, he crowns the gunwale or rim of the bowl, so that when the horn is steamed and spread (probably more radically in relation to the original width than a canoe would be), the ends come up, the gunwales drop and the carver has this characteristic shape.

The handle here was then reversed and bent backwards slightly, to give it a functional shape, as well as a nice contrast to the opposite curve of the bowl. Next the end was carved in the form of a bird's head, perhaps a raven, in a flat,

18

two-dimensional organization. Then the bird's body was compressed and conventionalized to fit neatly into the back of the handle. It was given long wings which also have meaning as a head-like form, an ovoid joint at the end of the tail feathers, and little feet, neatly expressed with a few lines, creating formline-like figures.

It's a fine representation of a bird in a conventionalized way, fitted into an unlikely space—a good illustration of the ability of these Northern artists to fit any kind of animal shape into whatever space they're dealing with.

REID: The genius of Northwest Coast design is that it adapts to any form. It was conceived of as decorative art, not in our sense of "decorative arts," but to express a symbol while conforming to the shape decorated.

It's a beautiful ladle—one of the great pieces that enhanced the enjoyment of feasts where it was used.

HOLM: The artist was concerned with representing some being or crest figure, and at the same time fitting it into a particular space. He must have been more interested in designing than in representing. I think aesthetics guided him. Otherwise I can't believe he would have done something like this.

REID: The two go together. Northwest Coast art can't exist without symbolism. I don't think you can take the basic structural forms, without the animal or mythical forms, and create a viable design. People have tried, but it doesn't happen, no matter how beautifully done. The focus is lost and I think focus is what it's all about, or at least a lot of it.

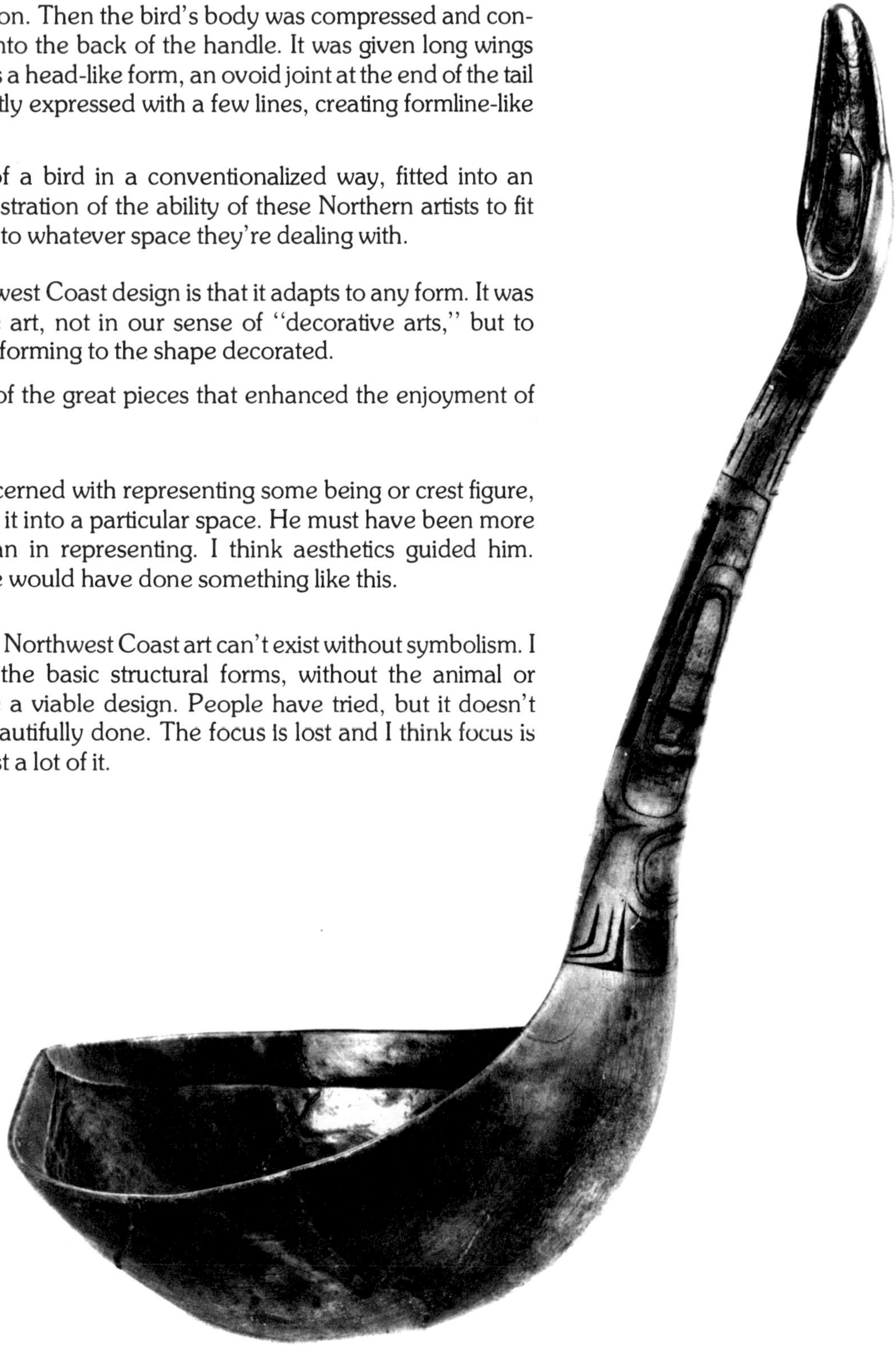

19

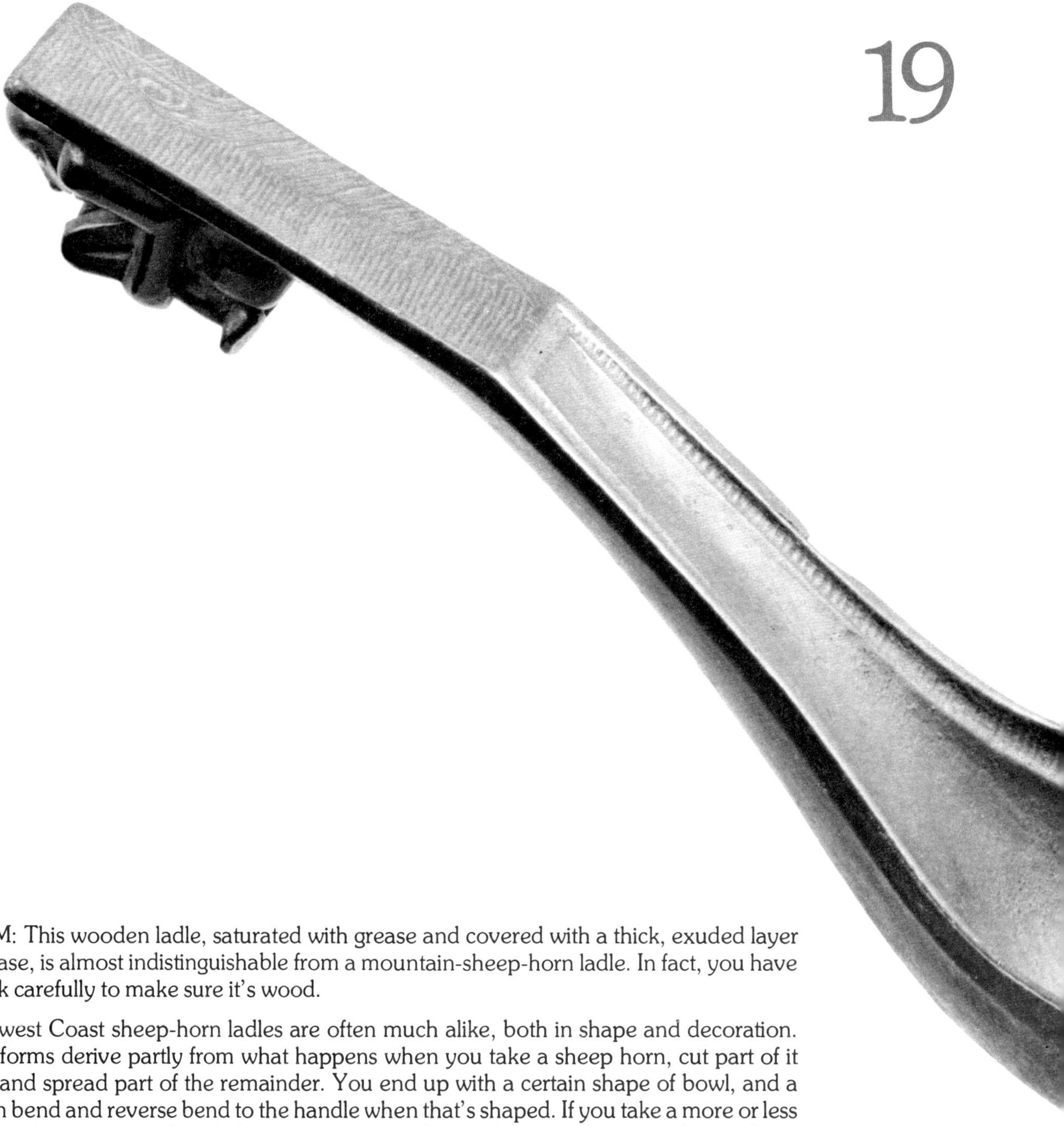

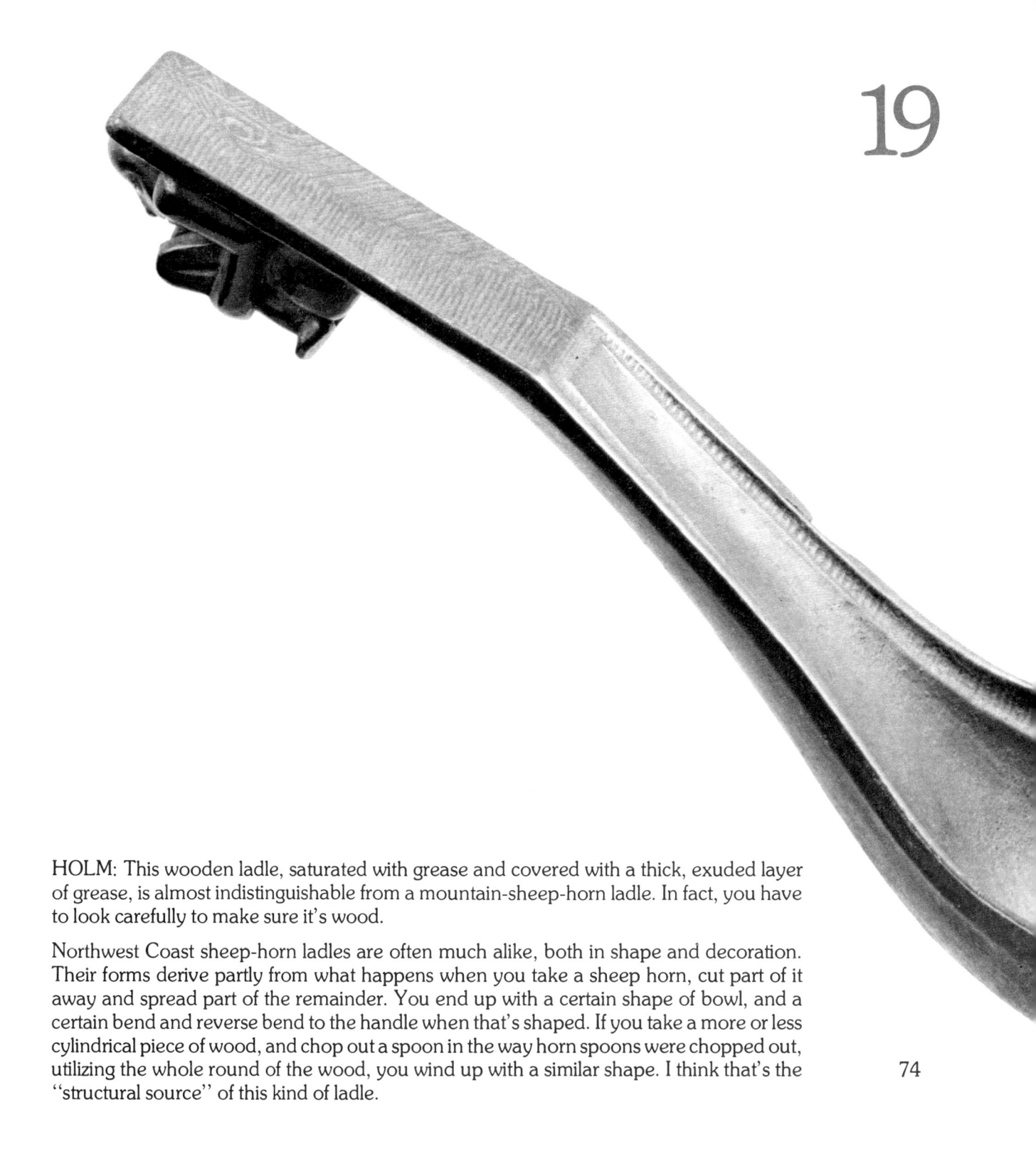

HOLM: This wooden ladle, saturated with grease and covered with a thick, exuded layer of grease, is almost indistinguishable from a mountain-sheep-horn ladle. In fact, you have to look carefully to make sure it's wood.

Northwest Coast sheep-horn ladles are often much alike, both in shape and decoration. Their forms derive partly from what happens when you take a sheep horn, cut part of it away and spread part of the remainder. You end up with a certain shape of bowl, and a certain bend and reverse bend to the handle when that's shaped. If you take a more or less cylindrical piece of wood, and chop out a spoon in the way horn spoons were chopped out, utilizing the whole round of the wood, you wind up with a similar shape. I think that's the ''structural source'' of this kind of ladle.

Function is another influence. Ladles were used, handled, balanced. I'm intrigued why people made things in the shapes they did when all sorts of other possibilities were open. Material was a great influence. Northwest Coast artists had the skill to alter materials in many ways, but generally followed the dictates of the material, modifying it just enough to do the job. That may contradict what we said earlier about the first pipe, but I feel it generally applied, especially in functional things like spoons and tools. This ladle illustrates that very well.

It's got a fine little man, with knees drawn up, who looks as if he were hiding under the handle. And it has a beautifully fluted rim on the inside with a little textural decoration on it. That rim is one of those features that seem so standard, seen over and over. I think there's an ancient prototype for that rim. Maybe someday I'll find it.

REID: Want a little guess as to that ancient prototype?

HOLM: I have some guesses—go ahead and say what you think.

REID: This guess stems from Buckminster Fuller's theory that all technology comes from the sea—that to build something on land, you just put enough material together and it holds up. But to build something to go to sea, you must use technology—it has to work and you have to do the most with the least. I think a great deal of Northwest Coast form, including that of these bowls and ladles—comes from the canoe form. You could get along without anything else on the coast except the canoe. It had to come first and it had to work. This rim occurs in canoes.

HOLM: Right. Many bowls are really canoes. They have all the features of big canoes and have been similarly compressed and widened in form. And they have this same rim.

But, beyond that, I think this rim is a remnant of birchbark construction or, in the case of a canoe, perhaps framing. I've been trying to find a prototype for that little groove running under the gunwales of big Northern canoes. I haven't found the exact one, but some birchbark bowls exactly reproduce these grooves. The problem is that there are no birchbark ladles, to my knowledge at least. But there are birchbark bowls that resemble wooden bowls with this feature. Yet the ladles often look like bowls with handles. They often have similar decorations, too.

This kind of thing intrigues me. Why did people choose to do certain things and then do them over and over? They became so important to a particular kind of object they were seldom let go, though they had no useful function. In fact, that little rim might have reduced efficiency slightly. Yet rims are so frequently seen, and have become so traditionally part of that form, they have to be there.

It's a super feature. It makes that ladle. It adds elegance you could hardly get any other way. But it has no use.

REID: One characteristic of Northwest Coast art is paradoxical: things were very functional, yet function was never permitted to interfere with aesthetics.

HOLM: Perhaps my narrow use of the word "functional" is the problem. I see the aesthetic aspect of this ladle as functional.

REID: This ladle is not too different from a canoe. Parts of the canoe are missing—it has no skeg on the front. But it has this little man crouched up there like a figurehead. The flat handle, which isn't functional, is the flat bow on the canoe. Aside from balance, which would prevent it from floating, it could be a toy canoe as easily as a bowl.

There were social pressures, sexuality, all sorts of inner drives that made this art necessary. But what made it possible was that its makers had to go to sea. The sea produced the aesthetic because the canoe not only had to be functional, it had to be beautiful to be.

HOLM: Its beauty derives from its function.

REID: Right. If it looks good, it's good. That's a primary rule of almost all technology, as true to our society as to any other.

HOLM: Ladle of wood. It's hard to determine the material at first glance, but if you look closely, you see the growth rings and grain of the wood.

REID: The main attraction is the patina, which gives the ladle almost the quality of horn. Its overall form is relatively pleasing. I prefer ladles with bowls tapering down a little more. This one rounds off at the end. It might have been different once. Perhaps it broke off when the artist was making it, or he may have decided to make it that way. But it hasn't got quite that canoe-like element of some of the other ladles here. This handle has a strange structure: the hollowness of the bowl extends right up the handle to the head, so that the handle is almost hollow. That has nothing to do with any function I can perceive. But perhaps he just carried out the adaptation of the canoe shape to the spoon.

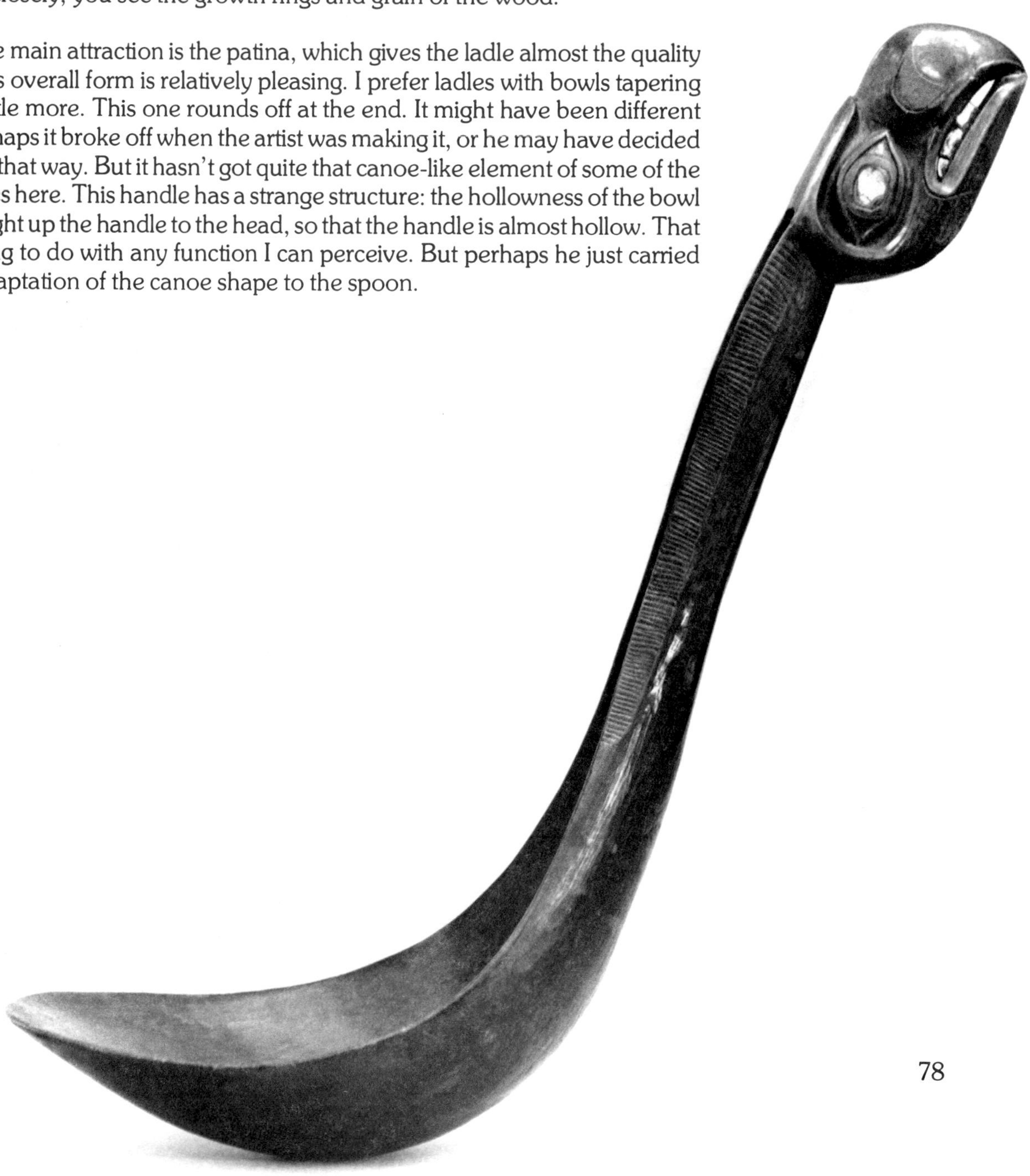

78

20

The eagle head on the end is well brought out and has abalone inlays for the eyes and teeth. Strange how a person who could do good carving on the head would get so sloppy with the striations on the handle. Why didn't he take an extra ten minutes to put those lines on straight? It was a simple thing to do.

HOLM: I agree—its color and general form are its high points. When he hollowed out that handle, he didn't stop at the eagle's head, but continued right through its mouth. I can imagine somebody looking at that and saying, "Gee, look at all that work—he's carved right down to there!"

The hole through the head doesn't seem to be anything, yet there it is. Maybe it was to lighten the spoon, or to prevent it from cracking.

HOLM: This sheep-horn ladle is similar to #18, with the same kind of flat design spread over the back of the handle and down a little on the bowl. It has a small, relief-sculptured face in the center of that design, and no rim on the inside of the bowl.

REID: It's extremely difficult to make such a bowl symmetrical. This one isn't wholly so, but it's close.

I won't attempt to interpret the design engraved on the handle, but undoubtedly it has meaning. In the center, just above the bowl, there's a typical Northwest Coast face, small, superbly executed. I think it emphasizes the courage which all the good artists demonstrated. For eyebrows he drew two parallel lines with a vertical line down the middle—and just left it at that. Looking at it now, that seems to be the only thing he could have done. He knew when to quit.

HOLM: Maybe that was one of his greatest skills—knowing when to quit. It looks like he did everything available for him to do, then stopped.

When you really get into pieces and examine them, you find over and over that the great pieces are examples of this ability to use the minimum, and to know when to stop.

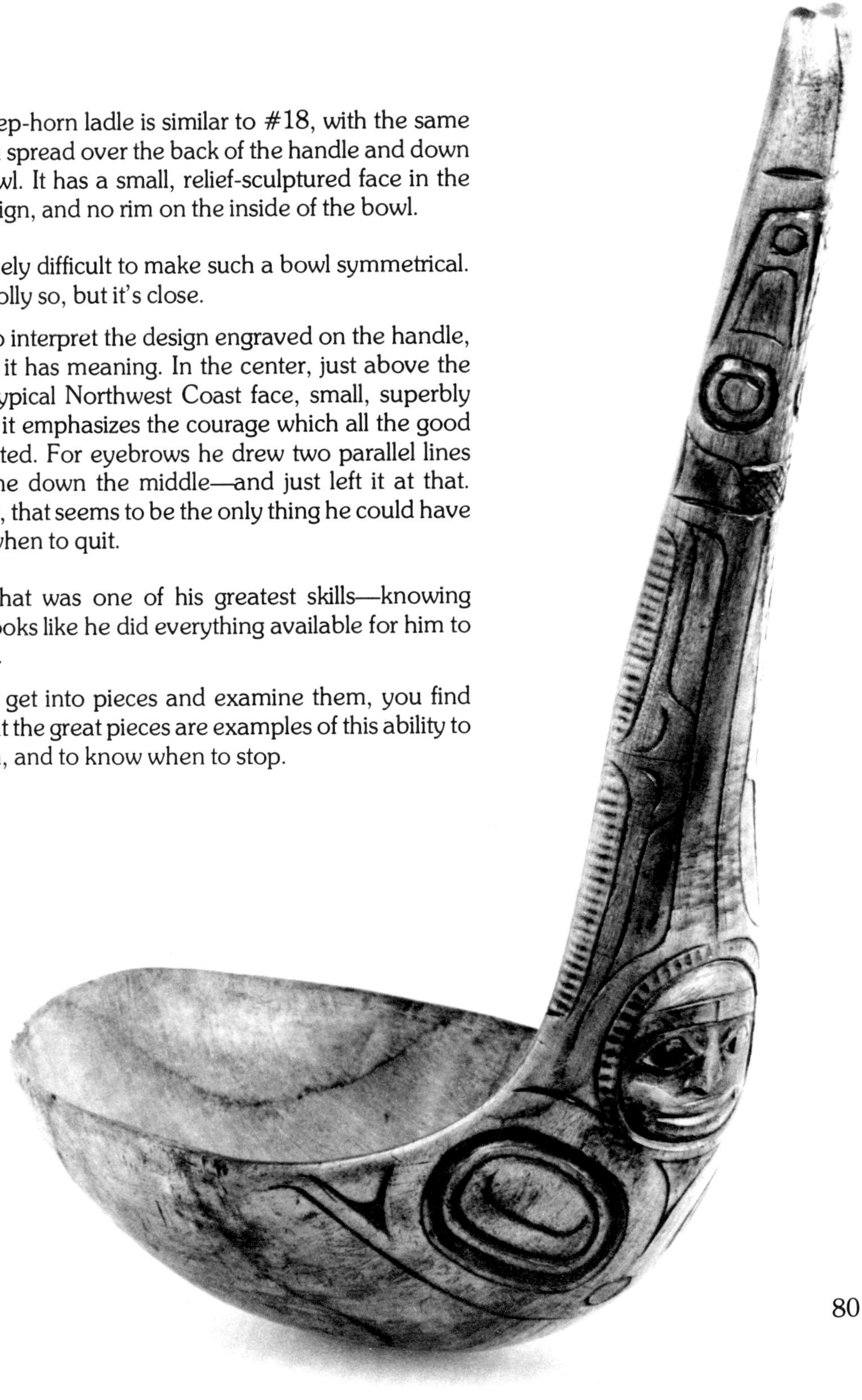

80

21

22

REID: An entirely different ladle from #18, infinitely more elaborate and highly decorated, but not nearly as beautiful, because the form wouldn't have the same elegance even if it had been carried out as I suppose the maker intended. Apparently he lacked the technique. Or perhaps it was impossible to give a real "bowl form" to this bowl. It's quite irregular. But the design is well thought out and not badly executed. Some kind of animal, a bear or something . . .

HOLM: . . . I'll go for a bear . . .

REID: . . . beautifully fitted to the form of the spoon. But the bowl is disproportionate to the size of the handle. And the handle is merely straight, without that elegant curve you were talking about. It's still an attractive thing because of this translucent quality, the color of the horn, and the really nice design applied to the back of the bowl.

HOLM: It's been said that the carved sheep-horn bowls of the Coast were made by Athabaskans and carved by Coast people. I don't believe that. Athabaskan bowls are different. But this spoon challenges my theory because it looks Athabaskan, though clearly it was carved by some Coast man. The shape of the handle—very thin, long—gives it the appearance of an Interior spoon, as does the large, rounded bowl. The horn was cut very thin and perhaps not put over a form when spread, but just bent upwards so the sides spread out, giving the bowl this irregular form, which also makes it look like an Interior piece. But the surface carving is certainly Coastal and very well done. Old-style work, probably early 19th century at least. And Northern, probably Tlingit rather than Haida, although it might be an Interior spoon traded down. A nice piece, though it doesn't match #18 in elegance of form.

REID: One nice thing about this design is that it adheres so strictly to the conventions. It's a classic example of what you do if you apply all the rules and use this basic, simple form in the inside areas. He wasn't very adventurous, but he certainly knew what he was doing. It comes off very well.

HOLM: He used up about two-thirds of the bowl for this creature's head, relegating the whole body and limbs to the remaining third. But everything works out fine. That kind of disproportion doesn't seem to matter because it looks so good as a design. You don't have to look at it as a figure with an enormous head and a tiny, misshapen body.

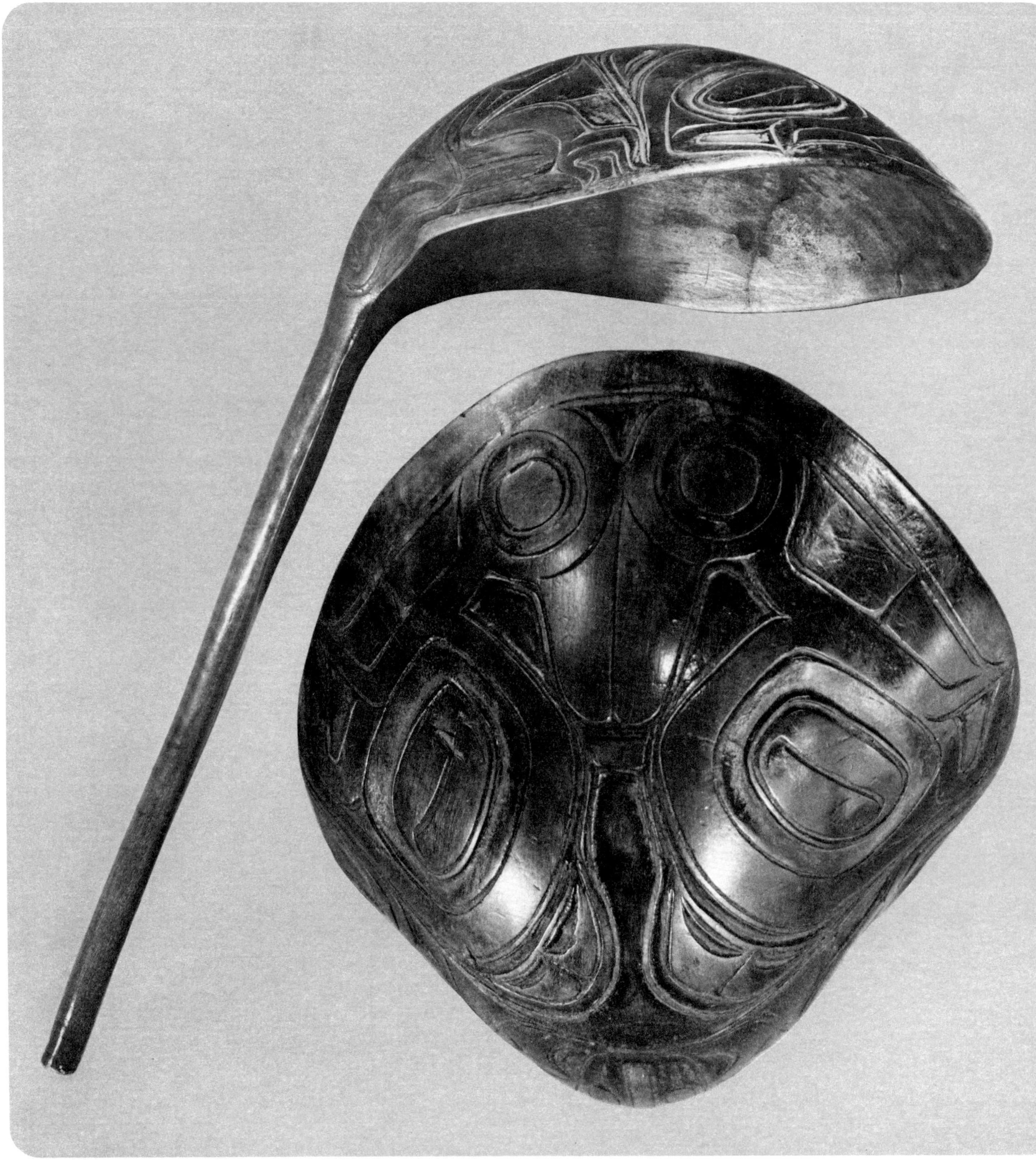

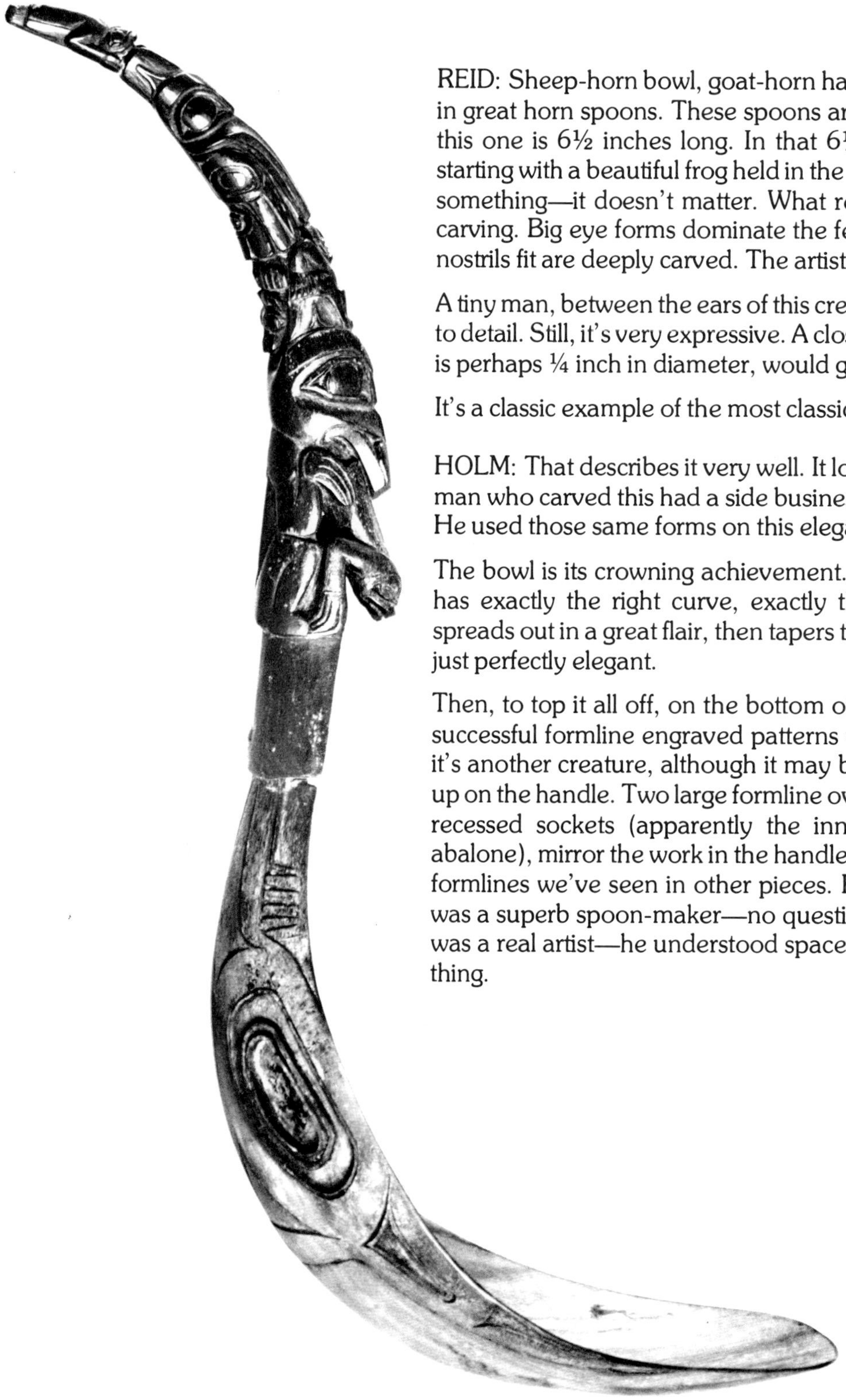

REID: Sheep-horn bowl, goat-horn handle. Has all the things you look for in great horn spoons. These spoons are very small. The carved handle of this one is 6½ inches long. In that 6½ inches, the artist put six figures, starting with a beautiful frog held in the mouth of some creature—a bear or something—it doesn't matter. What really matters is the boldness of the carving. Big eye forms dominate the features. The sockets into which the nostrils fit are deeply carved. The artist pushed his form to the ultimate.

A tiny man, between the ears of this creature, is too small for even this artist to detail. Still, it's very expressive. A close-up photograph of his face, which is perhaps ¼ inch in diameter, would give a strong sculptural image.

It's a classic example of the most classic of all Northwest Coast forms.

HOLM: That describes it very well. It looks very Haida to me. I believe the man who carved this had a side business carving argillite pipes for tourists. He used those same forms on this elegant feast spoon.

The bowl is its crowning achievement. The shape is absolutely perfect. It has exactly the right curve, exactly the right shape. The narrow neck spreads out in a great flair, then tapers to a long, smooth, rounded end. It's just perfectly elegant.

Then, to top it all off, on the bottom of the bowl there is one of the most successful formline engraved patterns we've seen. As nearly as I can tell, it's another creature, although it may be an extension of what's going on up on the handle. Two large formline ovoids, with deep, precise, boldly cut recessed sockets (apparently the inner ovoids were once inlaid with abalone), mirror the work in the handle. And it has the large, angular, bold formlines we've seen in other pieces. Really a superb spoon. This fellow was a superb spoon-maker—no question. But, he went beyond that—he was a real artist—he understood space and form relationships and everything.

23

24

HOLM: One-piece sheep-horn spoon. The whole has a deep, streaked, light-and-dark brown color. Very worn. This material is tough. It resists wear. So this spoon has been around for a long, long time. A couple of creatures are represented on the handle. The lower, main one is done in very flat form. A two-dimensional formline structure wraps around the handle, carved in relief. A more sculptural human figure, with a headdress, squats on top of that figure. The rather two-dimensionally organized main figure extends down the back of the bowl a little way, continuing the formline pattern into what appear to be flippers or fins. These flair out neatly and follow the shape of the spoon. Perhaps it's a sea monster. Fine carving, but much worn. From the way those engraved lines have been rounded by use, it's clearly been around a long time.

REID: The artist pushed a convention to its ultimate limits. The eye form, or the eye itself, of this lower creature, whatever it is, is extremely distorted.

HOLM: But you see this particular form on spoon handles. I don't know why it was done that way—perhaps partly because of the limited depth. To get as big an eye as he wanted, he had to drag the rear corners way down. It's very much distorted over the usual form, but it is seen on spoons.

REID: It looks perfectly natural, as if that were the right thing to do. It isn't that he didn't know what he was doing—he merely pushed it to its ultimate limits.

HOLM: I guess this is more extreme than most.

REID: This little man's anatomy is extremely distorted to fit the form, but it doesn't matter in the least. It's just the way he is. His anatomy is distorted, but when these things are right, they have their own extremes. Earlier this year I made a little gold bowl in the shape of a bear, with the bear mother suckling her cubs on the lid. She's kneeling, with a cub on each knee. Several mothers said this was a ridiculous position in which to suckle young. It is. It would be uncomfortable and strange. Yet it seemed natural for a lady whose function was to decorate a box lid.

HOLM: That's something you have to be aware of all the time. The artist has to recognize, when he's doing this, that it's a spoon handle, not a little man. If the figure has to be altered or has to pierce some other figure illogically, well, there's no great problem. A good example is the little figure, we often see, between the ears of the main creature on certain sheep-horn bowls. His legs and arms extend out on either side, within the ears. To be there and fill that space, he has to be a contortionist. Seen that way, it looks funny. But, if you forget about anatomical limitations and just accept these distortions, it works fine.

REID: This isn't a particularly important piece to be spending a lot of time on, but what is nice about it, to my thinking, is that the form of the horn has been retained, to some extent. There's a pleasing sharpness to the angle of the bowl in cross section.

HOLM: Right. For one thing, it was made out of a very small horn. The artist didn't have much material to work with. So he had to retain some. Original surface irregularities remain. But that adds to the spoon's quality.

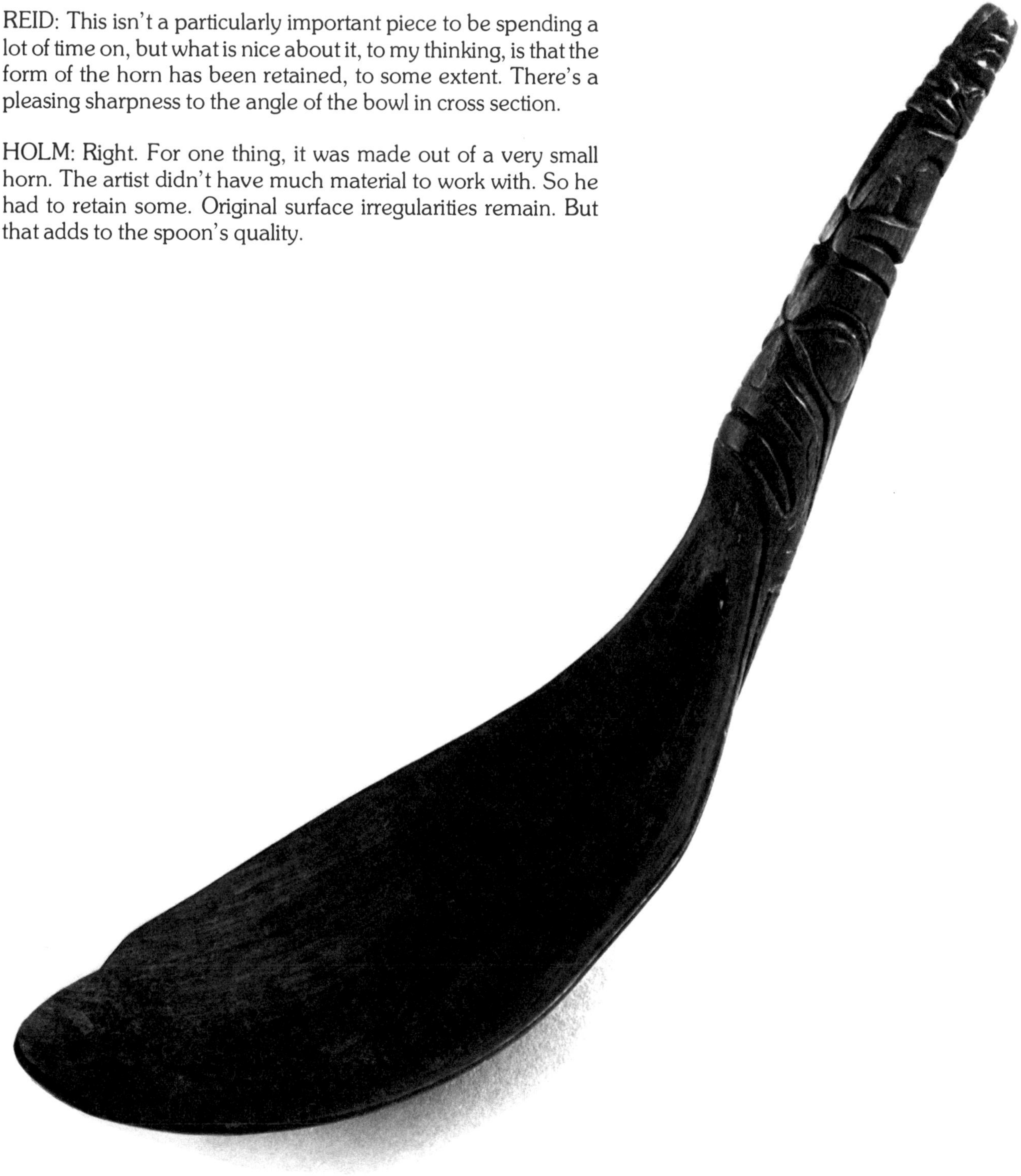

REID: Mountain-goat-horn spoon in two pieces—handle and bowl—its only virtue being minute carving which shows care. It's about as elementary a goat-horn spoon, with carving, as you find.

HOLM: I knew we'd get through with this piece pretty fast. I agree. But it has imaginative figures on it. One that strikes me is this creature with its mouth open. That's the most open mouth I've ever seen in Northwest Coast art. The fellow was doing some interesting things.

REID: He just wasn't doing them well.

HOLM: I'm inclined to see this as having a very Bella Bella quality—mostly on the basis of these extremely weird figures, but also on its structure, especially the eye of the main bird, or what appears to be a bird, and that odd little beaked frog, or whatever he is. The Bella Bella made many funny little monsters, apparently for no reason but to amaze people with the artist's imagination. Nobody but a Bella Bella could imagine these figures.

25

HOLM: Little goat-horn spoon of two pieces, the bowl made of one horn, the handle of the other. Handle delicately carved, different in style from the other pieces we've looked at. I'm inclined to call it Tlingit for several reasons: it has full sculptural or pierced figures which stand out as separate little carvings, as opposed to two-dimensionally organized designs covering a functionally shaped handle, and the little head looks very Tlingit.

The fragmentary figure (where the bowl and the handle join) might be a mountain goat; it has horn-like extensions over the eyes. There's so little there, it's hard to tell.

The next figure is rarely seen in most classes of Northwest Coast art, save in early argillite pipes. It's an insect, a dragonfly, naturalistic, with a big head at the base, very large round eyes, broad mouth, and tiny feet coming down from the bottom of the face. Over the head extend two pairs of insect-like wings with crosshatching, very lacy-looking and resembling dragonfly wings. Between them a narrow, segmented body runs through the spoon and back down the other side. A good, naturalistic image of a dragonfly's body.

A repair, or at least a modification, masks a break. The dragonfly's wings have been whittled off at the base so that the upper pair now separate. Originally they were joined to the head.

It's interesting why a dragonfly would be carved on a little horn spoon.

Above the dragonfly squats a man, very delicate, with narrow arms and legs, wearing a poncho-like tunic resembling ones worn by Tlingit shamans. He has a very Tlingit-looking face, surrounded by a cap resembling a shaman's cap and possibly representing a bear's head or some other creature with a long tongue.

REID: You didn't mention that all of this is fitted into an area about 5 by ½ inches. We get spoiled by goat-horn spoons because so many are so superb. Their maximum length is 6 or 7 inches, yet they compress, into a tiny shape, many figures, with all the monumentality of a huge totem pole or Egyptian monolith. They're as close to magic as you can find in the human artistic experience.

HOLM: It's best to hold one of these spoons in your hand and see its real size. But, in my classes, I show slides of them, magnifying some detail to monumental size. All 270 students gasp when they realize it's less than an inch wide and three inches long.

There're many examples of this in Northwest Coast art. It comes up often in my experience. Others mention it. A photograph gives no notion of size. This skill or style in using space so effectively, works in many sizes. I've often had the experience of

26

photographing a piece, or knowing it only from a photograph, and then, suddenly, years later, seeing it and being surprised that it's really half or twice as big as I remembered.

REID: The bear mother is a perfect example.

HOLM: There are many. And not just sculptural pieces. I was long familiar with a small painted box and kept photographs of it around. In my mind it enlarged to the standard size for most such boxes. But then, when I saw it again, it really was small.

27

REID: Bird bowl, short and stubby and pretty damned ugly. A young bird, I suppose, because its mouth is wide open, waiting to be fed. Made of wood, yet deformed as if it were made of horn. Not well shaped. Honestly, I don't know why the carver wasted his time.

HOLM: I go along with you. To really enjoy this, you would have to be a true "primitive" enthusiast. This really looks primitive in the sense that it's rough. I don't think it has much, but it can't be altogether dismissed.

REID: It can't be altogether dismissed, but it's quite all right for me to dismiss it.

28

REID: A nice, chunky seal dish with a strange decay on both ends which doesn't detract much from the beautiful, flat design.

HOLM: This illustrates all the typical attributes of a Northern seal-shaped grease dish—wide bowl shape with an extension on each end, one for the head, the other for the hind flippers. The rest of the body is worked out in a highly conventionalized formline pattern on the sides.

This is quite a bit like #35: formalized, massive formlines reduce the background to a minimum. The sculptured head and hind flippers combine with the rest which is two dimensional. The front flippers, for example, are flat along the sides. The flat design is similar in both bowls and so is the general form—the curved sides with lip or rim all the way around. It illustrates the Northern habit of making a dish, even in animal form, just like a dish. It's a bowl turned into a little animal.

REID: A good piece, made by a real pro.

HOLM: Knew exactly what he was doing, followed all the rules and came out with a successful result. It's also got a lot of age.

29

REID: Seal dish, not as typical or appealing as #28, but more lively, organic, interesting, a beautiful thing to hold. It's a functional object to hold grease, but has a life of its own—almost the appeal of holding a living thing in the hand. Obviously I'm not the first person who thought so, because the design, once prominent, is almost worn away by handling. It's heavily encrusted with grease, but even if you removed this, the carving would still be faint.

HOLM: The end of the nose has been polished until it's almost gone.

REID: It would take a long time for that to happen. It's old, obviously. It's been much loved. As you hold it, it's easy to see why.

HOLM: Several things come to mind about this bowl. Earlier, when we looked at the first bent-bowl, #34, we each called it a "bowl." I distinguish bowls from boxes by the undulating rim—high on the ends, low on the sides. That first bowl wasn't much higher on the ends, but it did go up and down. This bowl has the same thing. Yet there's really no reason for that to happen. If we just carved out a bowl, we could carve it straight across. It's natural for the seal's head and tail to come up, of course, but this feature is seen over and over on bowls that are not seals. The sheer of the sides (where the rim is higher on the ends than in the middle) is one of the structural details that gives such bowls their lively effect. The dip of the rim here is minimal, but still there and not needed at all. The natural upswing of the seal's head and hind flippers suggests it ought to be this way, but with #34, there's no obvious reason for it to happen.

REID: Seals lying on their bellies, resting on rocks, often arch their backs very strongly, with their heads and flippers in the air. That's where the shape of the seal bowl comes from.

HOLM: Sure, but this dip or sheer in the rim isn't confined to seal bowls. It's an obvious thing to do with seal bowls, but with other bowls there's no obvious reason. I have a theory about this, but we don't need to go into it now.

REID: These objects weren't merely used at ceremonial affairs. They were treated as art objects, passed from hand to hand, admired, fondled, examined closely. Everyone was a critic and connoisseur. Everyone probably felt some direct relationship with the objects in his immediate family, and maybe even with those in the whole community. These were communities of connoisseurs.

HOLM: No question that's true. Each piece was made by an individual artist expressing his own style, feeling, etc., and each was recognized as an art object. Must have been. They were made by trained, skilled, talented professionals. A professional artist requires a corresponding audience and body of critics. Otherwise there really can't be professional artists—men who produce things desired enough to be commissioned. There had to be this appreciation of art objects—the idea of the object as beautiful, beyond its function, perhaps having a ceremonial role, as well, or expressing rank or prerogative.

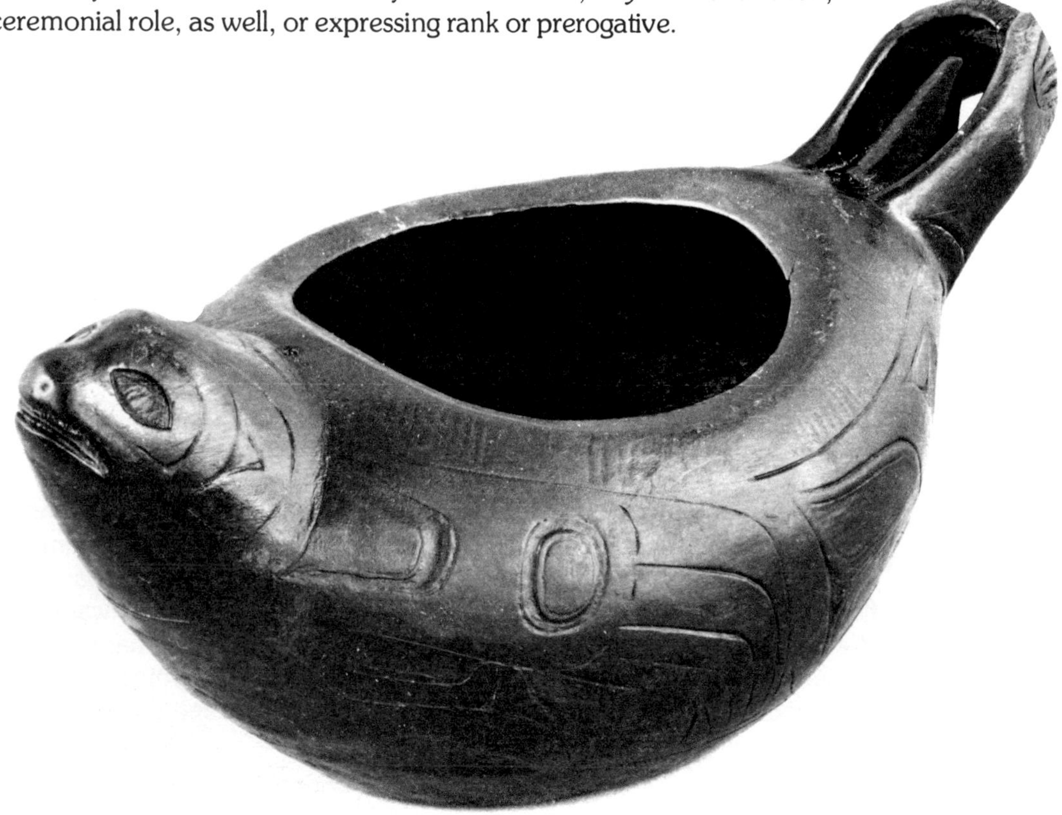

30

REID: Simply formed, undecorated sheep-horn bowl of absurdly elegant shape. The form may come from a number of places, but I think the canoe has influenced it most. Both ends are the same, but high and curved, and the general shape of the sides is that of a foreshortened canoe. It's just a beautiful thing. It's slightly cracked at one end, with a chip out of the other end, but this detracts little from it.

Beautiful color—translucent tones of brown ranging from almost cream to old meerschaum.

HOLM: What you say is absolutely true. It's a beautiful job of workmanship. Clearly the bowl was formed in a real mold. Some can be bent by pressing thin, steamed horn around a basic form, but this one was pressed into a real mold when steamed. That's the only way to get this flair on the sides and this regularity. Your description of the color was graphic. It's a great thing. We get so intrigued by decorative surfaces we tend to forget that almost every utilitarian thing we've looked at—bowls and whatnot—has a sculptural form of its own, quite satisfactory without decoration. This one points that up: there's no trace of engraving or anything else on it. Yet it's certainly satisfying.

31

REID: Sheep-horn bowl, much less satisfactory than #30. I assume this wasn't formed in a mold.

HOLM: It may have been, but it's not nearly as beautifully done as #30.

REID: The forms don't flow so gracefully into one another. Instead, there are abrupt transitions from curve to curve. Care hasn't been taken. Slight, irregular decorations—a striated border and what appear to have once been circle-dot decorations (the circle part has worn off)—add nothing as far as I'm concerned.

HOLM: I read the striated border design as related to birchbark basketry.

The whole bowl is more characteristic of the Interior than of the Coast. It has every feature Athabaskan bowls have. Perhaps it was collected on the Coast, since there was a lot of trade. I read recently that Northwest Coast carved sheep-horn bowls were actually made by Athabaskans and carved by the Haida. I don't believe a word of it. Haida bowls are different. You could never carve a bowl like this or #30 into the deep sculpture that some Haida bowls have. Athabaskan bowls just aren't that thick.

32

HOLM: Bowl carved of a single piece of wood. It has features that I believe relate to a couple of different kinds of objects. I don't want to make it sound as if Northwest Coast Indian artists were so devoid of original ideas they kept repeating everything from one category to another. But when they came up with ideas that worked and they liked them, they used them on other forms.

This kind of bowl has features uniformly followed from bowl to bowl. Variations are only in proportions and in arrangement of formlines. The structural form of the bowl remains the same. It has high, abruptly upright ends, closely resembling the ends of sheep-horn bowls of similar shape. And it shares with those sheep-horn bowls an interesting pattern of ridges on the inside, under the rim on each side and paralleling the rim, plus little vertical ridges running from the upper corners down to this ridge. Those ridges are also found in many carved sheep-horn bowls and ladles with very little variation. There's no reason for them that I can think of, aside from decorative function, and certainly they have that—they do a lot for the feeling of the bowl—but I find it hard to believe they would be followed that uniformly, with little variation from bowl to bowl, if decoration were the only purpose.

There are birchbark bowls with the same feature. They follow the same lines except that the ridges, instead of being carved into the wood, are made of bark folds and wooden reinforcing bands. They follow exactly the same shape. The folds are in the same place except that they're structural features of the dish.

I'm not altogether settled on this theory, but I feel these ridges are skeuomorphic—imitations of structural features from a similar kind of dish, copied or adapted, as a decorative feature, in both wooden and horn bowls. Artists recognized their decorative quality and used them elsewhere very successfully.

The bowl has a similar arrangement to #40 except that its corners, instead of being angular, are round. Formline face on each end—I think they're alike. Very simple pattern of little dash lines on the sides, typical of this kind of bowl. Traces of paint indicate a black primary formline structure with red inner ovoids. That's an unusual feature, taking the art as a whole, but common to these dishes as well as to the square ones. I feel it results from the color imbalance you get in this arrangement if you use the typical black inner ovoids.

REID: I think we've said enough about it. It's a pleasantly shaped dish with an elementary carving on it.

HOLM: Rough—very rough. They're often that way. To me, its great interest isn't in its impact as art, but that it illustrates features which, though maybe not important in many ways, say something about the life of the artist, about relationships between art and life, art and people, and particularly about the thinking of these people.

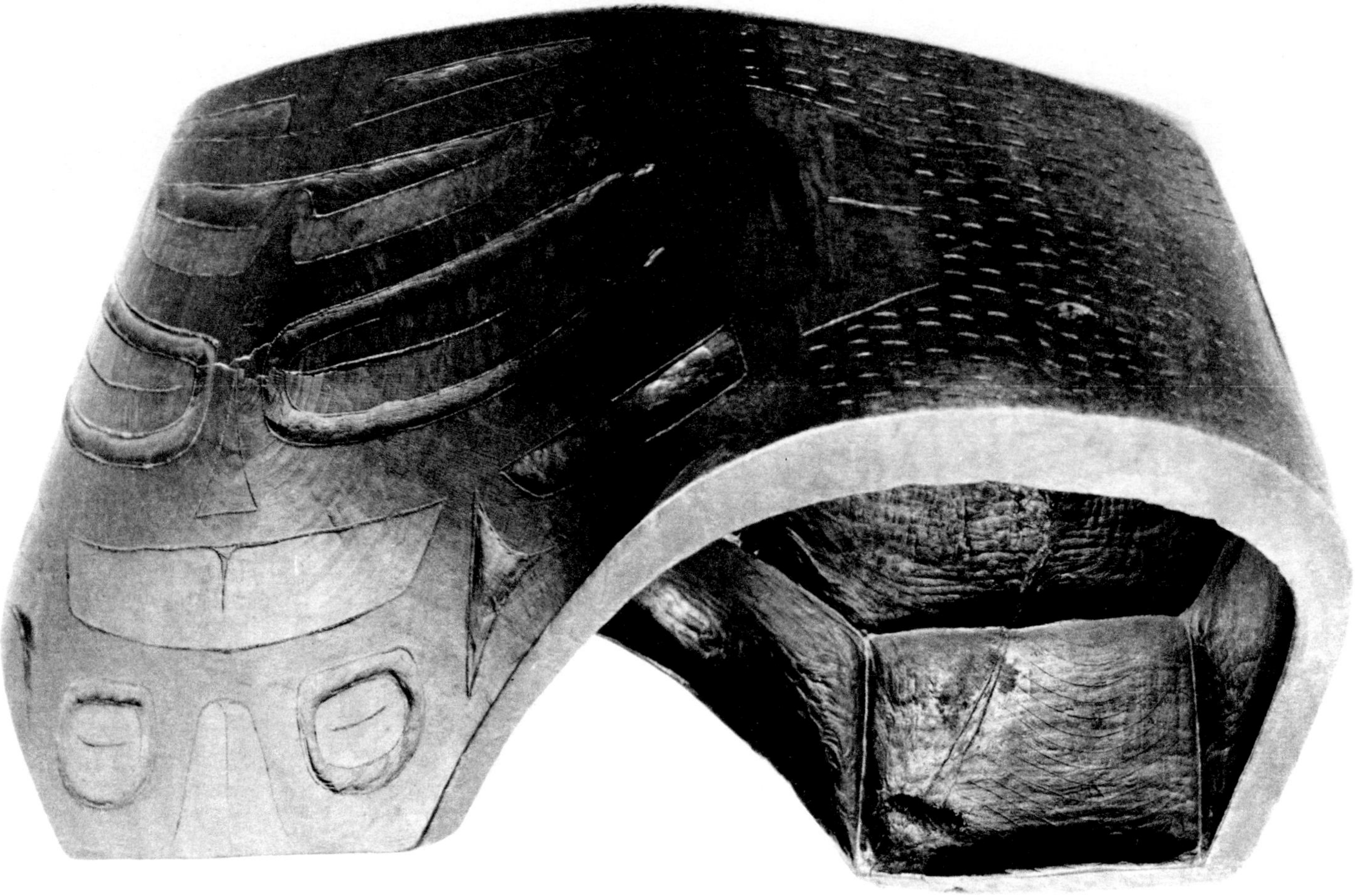

HOLM: Another grease bowl, almost round, with a really striking extension: a little man squatting on one end, his arms spread, grasping the bowl, his head tilted backwards, beautifully conceived. The work is pretty rough. A very strong thing. At the other end is an animal face—looks like a bear—sculptured into the end with his nose protruding a little. Some paint still shows on the sides extending back of the bear's large claws on each side.

I don't know how to interpret this thing. I'm not even going to try. But it's a very powerful thing. It's got the undulating rim of the seal dish, but not so pronounced. The little man's face is a beautiful carving—very Northern and naturalistic. That makes it hard to say where it came from. The more naturalistic these faces get, the more alike they become. They express human anatomy more than tribal or individual style. It could be Haida or Tsimshian, not likely Tlingit. It's got a lot of wear and a lot of years.

REID: The formal composition doesn't add up to much. It arbitrarily jams disparate pieces together. But the workmanship is true, and the face is beautiful.

Often an essential part, usually a face, is carved with care, while the rest is treated as elementary. I suppose the artist here didn't consider the rest important. I'd like to be able to project myself into his mind, to find out why he did it in this particular way—this strange combination of good and bad. The face is great in itself. It makes the whole worthwhile.

HOLM: This man may be holding his distended stomach. His ribs merge with the bowl as if the bowl were a great paunch. That may be what's going on. It's only a guess. I wouldn't want to defend that too strongly.

33

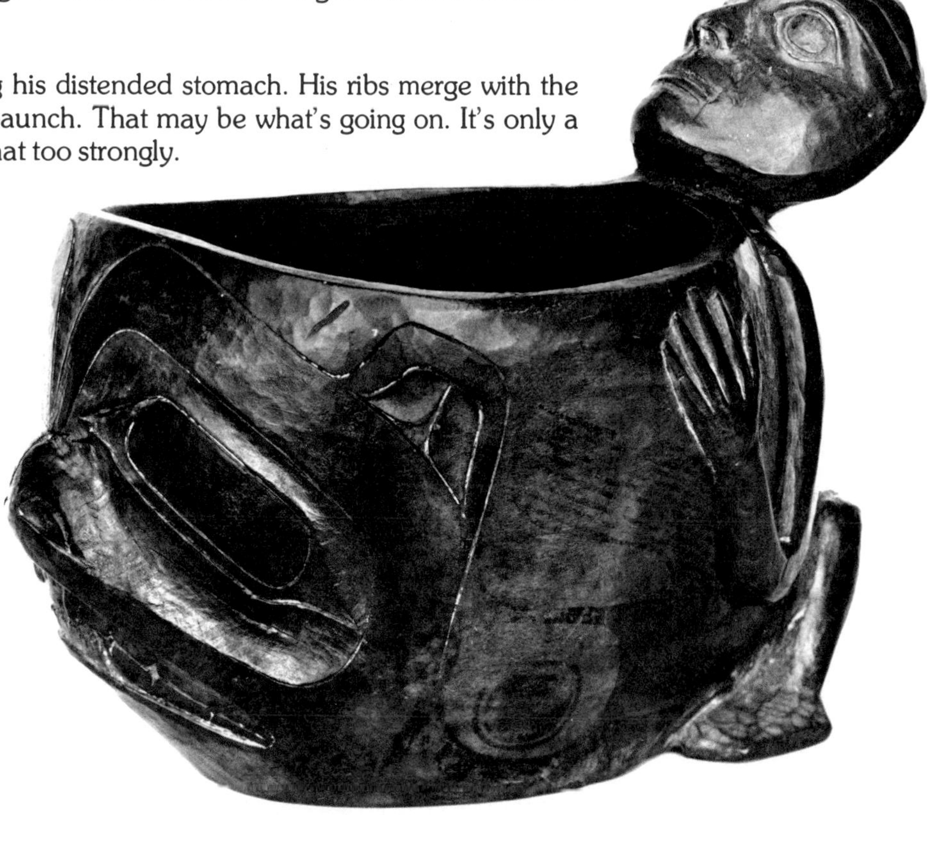

REID: We're now looking at what you call a "bowl"—a curved-sided, bent-corner box. Operculum decoration around the edge. Carved on all four sides and painted. The formalized face designs on the ends are directional, asymmetrically going from left to right. I can't identify the figures depicted. The carvings on the sides are each bilaterally symmetrical and one side differs from the other.

What appeals most is the overall shape. It's a superb sculptural object. It has a roundness—a combination of soft curves graduating from convex to concave on the sides. At the same time it has great strength in the forms which are carried through beautifully in the decorative carving. The flattened ovoids conform in every way to convention, yet there are new or different interpretations of the rules, particularly on the sides.

34

Assuming these are eye forms, the sockets are concave, of course, and the interior ovoids are very convex. This form is a perfect complement to the shape of the box as a whole. The side panels are perfect for the box. The end panels are beautiful in themselves, but aren't as complementary as the rest of the object.

HOLM: Let me make some general comments applicable to most containers of this kind and well illustrated in this one.

This is a bent-corner bowl, its four sides made from one piece of wood bent at three corners and sewn at the fourth in the conventional manner of Northwest Coast boxes. It has a bulge on each side, which is fairly common in bowls of this sort.

I think the bulges imitate the rounded surfaces of carved-out bowls. But bulging can't be carried past corners, which must be straight, so bulging surfaces reverse from convex to concave. I think that curve is simply a functional result of trying to have bulging sides with straight corners. Whether it is or not, it comes out great. It's a beautiful thing. The complementary forms, carved on the sides, also work very well.

One impression I get from these bowls is a feeling of organic form—this soft change from convex to concave surface somehow makes this thing very living. It has an organic quality flat boxes lack. Maybe this works along with its function as a bowl.

Two features here are unique, as far as I can recall. One I've never seen before and the other very seldom. The face-like designs on the sides resemble eyes, but I think are really the hip joints of the creature represented asymmetrically on the ends. But the whole has been constructed into a typical formline face on each side.

These long, convex ovoids lack tertiary lines—the fine lines that go around them. Yet tertiary lines are never missing on good pieces. The artist made up for this by putting two on the ovoids on the ends of the bowl: the eyelid line and the typical tertiary ovoid line. He followed the rules right down the line, then suddenly did this strange little thing, something no one would ordinarily do. In hollowing the sockets and tertiaries, he did everything exactly as expected; then he took a little fling at something different. It's a great little thing.

HOLM: I'm going to play the most dangerous game in Northwest Coast art—interpretation. No one has ever successfully done it. Early anthropologists tried and tried to get interpretations from the artists themselves, but got widely differing interpretations from everybody. That's all right.

This is a speculative fling. On one end of this curved-sided food bowl I see a bilaterally symmetrical formline design. On the opposite end I see a different design. The same formline figures extend asymmetrically on two sides, oriented so that corresponding ends of these figures are adjacent to the same end of the bowl (one side is the mirror image of the other).

That suggests to me that we have one big figure represented on this bowl, with his head at one end, his hind at the other, and his two sides swooping down—a fairly standard organization on this sort of dish.

I opt for calling this a whale. I looked at it last night for a while and tried to decide why I would say that, and the thing that really sold me was this end which I think is the whale's tail, even though the artist has characteristically doubled up his symbolism and made it look like a conventional face with big eyes and droopy cheeks.

I see the large "eyes" as joints on the tail; the "cheeks" as flukes on the tail; and the "mouth" as a conventional division between the two flukes on the whale's tail. This little face in the middle is harder to justify, but could

35

be there for a number of reasons. Skipping to the other end, I think this is the whale's head itself with eyes and mouth, the latter extending to the sides. The long lateral panels of the "dish" represent the whale's flippers and some other part. Maybe this little man in the corner is his blowhole.

This style—so beautifully represented in this piece—is one of my favorite versions of this highly organized Northwest Coast design. I don't know for sure its place of manufacture, but it's got to be Northern—Tlingit or perhaps Haida. It's very old; you find this sort of design on documented pieces from the early part of the 19th century. It has a massive quality: heavy formlines join in massive areas, with little suggestions of relief where they join. These are angular compared to many. There's a solidarity to this bowl, less seen in others. Background areas are minimized so there's very little true ground. There are eye sockets in hollowed-out form and tertiary spaces, but the slots between formlines are reduced to thin lines. There are no big, open areas of background.

This version looks different from some big, open, flowing formline things (say Edenshaw's 1890 work) but is actually the same thing in another style. These tiny, narrow crescent or T-shaped lines could be opened up to become large areas of ground, defining formline shapes, and still do the same job.

The persistence of this system, throughout all these variations, is amazing, thrilling. A formalized body of analytical, intellectual rules combines with great individual expression.

REID: We're speaking of the Northern style, of course.

HOLM: Sure. When we get away from the North, we'll designate it.

REID: An artist, in a rigidly structured society, must express his individuality to the utmost, but within that structure. Men utilize what they have at hand to express their personalities. Northwest Coast artists used the structure of art itself. So you get both very open and very concentrated formlines.

Here powerful, basic formlines, delineating the design, combine with delicate details, particularly in the elongated eye forms on the sides. These are narrow, delicate, exquisite, yet relate perfectly to what surrounds them.

HOLM: The same thing happens here as in #34—formlines take up most of the space, reducing ground areas to a minimum. Yet their elongation creates a feeling of delicacy.

If we take apart this long, elaborate ovoid (with a face like an animal head in profile or whatever), structurally it's exactly like these other more open, freely curving forms—put together the same way. The consistency that goes on and on through the whole "Northern style," for who knows how long, but certainly a *long* time, is tremendously striking. Yet with it you get great individual use of tools and art vocabulary.

This bowl also has that same organic feeling in its form, its bulging sides—its living shape.

REID: This may be unnecessarily critical, but I think he showed a little weakness here and there, particularly these segments of circles in the eyes.

HOLM: I think so. That leaves me cooler than anything else. It doesn't fit. The semi-angularity of the rest, which is so powerful, loses here. But it's an interesting departure. It's so different, I wonder if the carver didn't have something in mind significant to its "iconography." Just a guess. But it's certainly a departure from the rest.

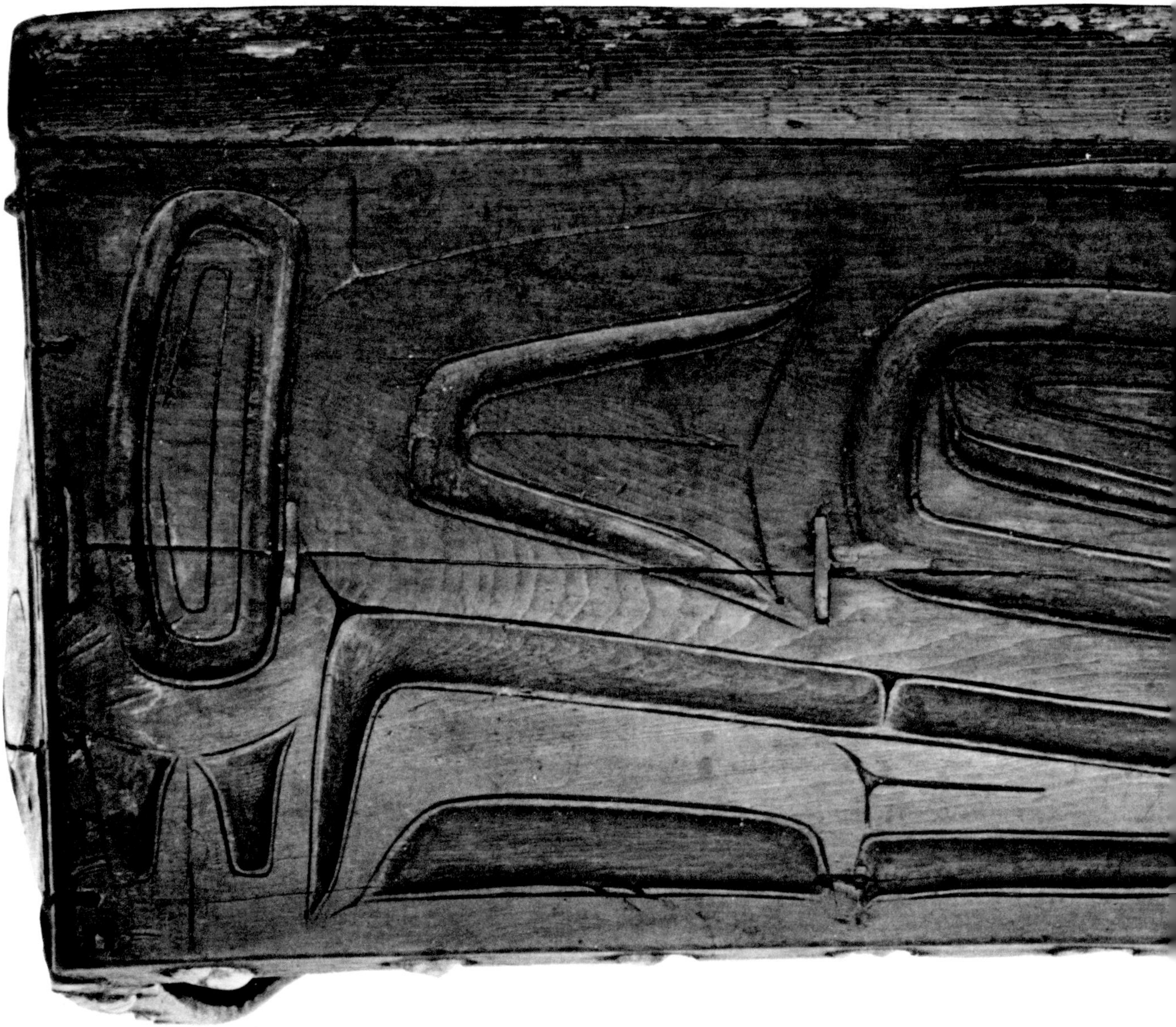

36

REID: Here we have one of the outstanding pieces in the collection—a bent-corner bowl with curved sides. I wonder what it's made of?

HOLM: Yellow cedar or yew. It would take a big yew tree to make a box twelve inches in height, though it could be done.

REID: Anyhow, it's a very fine piece. All these bent-corner bowls have such a lovely shape. It comes partly from the carving and partly from the method of construction.

The carving is very fine. It represents a bird—Emmons, who collected it, says a raven, which may be so. The beak is hooked, indicating an eagle or something else perhaps, but because of the form of the bowl, any bird, including a raven, would come out looking like this.

In the usual way it has the head of the beast on one end, the tail on the other, and the rest of the anatomy spread out on the sides. Emmons says it has a conventionalized bear's face on each side, but those decorations are probably wing forms. The "face" in the center of each side is symmetrical, but the flanking designs are not, and probably indicate wing and body forms.

It's a very powerful overall design with big formlines and then, in detail, exquisite little faces. The ovoids on the rear or tail side look like eyes, but I suppose are joint forms representing parts of the

bird's tail. I like the way the feet are indicated—so simply on the back of the bowl. One of the best examples I've ever seen of this type.

HOLM: I agree—the side designs aren't conventionalized bear faces but represent the bird's wings and parts of its body. On each side, along the edge adjacent to the raven's head, are outlines of the wings, around the shoulders. And at the tail or rear end, U-forms represent feathers. It makes an interesting arrangement. We have what first looks like a symmetrical design. Then we're surprised—but not surprised—when we realize the significance of these parts.

It's a beautiful thing, unusually large, but within the range of these bowls. It's a perfect example of decorating surfaces with a two-dimensional formline that merges, very slightly, with the sculptural beak of the bird.

I once ran into this same problem when making a bowl built on the general configuration of a raven rattle. At one end I mortised in a beak for the raven, but at the other end, where I had the kingfisher holding the frog, I bent the kingfisher's beak right up the joint between his eyes and ran it up the back of the bowl. So I can see that this certainly could be a raven—that the bent or down-turned beak is just a solution to a problem the artist was confronted with in making this bowl.

A very fine piece.

37

HOLM: Bulgy-sided bent-corner bowl with the simplest kerfs. About the only place you see this corner kerf is on a dish of this kind. The V-cuts form a regular mitered joint when the bend is made. That puts all of the bend at one point, and, unless the wood is very good, it breaks. So joints—that is, the bending parts—have to be very regular and even in thickness. This one is made that way. It has the standard bulging sides, slightly undulating rim, and flanges all around, all of which give it that living, organic look. It also changes in form very subtly from convex bulge in the center of the sides to slight concavity, as the side-bulges conform to the straight corners. I think that's another reason why these bowls have that living quality.

The design has been carved. It was probably painted once, but all traces are gone. I don't see any little reflections. Sometimes, if the light falls just right, you can see enough stain to distinguish between black and red. This doesn't show that. Instead, it's got a deep brown and black and amber color resulting from age and infusion of grease. That grease has oozed out at the corners and at the end-grain sections where the wood has been carved away toward the corners. Black, sticky gook encrusts the corners. But the color is gorgeous. Outside, in the sunlight, it's really great.

Offhand, I'd say it's pretty hard, close-grained wood, but not maple or alder. It's a whale design, naturalistic in many ways, though the formlines are very wide and extend to the extreme limits of the decorative area. So it doesn't have a clear silhouette. But it's easily broken down. I've looked at this box in detail: I have photographs of all four sides and have had a chance to examine it and think about it. On one end, there's a big whale's head with a broad grin, if you want to call it that. I think the "grin" is merely the result of developing a formline head into that space. The whale probably isn't intended to be happy. He's got big teeth, handled in the usual way—well, not usual for this art as a whole, but usual for pieces of this period, which I believe is very early 19th century or even before that. Teeth on such bowls were often outlined with little, raised tertiary lines, and each tooth set back in shallow relief.

The large round eyes are defined by heavy formlines, which almost take the place of background, if you don't look carefully. Between the eyes is a little ovoid with little crescent reliefs running out. I believe these define plumes of spray coming out of the whale's blowhole. They don't work for anything else.

Going around to the sides we have the whale's body extending along the top of the dish. It's developed into a long formline face with two eyes. Extending around the corner from the whale's chin is his flipper with a nice formline ovoid

joint which in itself makes a little face and mouth. Extending out from that is the rest of the flipper, shown in a U-form. Just after that is the whale's dorsal fin, shown downwards. Then there's another face, which may be another figure altogether. It becomes a bird's head as we go towards the back. The back shows the whale's tail. As it comes down from the rim, it spreads out to two flukes which occupy the two lower corners of the back. A real neat fitting of this single figure all the way around the dish. The nice detail of the operculum shell inlay—in singles and pairs—going around the rim makes it very elegant. A great example of this old-time, massive, angular, formline work developing the representation of a specific creature into a design on the whole bowl.

REID: It's very elegant. I like the treatment of the ovoids. About twenty years ago, when you and I began looking for rules governing this art, we based a lot of what we thought were the rules on the ovoid form and variations that grew out of it. Over the years, we've changed our ideas about that. The rules are still there, but seen differently now. We defined these ovoids as unmistakably the building blocks on which this convention is built. I think we were right. But the ovoids themselves can take more forms than we first conceived. This is a good example. In older forms you can have convex lines on the bottom of the ovoids, as well as on top, without losing anything in design strength or validity. Personally, I'd like a little more modeling in the patterning of this bowl; some of the formlines are so sketchy they're mere scratches. But it's a fine thing.

HOLM: The very, very fine little crescent reliefs define the corners of these large, massive formline areas. You feel they should have more substance. But this characteristic of very fine line and minimal use of ground areas is all part of this whole system. So it seems to me, and I've come to enjoy it so much I really think those are neat. What I like about them is that they depend on one's understanding of the whole system to explain them. You have to know what they are to know what they're doing. If you don't know what they are, they look haphazard; they don't look like they're doing anything. When you know what they're doing, they become important. They suggest more than demand. That's what I like about them. I understand what you mean, why they should have more strength, but to me, this subtlety is one of the great things about this whole style. It's not so apparent in later times—I shouldn't say later—it's just that they seem later. A more open style seemed to take over and this style went into disuse. But plenty of the early pieces show this very open style with large ground areas.

The thing about this particular version—epitomized in this bowl—is how much is left to your imagination—well, not imagination, but to your understanding. The artist only suggests—as if to assure you that he knows what he's doing—but never demands that you see this structure.

Here's a typical thing: the artist placed a little crescent scratch—not a scratch, but almost like a scratch—here and here, defining the corners of this ovoid. They don't demand anything: they just say, "Here it is. If you know what it is, you'll see it, and if you don't know what it is, you shouldn't be looking at it anyway."

38

HOLM: Another neat example of an abstracted animal spread around a geometric form. Very similar to #37, but more bulge, more undulation to the rim, wider flange—altogether more complex. And more difficult to interpret than #37. But certainly a quadruped, its head on one end, with "smiling" mouth, round ovoid eyes, and down-turned snout. An asymmetrical design, representing the animal's two sides, runs along each side, mirrored on opposite sides. Front limbs and claws under the body. Some strange, unspeakable thing comes along toward the lower rear corner. On the back end (I'm positive this is the back because the joint is always in the back of these bowls—no exceptions), the hindquarters appear as ovoids, looking like eyes, but clearly hindquarters, because below them are flippers or claws and, between them, a little tail. All this is worked out in angular, massive formlines. I think I see traces of red paint on the primary formlines.

REID: To me, there's more feeling in this box than in #37, where I felt a tentative quality.

HOLM: Compared to this one, #37 certainly has a tentative quality. There's no holding back on this bowl—it's strong.

REID: It has strength and balance between its angular forms and curved ovoids. Structurally, it's well made, but not beautifully made. With slightly more care, he could have come up with something a lot better. He wasn't up to the great master carvers. He had a good idea, knew where he was going, and just did it.

HOLM: He certainly didn't spend more time than needed. Some lines could have been made more neatly, without much more effort. One line is really hokey—much better on the other side. The two sides are the same, but the work is better on one. Yet the bowl's directness appeals to me. It adds quality.

Almost every great piece we've looked at has been left alone after carving. Hardly anything has been smoothed off with an abrasive. But knife marks are so finely made, so closely spaced, so carefully done, there's no obvious roughness. This is one of the neat things about old pieces made for Indian use. You rarely see this in contemporary work where carvers smooth surfaces with sandpaper. Sanding is much faster, but does something to surfaces, out of character with old pieces. That frontlet we're coming to, #70, is a good example where all surfaces, all planes and angles, are developed with the knife. When knife cuts are closely spaced and perfectly executed they're not apparent. Done that way, there's a crispness, a *finality* about the surface. But not when you sand. I've just about given up sandpapering. I don't mean that roughness helps. I overlook it here because the carving is so direct. I know people who think a rough, unfinished quality gives power. When that quality doesn't detract from Northwest Coast art, it can be overlooked. But it's never positive.

HOLM: Fairly large bent-corner dish or bowl made out of a hefty plank of yellow cedar, its four sides carved into a series of bulges, then kerfed at the corners. Nice kerfs. Broken, unfortunately, but once very neatly made. Grooved, bent, and joined with pegs at the last corner. The bottom, fastened on with pegs, appears to be red cedar, which is unusual. Surface uncarved; the whole decoration is painting. The design continues around the box, in the same direction, in a series of large, head-like shapes in a formline system. Very lightweight formlines, very curved, not perfectly done—quite irregular. It has a good general feeling, but its main quality is the almost sculptural form of its bulges and the typically undulating rim, low on the sides and high on the ends, with a little flange all around. A nicely decorated bowl but not in the masterpiece class at all.

39

REID: Perhaps the supreme virtuoso performance of Northwest Coast artists was in flat painting. But only a very few achieved that level of excellence and this fellow didn't. When it happens—I don't really know how—it's almost a miracle. They could produce absolute perfection of line and form on a rough wood surface.

HOLM: In a way, this bowl is interesting because it doesn't achieve perfection. The fellow used exactly the same system the next man used. He followed all the rules. Nothing here is out of line, in any way, as far as the system is concerned. That's interesting because after people realize that Northern flat design follows rules, they sometimes wonder if it's really art. But the rules are only part of the story. Here somebody proved that. A piece that obeys all the rules doesn't automatically wind up as a great thing. It takes something beyond that.

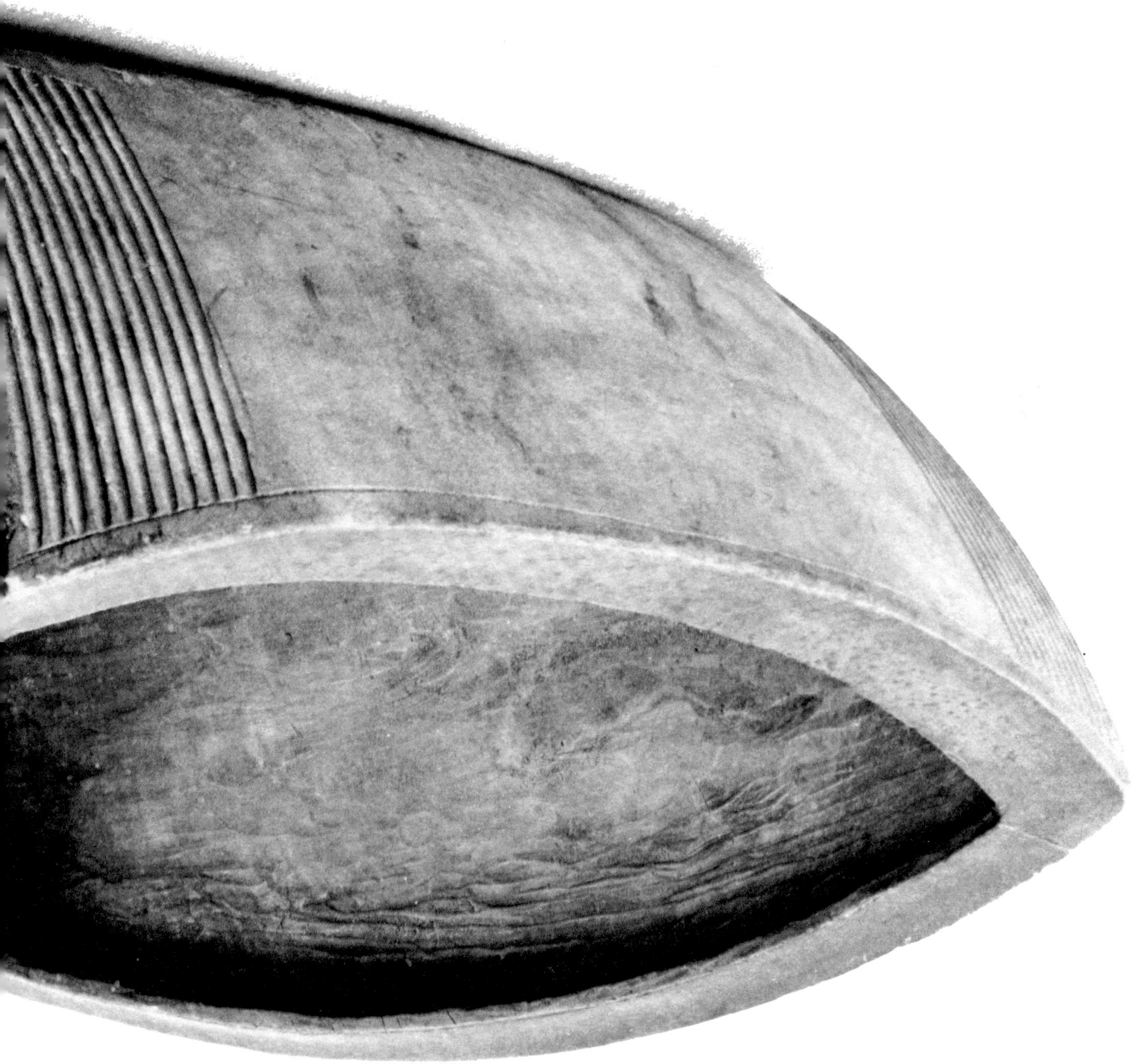

40

REID: Square food dish, like a bent-corner dish except carved of one piece of wood. Not only are the sides curved, but the corners as well, since it's carved rather than bent. Striations on the sides, for which you have explanations. To me, they're decorative. Has a lot of nice things going for it. Gratuitous lines parallel the top of the sides. There's no understanding the impulse of the man who put that design there, except that it looks better that he did.

HOLM: It's invariable—it's never missing from this kind of dish. If it's not there, it's not right. I'm sure that has something to do with its effect, but I'm also sure there's more reason than that for it to be there so uniformly.

REID: The top is lipped, as in all these dishes. Here the lip has a concavity which adds to the organic quality of the dish itself. The only carved design is on the ends, which puts it on the end-grain. That makes it a little difficult to carve. If you've ever tried this, you know it's not easy. This carving falls slightly short of being the work of a master, but not very much. It's darn good. A straightforward design of a bird's head spread out with a double-eyed face in each of the bird's eyes. Those faces themselves seem to have beaks and are bird faces. It doesn't matter. It's a convention used for eyes in many of these designs. It's classic Northern-style design found in variations on chests and boxes, etc. The artist didn't attempt to create anything new or different or radical. He just wanted to make a nice dish. As far as I'm concerned, he succeeded in every way.

It's well finished on the outside—not so well on the inside—but perhaps that doesn't matter. Heavy. Typical red and black paint. The only possible variation is that the main formline is red, rather than black, and the secondary formlines are black. Standard, utilitarian piece, but a fine example.

HOLM: I've had a lot of chances to look at this piece because I have slides of all its sides and use them in lectures. So I've thought about it quite a bit.

I agree with everything you say. It's unusual in still another way. There're literally hundreds, maybe thousands, of these square dishes carved out of single blocks of wood, with designs on the ends. The red formlines aren't as common as the black formlines but are still frequently seen. What is unusual here is the double-eye structure of the end. Of all I've examined, only a handful are done this way. Most have the standard, single-eye end. One reason for this, I think, is that it's a large dish. The artist had the room and used this slightly more complex arrangement.

About the workmanship. It's hard to carve on the end-grain, and often these bowls aren't well carved there. But I don't think it's *that* much harder—a little harder, yes, but a lot of these dishes are less well carved on the ends than they ought to be. This one is that way, though it's better carved than most.

I agree 100% with you that these little panels on the side, with vertical striations, are a great decorative feature. They're so much a part of these dishes that I'm sure we'd miss them, if for no other reason than that we're accustomed to seeing them there. They do something for the dish decoratively. The reason I'm concerned about them isn't that they're needed for design, but that they're so unlike anything else here, yet always on these dishes. I don't know a single dish of this kind that doesn't have them. Even some that have elaborate formline carving in the middle still retain this form. And there are little features to it, uniformly followed, which don't seem to make sense, except that they work all right in the design. One is the line you mentioned that parallels the upper rim. It's always there. The other feature that's unusual, and seems to lack logic, is that the lower border of this striated panel runs up from the corner slightly, at an angle, rather than straight across and parallel to the bottom rim. This, too, is a universal feature. Out of all the boxes I've looked at, I've seen only one or two that had this line paralleling the bottom. All the others bend at an angle. My theory is that this little panel is more than just a decoration; I think it's a useless remnant of a functional detail—or rather structural detail—of another kind of container.

There are lots of these skeuomorphs in Northwest Coast Indian art. We've already spoken about the interior rim of certain ladles and bowls. I'm convinced this little panel is an imitation of a pleat in the side of a birchbark dish, typical of the Athabaskan peoples of the Interior (of northern British Columbia and Alaska). When birchbark dishes are cut in a rectangular shape, pleated and folded in this way, they come out, not only with the little panel on the side, but with the undulating rim, which may or may not mean anything. But take a piece of cardboard, snip it out square, make a couple of pleats—and you have a model of this dish.

I feel that's what this is. I don't know how to explain the texture formed by the vertical grooves, a detail that is uniformly followed, but it may also have significance. Some dishes have little horizontal notches on the corner. Exactly what they represent, I don't know, but they, too, probably go back to some Interior feature.

REID: This dish would be fine as a contemporary, functional object—a salad bowl or something like that. It gives the feeling it needs to be used, not stuck on a shelf. Unfortunately, with the economics of the situation the way they are these days, that can't take place unless you make one yourself.

HOLM: Square storage box with thick lid. Nicely made. Carved and painted all around—I'd better say painted and carved, if I'm going to be consistent with my theory that the painting comes before the carving. It has what first appear to be standard formline decorations and structure, but it's very odd in lots of ways. A typical box of this design arrangement consists of two big heads, each occupying two adjacent sides divided at the corner. That is, the symmetry divides at the corner of the box. In every one I can think of, aside from this one, the two halves of each head are alike—mirror images of each other. That isn't happening here. They're different all the way around. The basic, big formline of the head is the same, and the details of the main head are the same. But from there on, especially in the lower half of the box, different things happen on the two sides.

This fellow apparently got bored doing a thing twice or he wanted to do some different things. He sure changed it around. As you look at the other side, the same thing happens . . . a lot of different little things happening . . . the lower corners are different . . . the two sides of the head are different . . .

REID: . . . probably drunk . . .

41

HOLM: . . . could be. It looks like a standard, fully carved, square box, but it turns out to be something else. Dark red paint (not the vermilion we've seen, nor just dirty vermilion, but another paint—maybe made of red ochre) and, in the tertiary areas, traces of blue—most of the blue being gone, which isn't unusual. The carving is a bit rough and the lines aren't too straight.

REID: All I can contribute is a lot of silence. If you wanted to take the time, you could play his game along with him.

HOLM: Maybe that's a good thing to do with this box. I think he was playing games—that seems to be primarily what was happening here.

REID: I think we're right: he was having a hell of a lot of fun and the people who handled this box, after he was through with it, just sat there shaking their heads.

42

HOLM: Small chest with bent corners. Rich red-brown in color. Probably of yellow cedar, with a red cedar bottom and lid—typical for Northern chests. It's been identified as having belonged to Chief Shakes of the Stikine Tlingit, at Wrangell, Alaska.[37] The name "Shakes" was held by a number of succeeding chiefs of the Nanyaayi sib.

It's an old chest, judging by the style of the design and the appearance of age. I believe it dates back to at least mid-19th century. There's no trace of paint, but I'm sure it was painted originally. The carved designs on the two long sides are nearly alike, which is somewhat unusual. The ends aren't carved—this is typical of many chests. I think there were probably painted designs on the end panels, but there's no sign of them now. The formlines are broad, so there is little background, only narrow slits—an early style. This old style of design is one of my favorites. It leaves some detail and structure to the imagination: the viewer has to have an understanding of the design system to appreciate fully what's happening, and that's a satisfying feeling. Small chests like this were used to hold ceremonial gear and also sometimes as coffins for the cremated remains of a chief.

REID: The interesting thing about this little box is the—what would you say?—*casualness* of it. It's as though the carver were commissioned to do something, but he certainly wasn't going to expend very much imagination or care on it. So he just copied one side on the other, which as you say, is pretty unusual, and reduced his design to elementary forms. This same casualness seems to enter into his execution of the inner forms as well. The ovoids are soft, without the tension this form usually has. And yet it's so competently done, obviously with so little effort, that it has the pleasing charm of a casual sketch by a good artist. Which, I suppose, is what it is.

HOLM: I have ideas about the origin of this chest. I'm reasonably sure it's Bella Bella. I think we're going to reach a point where we can possibly even know the name of its carver or painter. Several chests, in collections here and there, are amazingly like it, in detail and organization. Yet all are different. Either the same fellow or the same school of painters made a lot of square, painted boxes, consistent in style with this one.

It's painted with black, red and blue-green. Shallow relief carving. Carving reasonably good. Well conceived. It must have once been bright and rich. Now it's badly worn, even scorched in one place, and has lost some of its original elegance. Has a look of artistic ruin.

The formlines are light—that is, narrow. It's very open—lots of background, lots of open areas—unlike the bowls we've been describing with their massive formlines, heavy intersections, and thin little relief slits. It's at the opposite end of the scale from those, yet the principles of putting all these parts together are exactly the same. It's just an exaggeration, in another direction, of the formline style—of representing creatures in these very organized, very conventionalized ways.

It's hard to know what's represented here. The end panels look like bird profiles, with down-turned beak, ear, long eye, and wing feathers below. We have the fun of looking at two ends which, at first, look the same, but turn out to be different in every way, every part—nothing is the same.

REID: There're some interesting little details here and there which, if we had a little time, we could try to figure out. Notice this formline extending from the main face on the flat surface. It seems as though it might be an extension of the finger of the hand, but the hand is complete without it.

The concept of these chests was pretty rigid. Someone figured out how they ought to be done, then everyone did them essentially the same. But everybody brought to that essential form his own concept, his own individuality. In many chests you see unexpected, interesting details that take a lot of looking for, but are pleasant surprises to find.

The carved ends, I feel, are the most pleasing parts. Also, it has a sculptured lid, rather than just the ordinary slab lid, which goes well with the scale of this particular box.

HOLM: This same fellow—I'm sure it's the same person—made many chests and boxes. I think he was practically a full-time chest- and box-maker. The large chests are 100% normal, as far as basic design structure—front and back, painting on the ends, standard lid, etc.—and, along with all that, little individual quirks and details.

He made at least three chests that I know of, and undoubtedly many more. One is illustrated in Niblack[38] and now in the Smithsonian. It was collected in the Queen Charlotte Islands, but I believe it's Bella Bella work. It has the same kind of lid, carved ends and stylized face seen here, rather than the big, formalized formline face. Apparently for this kind of chest, of this size and with this kind of head, artists did fully carved, asymmetrical ends and this overlapping lid. It must have seemed the right way to do it, for they consistently followed that pattern in smaller chests.

43

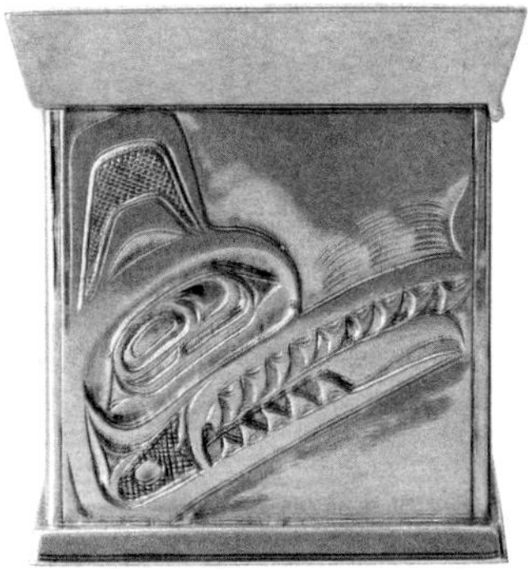

REID: This little chest is a living "arti-fake," made by myself. It sets out to do nothing but be a miniature Northwest Coast classical chest of gold. Made by conventional European goldsmithing methods, in which I've been trained. Differs in structure from a real chest in that it has a hinged lid. Reasonably well made. The typical split-image designs on the front and back are original, insofar as they've never existed before. But they conform to conventions.

If you have two opposite sides of a box, which can't be seen at the same time, you design them so that superficially they look alike, but when you look again, you discover they're different. I think of such designs as a joke or device to add interest. Here the ends represent different versions of the same wolf. I think they are the least successful part. Too realistic. They don't go too well with the rest of the box. If I were to do it again, I'd do it differently.

HOLM: It's a great thing. The two faces of the chest follow the very conventional

44

form of these chests. I can't criticize the arrangement of this kind of thing. I disagree with your analysis of the ends. The semi-realistic representation of the wolf head works very well. The scale is close to that of the main faces. Stylistically they're alike. It doesn't bother me that the wolf head is more realistic. In many boxes the shift in gears between main faces and ends is drastic.

I agree wholeheartedly about the "surprise" worked into these designs. At first they appear symmetrical—exact repeats or mirror images. But turn the object in your hand or walk around it two or three times—you'll find differences. I have fun in my classes with a sequence of slides showing opposite sides of an object which, at first, look alike. I mention that something is going on and ask students to fix their eyes on one point and hold it in mind. Then I show another slide. A gasp goes over the whole place. Then I say, "Now look at another spot—any spot. Fix your eyes on that and hold it in mind." It takes two or three times before they believe this change has happened. It happens very successfully here.

HOLM: Square bent-corner box with simple decoration of painted red corners. Geometric design on the lid. Tlingit. Good example of a storage box from the Northern part of the Coast, made of one long plank, kerfed at three points and bent by steaming into a box form.

These red-corner boxes are of a special kind. At first glance they look plain and not too exciting because of their simple decoration and the plainness of the wood. But, when we look at them in detail, they're really pretty grand. From a structural point of view, they're sometimes the best of the bent-corner boxes. Some have very thin sides, beautifully made kerfs, and beautifully fitted corners—the kerfs close themselves in the bending of the corners. Often the sides are made to bulge outward slightly, in the same way that the sides of the bent dishes are carved into bulges, but much more subtly, so that there's only a very slight curve to a side. This almost looks as if the side was bent rather than carved out. But it can be seen that the surface of the board crosses lines in the wood grain, which then appear almost like contour lines on a map. The board, in fact, isn't flat, but carved into a series of slightly curved surfaces, one bulge to each side. This curve is repeated on the inside so that the inner wall of the box parallels the outer, very thin, slightly bent side. Often the bottom is hollowed slightly on its upper surface to correspond, so that the box has no flat surfaces on the inside, but curves gently all around.

I used to have several of these sitting in my living room, by the front door. Friends who had come to visit, and who had put up with an hour or so of propaganda on the quality of Northwest Coast art, after having been shown the subtlety of the construction of the bent-corner box, would sometimes say, "I always wondered why you had those packing crates by your front door."

But the packing crate similarity ends pretty quickly after you begin looking at these boxes. The design, though simple, is interesting and very successful. The lid has a typical geometric design, incised lightly, then painted with red paint. The pattern of the corners parallels the cord-ties often seen on these boxes—a network of cord, one continuous line wrapped around the box in an elaborate pattern of bends and ties, forming a protection for the box, as well as a means for fastening the lid. The red lines parallel this cord design and bring the cords into the structure of the pattern itself.

REID: The geometric pattern on the lid is integrated so beautifully with the red corners, that lines drawn from the edges of the red corners on the vertical sides form the outline for the geometric patterns on the lid. It makes a very pleasing and unified whole. A very simple, very beautiful thing.

45

46

REID: Bent-corner box in traditional shape—that is, considerably higher than wide. Typical thin bottom and heavy slab lid, decorated with operculum inlay. Offers a nice contrast between an elaborate, painted design, on two opposing sides, and little calligraphic lines, on the other two sides. Straightforward flat-design painting, beautifully conceived and executed, but not particularly original. What one expects in a competently made, well-decorated box.

The artist divided his surfaces into three areas and used all the familiar patterns of ovoids, curves, and so on, to fill his spaces. I like the little forms on the almost blank sides where just a single line outlines a flattened ovoid. He's added what look like claws or something—a bit of delightful calligraphy.

HOLM: Certainly a standard box for its type: the division of space in the main designs and the general layout is the most common arrangement for boxes of this kind. They seem to fall into a limited number of compositional types. This one has the large, single-eye, structured head at the top third of the box. The body is in the rectangular central area. Flanking that are perhaps the front appendages. And on the bottom are a pair of joint-like designs. The primary formline is typically in black, with secondary details in red. About half of all painted boxes seem to be in this arrangement. No two are exactly alike. They even differ from side to side, though the main arrangement is the same. I share your interest in the little side panels. I'd like to know a lot more about them. They don't fit in with what I expect of decorations on painted boxes. But—there they are.

HOLM: Box very similar to #46. Taller than wide. Essentially a square box with elaborately painted designs on the front and back. Spare or very simple designs on the other two sides.

This box, although it has the same general configuration as #46—head at the top, body in the center, appendages flanking the body area, and joint designs at the bottom—is very different in other ways: it is much simpler, with a good deal less detail.

Some details are extremely unusual: the mouth form on one face, with large, U-shaped snout hanging down, is rarely seen on these boxes. And the inner ovoids of the lower joints are just simple, solid ovoids with a C-shaped

47

relief, rather than a profile-like relief head form, typical on these boxes.

But where it's strikingly different is in the side patterns, which are complete formline designs of red with red inner ovoids. The artist didn't follow the ordinary system. He wanted to make some variation on it, to come up with something different.

It's a beautiful box and very well painted. Missing the lid.

REID: Pleasing design, very open, beautifully proportioned—a fine example of Northwest Coast painting.

HOLM: This box is another thing altogether. It's unique. There's not another one like it, as far as I know. A very fine piece.

REID: Oh, it's just wonderful. I've been admiring this box for a long time.

It's a bent-corner box, pegged on one side, roughly square in cross section, taller than wide. A lid with rounded edge gives it a soft, pleasing character which goes with the curved, rounded corners of the box. If that were all, it would be just another box. But the painted design is really exceptional. It consists of two highly decorated sides, each with a circular field surrounded by a halo of U-forms, with very different designs on each side. These may actually be reverse or opposite sides of the same creature, because one definitely has a face, and the other could represent hip joints or a tail or something else.

What intrigues me, more than anything else, is that it shows the unlimited imagination of an artist pitted against the conventions he's forced to work within. It also shows that he didn't let reality interfere with his design or aesthetic concepts. This is particularly evident in what I suppose is the front of the box. There crosshatched fields or planes surrounding the eyes and representing, I suppose, the eye sockets, project considerably above the eyes themselves. The eyebrows are put right through these eye sockets, which is anatomically crazy, but works beautifully in the design. The design has an arresting quality as soon as you see it.

Again, very elementary, flattened ovoids and thin formlines mark the sides.

HOLM: I think this box is one of the really great examples of the art we've been dealing with. It's full of surprises at every view. The lid has a slight lip at one end, resembling lids from the Southern part of the Coast. Yet it's clearly part of this box and this box is clearly Northern. And then, of course, the altogether unique handling of the painting of the box takes this piece right out of the realm of the ordinary.

I've recently been analyzing box designs and I've tabulated the details and compositional arrangements of 140 boxes and looked at a couple of hundred more. Not one comes close to this. It's a completely different box. And it's fantastically well painted. The technical quality of the painting is just out of this world. Look at the mouth of the inverted face. Look at those little lines defining the inner edge of the mouth and the region between the teeth or whatever you want to call them—so perfect! Those tiny tertiary lines parallel the formlines and then divide the area in the most subtle way. They come almost to the end, then turn around and come back. That kind of thing sends shivers up my spine—it's so perfect and works so well. It's not just a matter of great precision but of great sensitivity. You see it all through this box. Look at the other side: the same kind of thing is happening. Little, thin tertiary lines border some of the spaces between the formlines and subtly set off one space from another. It's just a remarkable thing.

Each side panel has a calligraphic form in its center. The diagonal, opposite corners have another feature: red stripes pass right through them. This fellow just couldn't quit. He had to make this box a completely unique production. And he was certainly an expert painter. A wonderful thing.

48

HOLM: This box is even wilder than #48. In my box composition study, two boxes were completely unique. This is the second one. The lip on the lid and the rectangular panels, especially those that aren't centered, are very strange. The painting, confined to these rectangles, is unique. Nothing like that, as far as I know, in other Northern boxes. And the organization of the painting is unlike box designing. Not the same setup at all.

It resembles a Southern box, Kwakiutl or Nootka. But the corner kerfs and some of the other construction details are like a Northern box. Beautifully painted in pure Northern style. So I don't know what's happening here. Perhaps the box comes from along the border in Bella Bella country. The painting resembles some documented Bella Bella pieces. Maybe it comes from the border between Northern and Southern styles. In an area where

49

boxes usually follow the Northern system, somebody may have picked up suggestions from a Vancouver Island box he saw or owned.

REID: It's a startling piece.

HOLM: There are some Bella Bella boxes with borders like this and even with this U-shaped or lobe-shaped painting. But the combination of that and the very odd composition, and then these little asymmetrical rectangular compositions on the sides, makes this unlike any other design. Individually the form patterns are just what we might expect. All the rules are followed. But the larger compositions are completely unique. We've certainly seen a remarkable bunch of boxes here, showing great range of style.

REID: Damned nice basket. Tlingit, I presume. Geometric design in false embroidery—gold, in zigzag pattern, and a very soft brown. Perhaps most appealing is the textural pattern worked in. The different colors and textures work together—a beautiful thing.

HOLM: Its proportions—its basic form—is very pleasing. The slight, regular taper is a technical achievement. Baskets are relatively easy to make straight up and down, but variations from a straight cylinder cause technical difficulties. This basket expands uniformly as it goes up.

50

51

REID: My knowledge of baskets is elementary. Heavy basket with painted design of a bear. Very nicely carried out. It's almost as if each individual stitch was painted, creating the effect of woven pattern.

HOLM: This basket is particularly coarse, so you really see that effect. It's a storage—or whatever—basket, probably Haida. Has the Haida, instead of the Tlingit, "jog" in weaving. I'd say the painting is also Haida. Made of split spruce-root twined in a variety of stitches. This material is extremely brittle and fragile when it gets dried out.

52

HOLM: Finely woven Tlingit basket with nice little textural details; skip-switch twining; row of scattered birds and row of eye forms. It's decorative, interesting, but doesn't do what a really good Tlingit geometric-design basket should do.

A tag identifies this as coming from Yakutat—could well be. That's one of the places where Northwest Coast Indian craftswomen tried to interpret painted designs in woven basketry. I've never seen one that, to me, was successful, and I like Tlingit baskets very much. But that kind of design just doesn't lend itself to the basketry technique, though Chilkat blankets readily bring it off and are related to it.

53

HOLM: Small, lidded basket with rattle in lid—fairly usual for this kind of basket. Lots of background left plain. Small geometric designs in false embroidery. Nicely shaped lid with hollow knob on top and seeds in it to make it rattle. Probably a trinket basket made for sale.

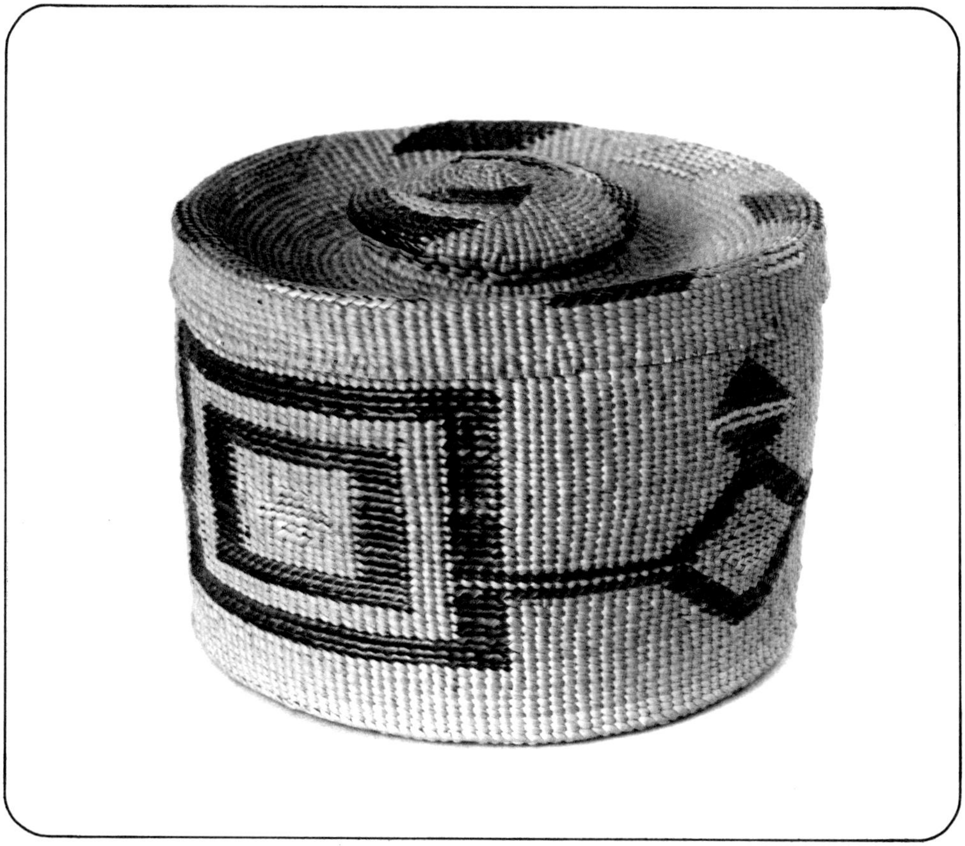

54

HOLM: Basket probably made for native use—I'm not sure what it was—a drinking cup, or perhaps half a double basket made to store, say, eagle down. Heavily, almost entirely, covered with false embroidery in a geometric pattern. I don't know the pattern names in Tlingit basketry, but they had names. Nice colors—soft now, but probably brilliant and gaudy when first put on. The orange and green, I believe, are commercial dyes. The black appears to be maidenhair fern stem. The white is bleached grass. Originally, it must have been more contrasty, but not too gaudy. Age has softened it. It's very pleasant now. Nice proportion between the heavily decorated part and the more simply decorated bottom. Tlingit.

57 56 55

58

HOLM: Chilkat blankets are certainly among the great accomplishments in Northwest Coast art. In addition to their great decorative and aesthetic qualities, they're powerful examples of human technology.

Their production is tremendously involved. It's the hardest way I can think of to come up with this kind of design, involving extremely complicated techniques. Yet, when complete, the blankets look as if they were meant to be that way.

REID: Traditional Northwest Coast flat design depends so much on precision of line and beauty of curve that, when the materials themselves militate against this treatment, the spirit of the design is largely lost. Bead and button designs seem to leave out an awful lot.

This doesn't seem to be the case, however, with the Chilkat blanket, in spite of the fact that the weaving technique doesn't lend itself entirely to precise definition. The Chilkat blanket is, in itself, such a powerful thing, so beautifully thought out, so exquisitely made, you never doubt its reason for existence. It's as strong and complete as the whole other group of flat-design techniques—painting, low-relief carving, etc.

HOLM: A blanket looks quite different on a wearer than on a wall. Some button blankets may be more successful when worn, but the Chilkat blanket seems to work beautifully either way. Spread out, it makes a perfectly satisfying flat design on the wall. It also works perfectly when worn, as it was intended to be seen, draped over the shoulders of a dancer or chief, in motion with its heavy fringe. Of course, the pattern that's so clear and symmetrical when spread out, is altered by the draping when hung on the shoulders. In olden times, the only occasion, to my knowledge, that Chilkat blankets were spread out flat was at a memorial or funeral, when they were placed over the lower body of the deceased chief or hung on the wall, displaying his crest articles.

In the dance, the symmetry and continuity of the design are broken somewhat by the way the blanket hangs over the shoulders, yet this richness of overlapping folds of color and pattern enhances the ostentatious effect. The central pattern in this blanket can be interpreted as a diving whale, with the whale's head, eyes, jaws and nose at the bottom; the body in the center; the tail, with upturned flukes, at the top; and the flippers flanking the body. The side panels are much more difficult to interpret. In fact, in the early years of this century, when Boas, Emmons, Swanton and others attempted to interpret blankets with the aid of Indian artists of the time, they got widely different interpretations of the same patterns. Designs had become so abstract and conventionalized that the meaning of their symbols—their representations—were essentially lost, especially in the side panels, though these can be interpreted with a wide stretch of the imagination (figures can be seen in them).

This blanket is the most typical Chilkat blanket form. It's in practically perfect condition and the weave is of high quality, though not as fine as some in terms of thread count.

REID: Of all the fabrics done throughout world history, I think these rate very high. They're one of the great achievements of mankind in this field of art.

59

HOLM: The design on this blanket, although very abstract, is a bit more naturalistic than #58. It's a killer whale, with tail spread out along the upper border and head down toward the bottom of the blanket. The long dorsal fin is divided and extends laterally from the body (the upper face design) into the centers of the side panels. Because of this representational fin, the side panels aren't so distinctly set off from the central design as they are in the usual blankets.

HOLM: Chilkat woven dance shirts are a good deal rarer than blankets, and this is a particularly fine one. It's classic in design, very nicely worked out, and in beautiful condition. It's much narrower in proportion to its height than a beautifully woven shirt with a nearly identical design in the Burke Museum collection, and yet the same elements are expertly adjusted to the space so they work out equally well in each shirt.

All these Chilkat shirts have designs on the back consisting of bands of geometric patterns crossing an open white ground. Maybe these bands are related to basketry, or even to quillwork designs. The checkerboard pattern at the bottom border is typical for the back of a shirt. It's done in a two-color twining technique which is also used for teeth in the small faces on the front.

The front design has been interpreted as a beaver, but it's hard to find the beaver's symbols here. This same shirt appears in some old photographs of a Tlingit family who have the right to the beaver crest. One shows the shirt displayed at a funeral, another when worn at a ceremony, both events probably at Angoon, about 1890.

REID: A Northwest Coast chief in full regalia must have been about the most gorgeously panoplied human ever to strut the face of the earth. These costumes weren't as colorful or elaborate as, say, a Chinese emperor's brocade robes, or a Renaissance churchman's gold and velvet, but the power of these designs more than makes up for that. The combination of a garment like this with the right headdress and the rest of the outfit would be overwhelming. Even hanging lifeless by itself, it's a gorgeous thing. Saville Row, eat your heart out!

60

61

REID: Dance shirt or tunic made of blanket cloth, with two large bear heads outlined in dentalium shells arranged in rows of 1, 2, and 3 shells each, producing a bold, striking pattern against the rough, dark texture of the cloth. The bear heads are made very colorful by the use of large pieces of abalone.

Northwest Coast design is often destroyed by the use of beads and buttons and materials which don't adapt too well to that type of expression, but this shirt, just by its boldness and simplicity and use of materials, retains a lot of the austerity of the basic design and provides a striking, colorful garment.

HOLM: Another imaginative use of available materials. Dentalium is certainly native, probably long in use on the Northwest Coast. And abalone was used on the Northwest Coast in ancient times—perhaps for appliqué, just as, later, imported abalone was used on this shirt (I'm sure, from their thickness and depth of color, that these particular shells were imported). There was a succession of adaptations of available materials to a design system developed in painting, wood carving, etc. Designs made of native shells carried over to designs made of trade buttons.

It's a striking piece. On the dancer or orator, with an elaborately carved and decorated headdress and staff, it would be part of a very rich ensemble.

62

HOLM: Pair of leggings made of brownish woolen trade cloth, edged with a cloth binding and beads. What appears to be a frog is spread across the bottom and above this is an elaborately colored, detailed sea creature, maybe a sea lion, maybe a sea monster, swirling around an un-Northwest Coast-looking rosette.

REID: Great as costume pieces. They'd look magnificent being worn. But they have to be judged simply as colorful, decorative objects. In terms of Northwest Coast design, they don't come off well. When you try to do this kind of thing with the conventions of Northwest Coast art, you lose all that gives this art validity—its crispness of line, its subtlety of form. It becomes something else—the sort of thing we decry in the non-Indian adaptation of Northwest Coast design.

HOLM: For a long time I didn't like any of the so-called "totem" designs in Tlingit beadwork, only the floral patterns, some of which are gorgeous. But, more and more, I've come to see these as another kind of thing. They can't be looked at from the same point of view as typical, classical box-paintings. The beadwork techniques and the range of colors completely alter this art. The same shapes and design elements used in boxes are found here, but they've become something else. We can enjoy a piece of this kind if we see it in terms of itself and not compare it with a painting. But I still have trouble with it. I want to see that frog—if it is a frog—with nice formlines and ovoids and U-forms, all working together as they should. It's hard for me to forget that and see this as a beaded item with a different tradition behind it, although basically the design rests on the same system used in painting.

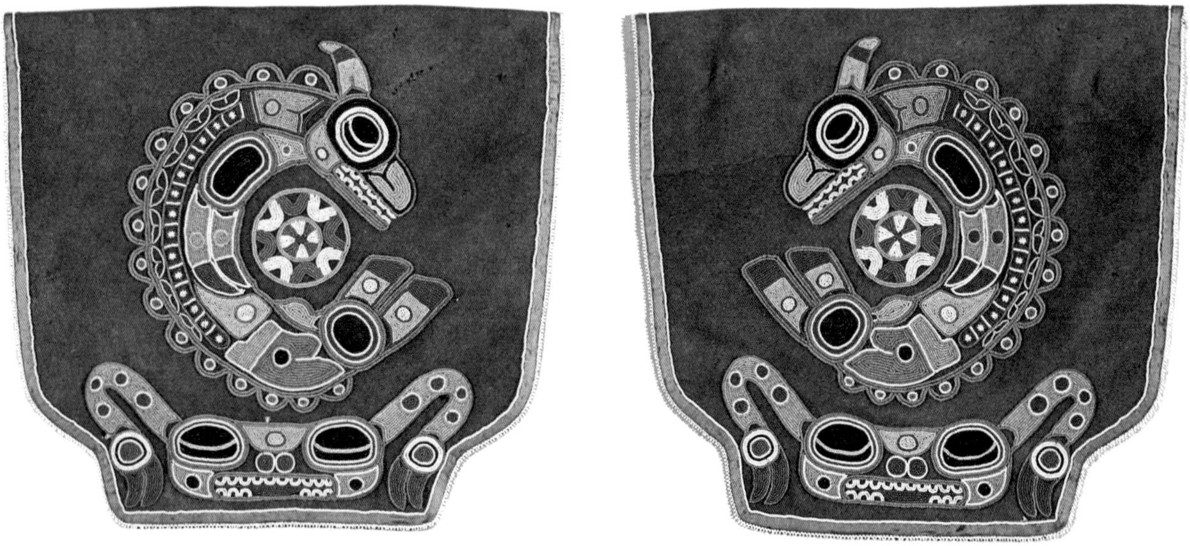

63

HOLM: I'm not going to comment on what might or might not be going on—I'll leave that to you, Bill, or to anyone who might want to give it a try. I do know that whatever is happening, it's in about the most elegant way possible! There are a few of these fantastic combs around and they are among the most exciting small carvings I know of. What is it about combs that inspires artists? I've seen combs from practically every part of the tribal world that are just like this one in their arrangement of an elaborately carved figure above a row of teeth. Most seem to have been made as hair decorations rather than as combing implements. I'm not sure how these Northern combs were used, but they are often fine carvings. This one is typical—a large figure in high relief on the front, and a compact formline design on the slightly hollow back, maybe representing the back or even the insides of the creature. I can see the vertical design as a tail; if it is, the animal is probably a wolf. Most that are well documented are Tlingit, and this one reads Tlingit to me. It's an early one, judging by the style of both the sculpture and the flat design.

REID: I'm supposed to belong to the wolf clan, but I sometimes wonder if it ever really existed because the wolf shows up so seldom as a crest on totem poles or food dishes or anything else. Maybe we're just not very good at identifying it. I've come to believe that, if it's got a tail, it's a wolf, and this has what might be a tail along its back. Otherwise it could be a bear.

Another somewhat unusual feature is the presence of sexual characteristics. The wolf, or whatever it is, seems to have female breasts—very rare in Northern carvings, and the little man's masculinity is hardly in doubt. This comb is loaded with wonderful Freudian possibilities. If the man is being eaten, which is certainly indicated, he sure isn't finding the process unpleasant. And if this is supposed to imply that something else is really going on, it says a lot about a people who could visualize such things in such a strange form. This little comb could give thought to curious and voyeuristic minds for a long time. It's also a beautifully tactile, powerful little piece.

HOLM: Beautifully made spruce-root hat, in excellent condition. Fine three-strand twining at the top. Nice painting all around in the classic style of an animal spread around the whole hat. Looks like a frog. Cute little face at the back—nice job, but weaker. Its *parts* are in keeping with the concept of the piece. But it divides into parts, rather than belongs to the whole, maybe because its red outline doesn't contrast enough with the background.

I know of other pieces, apparently by the same painter, but I don't know who he was. Here the painting is technically beautiful, even though applied to a rough, woven surface. The bottom half was far more difficult to

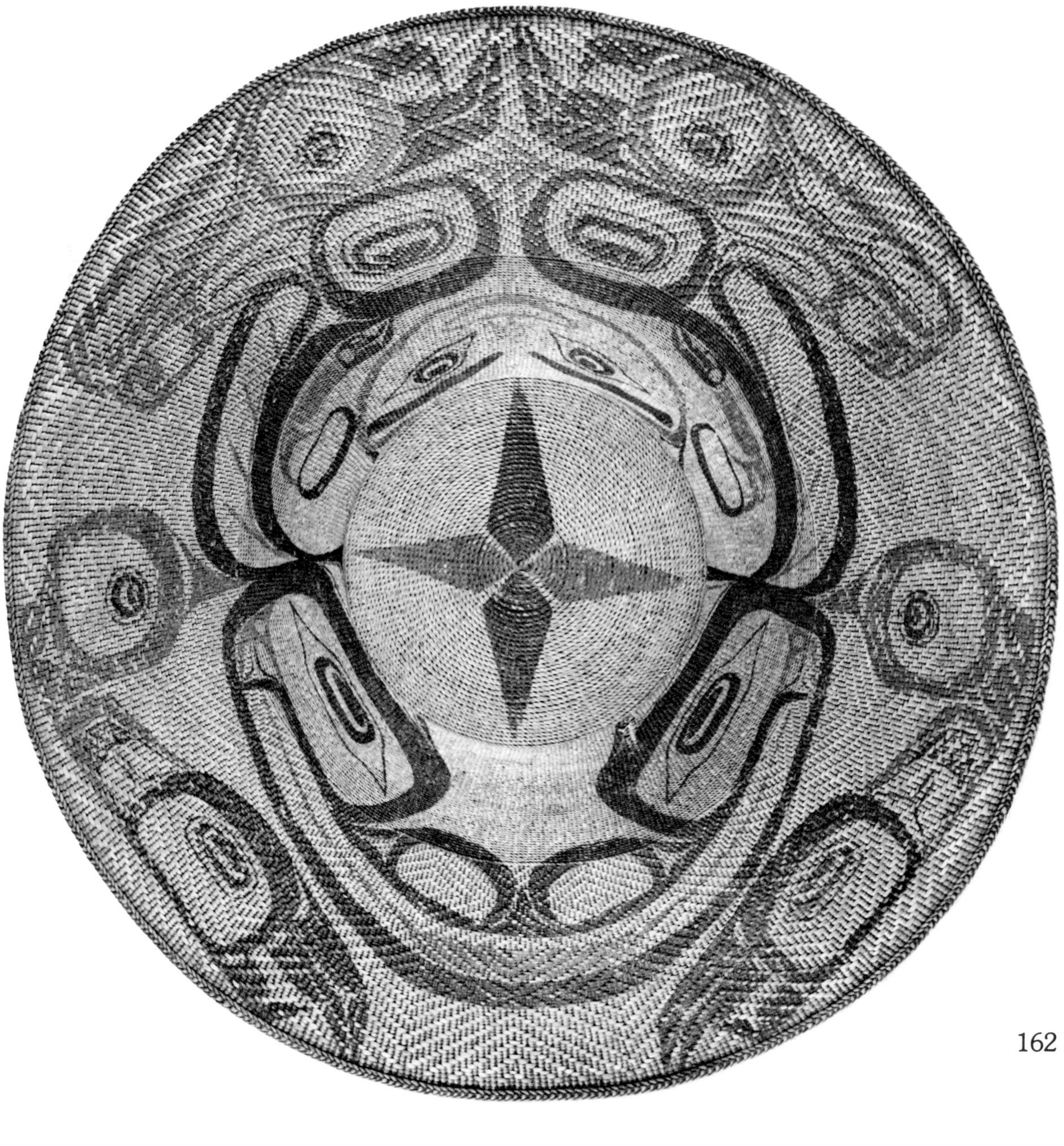

162

paint than the top half. Skip-stitch twining leaves a rough texture, while three-strand twining is relatively smooth. Many of the really old hats confined painting to the top part. Later, people ran painting down over everything. It's hard to do. Maybe hats had three-strand twining at the top just to make a smooth place for painting. When they started painting all over, weavers forgot they should make it all smooth.

REID: Beautiful shape. What really makes Northwest Coast art—from canoes to spoons to hats—is the essential form. Of all the elegant headwear conceived in the world, the spruce-root hat comes close to the best.

64

65

HOLM: Head of a sea mammal—maybe a sea lion, although he has no little pointed ears or whiskers. Maybe a whale.

Headdress or ceremonial helmet. Too light for a war helmet. Little holes for sinew ties through the rim on the sides and one hole in the back. I don't think they were intended to attach a visor, but to tie chin straps when the helmet was worn as a headdress.

This is one of the best examples I know of the ultimate expansion of the formline system. The entire head is covered with big, black, primary formlines so broad, so expanded, the helmet ends up looking like a black head with little decorative lines. These are, in fact, big formlines joined and merged in the usual way. I think it's just absolutely super.

REID: This represents something I admire tremendously—something I can't do myself. If I can't make a thing work, I just add—put a bunch more junk into it—until finally the space is completely filled, and there's nothing more I can do about it. This guy did the most with the least. I know some chests where this is done and I think they are among the most beautiful objects in Northwest Coast art.

This is a very simple, elegant form which conforms in a three-dimensional way to the two-dimensional convention of the Northwest Coast. The artist did what he had to do and quit when he was way, way ahead. What you say about the formline is absolutely true. Well, it almost makes one want to weep, or something.

HOLM: I'm certain this isn't a war helmet, although conceived and shaped like one, with this animal head sticking out and around the top. I see this whole form as derived from armor and made into a crest headdress, with that band around the bottom as a modified visor, though worn above the eyes. The band extends all the way around, unrelated to the upper piece, although it does complete the animal. It shows its flippers there; I'm sure that's what they're intended to be. But the band doesn't merge with the animal at all. It's separated all around. Then, right at the back, it has a little dividing line. This works well in the design, but also suggests the closure at the back of the visor, just on the side.

I don't want to defend that very much. The helmet just suggests that to me. Were the helmet and visor taken together and modified into a crest hat? Anyway . . .

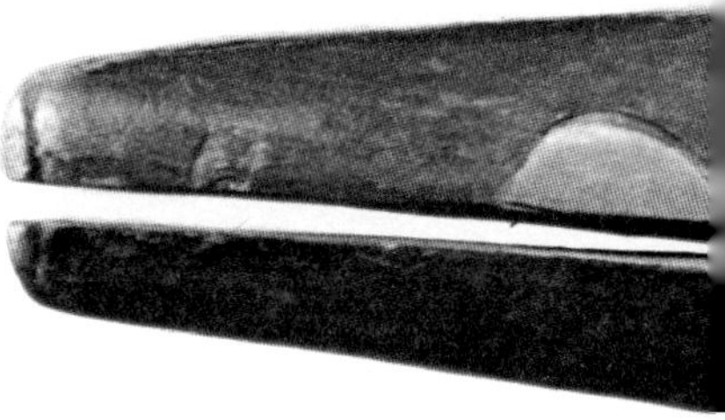

HOLM: Tlingit crest hat. I've known this piece for a long, long time. I first saw it perhaps 12 years ago and had seen a photograph of it before that. At first, I could take it or leave it. It didn't do much for me. Now I like it very much. Perhaps that says something, I hope, for my increased maturity in these things. Part of what first bothered me was the brilliant blue paint. I thought it wasn't the right color. The color certainly is striking. A lot of very intense blue contrasts sharply with brilliant vermilion and graphite black.

It's a bird, said to be a crane. I'm not sure of the native interpretation, but anyway it's a crane-like bird with a long bill. The body serves as a cap fitting over the wearer's head. A broad, stylized thunderbird or hawk-like face stretches across the front—very Tlingit to me. Extending along the sides are what I interpret as the bird's wings. Although they lack separate feathers, they're done in typical Northern formline style. The carving is good—not the cleanest ever, but strong and direct. You can't really complain about it.

The hat is conceived as a close-fitting cap in the form of a bird with a broad, strongly sculptured face on the breast, and then, thrusting right up out of the top, the bird's head, its great beak coming forward. It successfully illustrates the idea of a mythical bird in the ancestry of noblemen wearing this hat.

A wooden band goes around the back of the head to hold it in place. Everything is hollowed out, even the neck of the bird, to make it reasonably light. I think it's a very strong, effective piece—a true crest hat, of great value and importance in the family from which it comes.

REID: I wonder if that's all there ever was, or if leather or feathers or something have been cut off.

HOLM: It's chopped off in the back rather abruptly. It seems incomplete there. It could very well have had a leather flap, with more detail, coming down. Many Tlingit clan hats did.

REID: It's a very graceful object, pleasing in all respects. There's a bit of abalone inlay in the hawk face in the front and in the eyes of the bird itself. Rather interesting red eyebrow forms which I suppose aren't eyebrows but have to do with some actual characteristic of the bird depicted.

HOLM: I think so, too. It's been called a crane, but it might not hurt to look through a field guide to southeastern Alaskan birds to see if there's one that really looks like this. I think the stripes on the neck, as well as the red stripe over the eye, are identification clues. It may represent the red-throated loon.

66

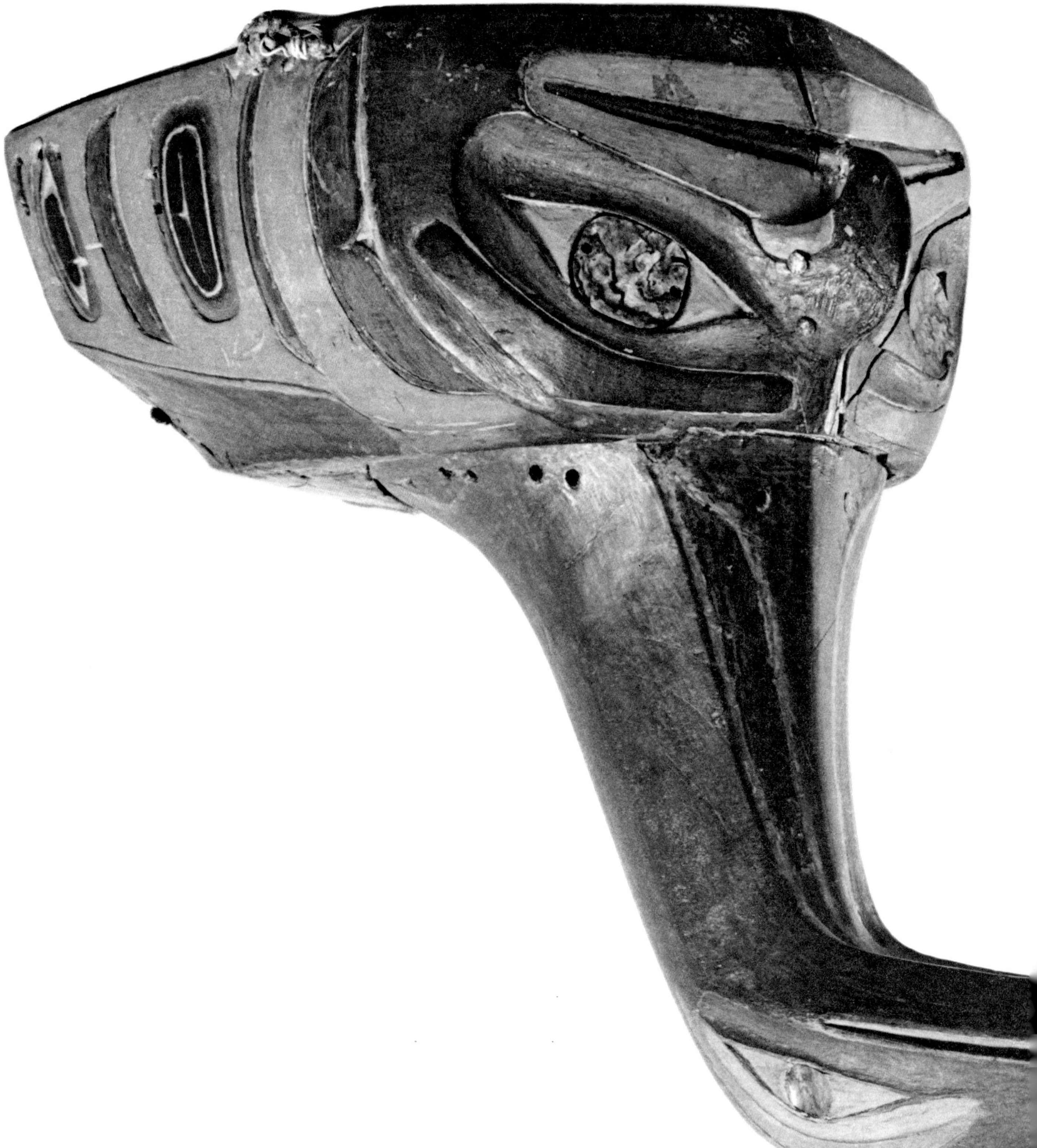

REID: Headpiece with carved skullcap, very ingeniously made. Are there many of these around?

HOLM: Quite a few. Most that I've seen were well-documented Tlingit pieces, although I don't think this one is. It's Alaskan, I think, but probably Haida, or from that same problematical little corner of Alaska and British Columbia.

REID: It was problematical, but it sure was rich. This is a very nice example of things that came out of there.

Although a tradition has grown up of calling representations of birds with this kind of back-curved beak hawks or ospreys, I suppose that it represents a thunderbird. Marge Helpin maintains that there are no hawks in the mythology or the art.

It's in beautiful condition. Has it been restored?

HOLM: Yes. It was completely covered, badly, with shiny commercial paint. That's been removed.

67 REID: So that's the reason for its "new" appearance. The abalone is all intact now. Anyhow, it's a beautiful carving. It has some of that "out-thrust" quality—that explosive force associated generally with more Southern groups. As always in these Northern pieces, the thrust may be outward for awhile, but it comes back into itself again instead of just continuing outward—as with Bella Bella, Bella Coola, or Kwakiutl pieces.

HOLM: This piece is in direct contrast to the wolf frontlet, #71, which thrusts right out and can go right on from there.

REID: A simple depiction of the form, yet nicely done in detail.

HOLM: The faces in the ears are a nice touch—typical of that region. Frequently a little profile face or full face in the ear is worked out in the same sculptural style as the rest of the figure.

The art conventions are carried through here. This artist seems to have had more control than the one who made the wolf frontlet, #71. And those conventions, working together, make this thing a unit. I'm looking at the curve of this beak coming back, returning into the composition. That almost repeats the shape of the ears. These "near" repetitions—semiangular forms which work around and around in the thing—keep the movement going. It works very well.

REID: What about that green paint?

HOLM: That's what was there. I don't know what to say about it, except that it's green.

REID: Commercial paint.

HOLM: Maybe. There was a layer of quite blue paint over it that was real enamel. What this is, I don't know. But the blue enamel came off of it. It's always hard to know what to do about that. I'm pretty sure the blue paint was put on by some Indian who had a legitimate purpose in doing so.

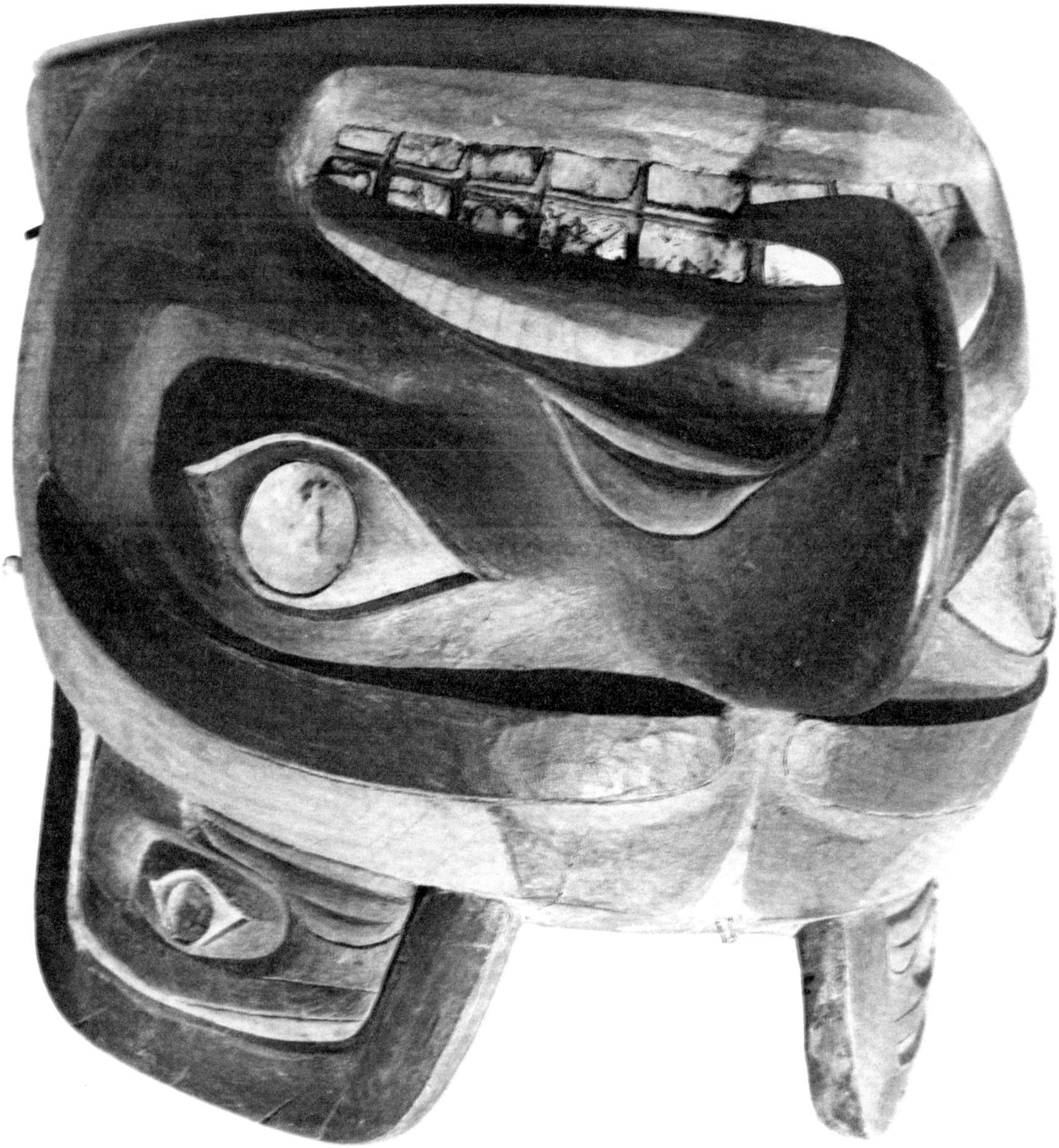

68

REID: Tlingit frontlet of some kind?

HOLM: Might be Tlingit. There could be a question. I tend to go for Tsimshian. Frontlet, anyway.

REID: To me, it's not a pleasant thing. Nicely made, a piece nobody would be ashamed to wear. Unusual and for that reason perhaps valuable. But it really doesn't do that much for me. About all I can admire is its fairly proficient technique. The face is well modeled but not very expressive.

HOLM: My guess is that your feeling is partly based on the facial expression. But, eliminate the mouth and the top part looks different. Maybe that's the problem. I don't share your feelings about it. I think it's very nice, more than nice. I like it a lot.

It seems never to have had a rim. That makes it unusual, though I know of other examples. Other than that, it's a typical dancing headdress frontlet. I find the carving expressive and not unpleasant. The face has been given the most attention. The body and arms and legs are much simpler, almost crude. The features and structure are Northern style, and, to me, Tsimshian, especially the open skeletal structure with nice, firm or taut, flesh and skin over it. Then it has an interesting painting on the face. It reflects the whole painting and relief-carving tradition we've been discussing all this time. Here it was applied over a very irregular surface, yet it's related to that surface.

REID: Let's face it. We're not talking about bad things and good things. We're talking about good things and great things.

HOLM: No, I don't mean to give that impression. Our likes and dislikes are subjective. Some pieces one of us likes, the other doesn't. That says nothing about the piece itself. It merely says something about the people looking at it.

But, I really feel that, if the fellow's mouth had been different, you would feel differently about it, too. But—that's a guess.

69

HOLM: Fine little frontlet. Very Tlingit. Has many characteristics I think of as being real Tlinglit: the shape of the plaque itself, almost rectangular with a very slightly curved top; flat, blue-green painting over all the plaque; the carving style of the bear and the cub—I presume it's a cub.

It was once painted solidly Tlingit blue-green, with details of the faces and limbs in vermilion. A lot of the blue has worn off. That's typical. Somehow, that particular paint just doesn't hold up.

REID: How was that paint made?

HOLM: I don't know. I've made blue out of copper and it looks something like this, but it's always a little brighter. This is quite bright where it hasn't worn away too much. I've an idea there was some chemical problem with the combination of copper-derived paint and the binding medium.

In some ways this frontlet is similar to #70, but stylistically it's very different. With #70 there's a depth and definition to the carving of the eye sockets and other parts that suggest Haida attribution. But this one has the roundness and flatness of the typical Tlingit frontlet, though its general configuration is the same.

REID: It's better than it looks. If you look at it superficially, the flaking of the paint makes it look as though the carving wasn't particularly sharp or well defined. But if you examine it closely, you see that it's actually well worked and beautifully detailed.

It's not one of the most exciting pieces because it's such a straightforward approach. The carver didn't want to do anything except a good, competent job. Everything is laid out in a traditional straightforward way. There's nothing wrong with that. It's well designed, well constructed—an attractive piece. For its size, it enjoys a lavish use of abalone. Very nice.

REID: About as classic a frontlet as you can get for its style. Bear with small human faces in the ears. The human faces have little three-fingered hands projecting over the bear's forehead. This is one of the great things about Northwest Coast artists—logic as we understand it had no relevance in their way of doing business.

Lots of abalone inlay in the piece: nostrils, eyes, forearms. Like all Northwest Coast creatures, this has humanoid characteristics as well. Its arms and legs are more human than bear-like. Red lips. Lots of red painting. The painting is elementary, but well done.

It's been suggested this is a Charles Edenshaw piece because it resembles an unfinished frontlet (C) directly attributed to Edenshaw in the American Museum of Natural History [16-241]. If it isn't, it's very similar. In any case, the artist wasn't taking any chances on being very radical. He made a straightforward frontlet and certainly did a good job of it. Of its type, it's as good as you could find.

70

A

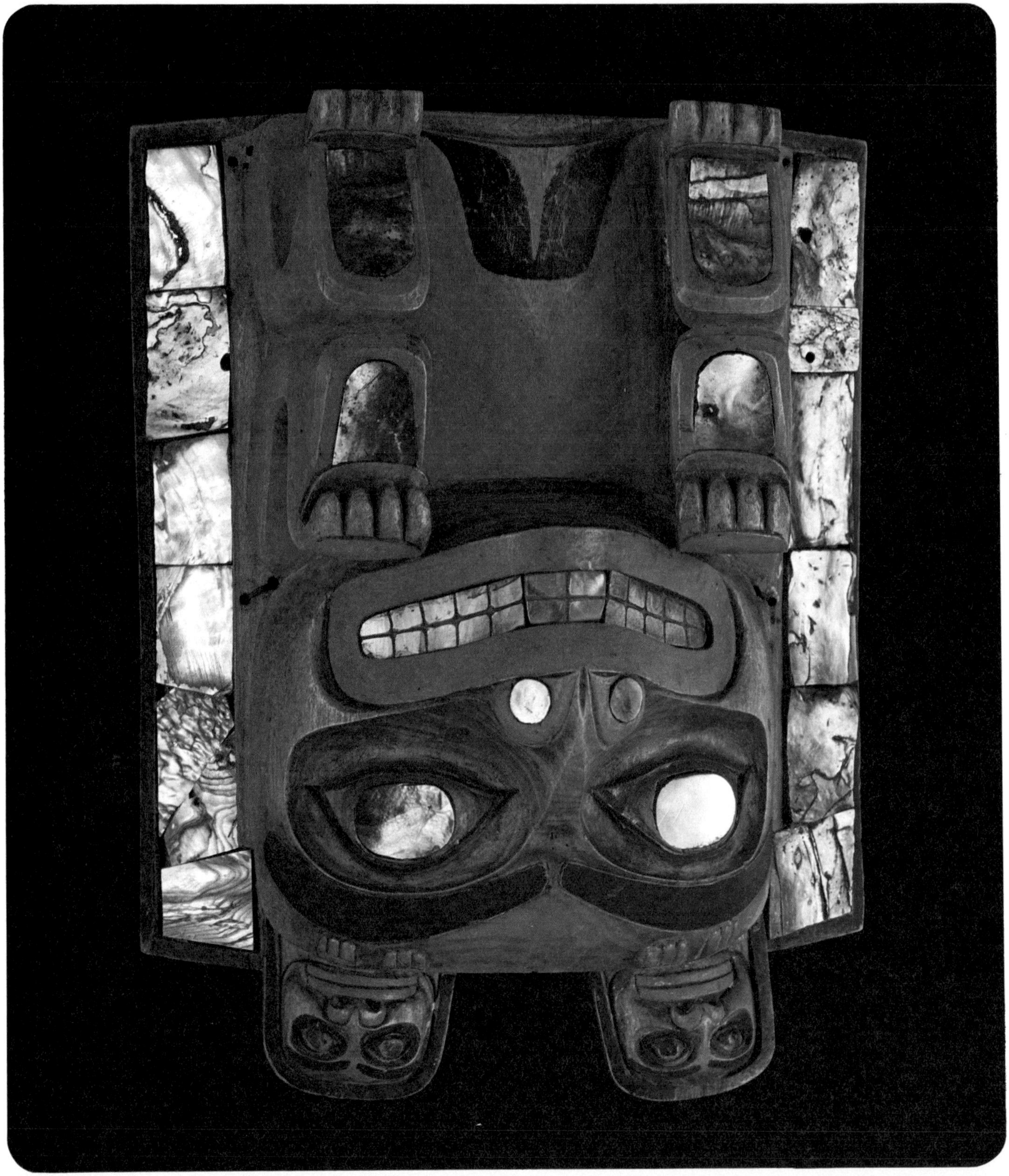

HOLM: I agree with everything right down the line. Personally I'm not strong for an Edenshaw connection here. The unfinished frontlet is different, especially in the structure of the eyes. Its limbs are rounded and modeled, not flat and angular. The only thing here that suggests Edenshaw to me is its similarity in structure to another bear frontlet (A), belonging to Mrs. Morton I. Sosland, with little naturalistic faces, in the ears, that look like Edenshaw faces. This frontlet also seems to belong with a dogfish frontlet (B) in the Denver Art Museum [QHi-119]. I think all are classic Haida frontlets and the work of one man. They show more real Haida characteristics than almost any Edenshaw piece. They're right down the middle—classic Haida style—while Edenshaw's work skitters around the edges, devolving from it but going off into another thing.

To me, the crispness of it, the definition of eye sockets, the spiral nostrils, the rather geometric or formline limb structure, and the almost self-consciously structural form of the whole thing make it classic Haida—maybe not Edenshaw. I'm always worried when people get concerned about

B

whether a piece is Edenshaw or not—when they think that means something about its quality. We know it's likely to be a good one, maybe a great one, if it's Edenshaw, but that certainly doesn't make it better than another one. Personally, I don't want to stress that possible connection here at all. It's a great piece in itself. I felt that from the moment I saw it. It doesn't need to depend on any other characteristic.

Almost without exception, the red paint on these pieces appears to be vermilion. A few are so dark, it's hard to tell, but that seems to be the paint we see. Right now I'm having a person, knowledgeable about these things, analyze the pigments of several hundred pieces. Hopefully we're going to come up with some knowledge about Northwest Coast paint pigments. I think we're going to find a lot of very refined, perhaps commercial, vermilion paint. This is no problem—we know vermilion came into the trade on the Northwest Coast very early. It was highly desired by artists. They used a lot of it. There's sure a lot of vermilion in this bunch of stuff. That's a very fine frontlet.

177 C

REID: Bella Bella frontlet, probably maple. Upturned beak or, more accurately, radically uptilted beak; upper part very long, lower part very short. Domed metal eyes. Abalone inlay border. Little man at top. Teeth. Beautifully made. Concave, convex surfaces blend perfectly. Variation in line adds great interest to the whole design. Power with subtlety. A damned nice thing. We can only imagine what it would look like worn, but it would be no disgrace, to anybody, to appear at any occasion wearing this.

HOLM: Let me look at the wood with my lens. All the masks we've talked about so far, I think, are alder. I think this is maple. Anyway, it's a hard, dense wood.

I'm inclined toward a Bella Coola identification or, if I have to specify beyond that, to Bella Bella. I base that on: the structure of the planes of the face; the shape of the orb of the eye and the structure of the cheek around it; the handling of the nostrils; the bold eyebrows with sharply back-slanting, clearly defined forehead planes; the eye socket running on to the beak; the little T-shaped relief defining the border of the eye area on the cheek—here barely discernible because a lot of the blue paint has rubbed off (as is usual, although this is a different blue from the one we talked about before and doesn't fall off as readily as the other). There is also the very Bella Coola color arrangement—a blue as a main color that has almost come to be called "Bella Coola blue," vermilion, black, and natural wood background.

The little head protruding over the angular rim is a familiar feature of Bella Coola/Bella Bella frontlets, as well as of frontlets all the way down to the southern Kwakiutl. Another characteristic is abalone inlay spaced out on the rim, rather than in a solid or closely set band. And the swept-back side panels and the upswept beak are also characteristics of frontlets of that region.

In complete form, this frontlet was tied or sewn to a cylindrical frame, the upper rim of which was set with sea-lion whiskers in the form of a picket fence. The back of the frame had a long pendant trailer, a foot or more in width, covered with rows of ermine skins, extending down the wearer's back, sometimes to his knees. The whole headdress was extremely rich, combining many materials, each doing its thing in the dance. Along with this headdress, the dancer wore his dancing apron and either his Chilkat blanket or his button blanket. The whole was spectacular.

The headdress is meant to move. As the dancer performs, he shakes his head, bobs, dips, throws his head back. The sea-lion whiskers, standing as much as a foot above the headdress, whip back and forth . . . eagle down, put in the center of the headdress, scatters and flies through the air . . . all the ermine skins flop up and down as he bounces and jumps . . . and the abalone glitters in the firelight. Alone, right here, this frontlet is a powerful thing, but seen together, with all the rest, it has an impact hard to imagine. This would be a great frontlet. I'd be proud to wear it. It's a great piece.

REID: I think what appeals to those of us interested in Northwest Coast art is the enormous number of levels of aesthetic appreciation involved. A piece can become part of a costume and, as such, disappear into an overall effect. Or it can be held in the hand, a thing of beauty in itself. And beyond this, there are many other levels of meaning and expression in every individual part. This can be said of great art of all periods, but it's such an obvious, pleasurable thing with Northwest Coast materials.

71

72

REID: Frontlet. Bella Bella? Bella Coola?

HOLM: Could be either. It has a wildness that suggests Bella Bella, but it could be either one.

REID: Whatever it is, it's pretty great. I've known this piece for a long time. A friend owned it and was justifiably proud of it. At that time it was badly damaged, with about a third of it split off completely. I presume it represents a wolf or some kind of wolf figure.

HOLM: I think it's a wolf.

REID: It has a lot of strange things going on. It's got that nice shape of a copper shield. I think that's one of the most attractive of all frontlet shapes. It's exquisitely carved, in a bold, straightforward way.

There's an entirely different feeling about Southern and Northern carving. Both the Haida frontlet, #70, and the Tlingit frontlet, #69, are contained and circumscribed by the shapes and the forms of the plaques they are on, whereas this thing seems to be rushing out of the background—as though it had so much energy, it was impossible for this plaque to contain it.

It has some very interesting things. The ears, which are vaguely humanoid, seem to have been put on backwards.

HOLM: They're really different.

REID: They grow out of the border of the frontlet, rather than out of the head of the beast. That kind of crazy approach, I think, is one of the delightful things about some pieces of Northwest Coast art. It represents a kind of imagination impossible to conceive of in our more circumscribed lives.

A couple of other little faces are very Bella Coola-ish or Bella Bella-ish.

HOLM: It certainly is a powerful thing, and it does rush right out of the background. It has inlaid metal, apparently copper, for the teeth, and the washer-type of eye where a metal disc with a hole in the middle has been domed out and placed over the eye with a mirror behind it, so that it flashes a little glint from time to time as you move it. The eyes of both the other figures, above and below the main figure, are also made of mirrored glass. That's fairly common in this central area of the Southern Coastal region. Also common to these thrusting frontlets from the Bella Coola – Bella Bella – Kwakiutl area are added pieces like the paws or hands that jut out below the main figure.

The big problem in restoring this has been the copper-shaped, bowed recesses at the top. We concluded that they must have been little rattles made of real copper, shaped in the form of "copper shields" and domed out to hold some rattling material. That's a guess. It's a strange, strange thing.

A very strong headdress. No trace of paint that I can find. I don't know if it was ever painted or ever finished or what the story is.

HOLM: Frontlet. Northern style. I'd call it Tlingit, but it could be Haida or Tsimshian. In a photograph, it looks like an ordinary, straightforward frontlet, but when you see the actual piece and hold it in your hands, you realize it's not an ordinary frontlet at all, but about twice as big as most. Another frontlet-like headdress, #74, is very large. But it's unusual in other ways as well. This one is like a standard frontlet except that it's very much enlarged. Though the design and carving are reasonably nice, its outstanding feature is its size. It has no abalone inlay, but that's not completely unknown. Quite a few frontlets have no abalone. This one has strange, striped painting on it, much obscured by what looks like varnish.

REID: It's one of those funny, interesting pieces which, to me at least, aren't terribly pleasing aesthetically. It represents some kind of bird . . . and well, it leaves me completely unmoved. The bird seems to be well contained within the border. In places on this border, it almost looks as if the frontlet were molded—and not particularly well—out of some plastic material, rather than carved out of wood. There're dips and hollows in what should be flat areas, which is inexplicable, unless the carver had a terrible piece of wood which split the wrong way on him. I can't begin to speculate on the reasons for these things.

The face at the bottom—which this bird sort of perches on—has tremendously exaggerated eye sockets that almost consume the whole face.

HOLM: That's a Tlingit characteristic, of course. It's one of the things that makes me feel this frontlet is Tlingit. Strong little face. And the feet are nice, too—as they come down and emphasize that point between the eyebrows. The toes converge in a strange way, but it works well.

REID: Well, it does seem to work as a design in some ways. The little feet repeat the pattern made by the beak, and these two features correspond very well. Too bad it's lost its color. I imagine it was spectacular when it was new and all dressed up with the rest of the rigging on it. The wearer certainly towered above his compatriots with smaller headdresses.

73

REID: Fantastic frontlet. It doesn't conform to any style of Northwest Coast art, as far as I'm concerned, yet when I first saw it years ago, it immediately had a Haida impact. I think it's one of those funny Haida things that happen now and then. Haida artists worked mostly within a rigid, formal system, but occasionally burst out and did crazy, wild things which out-crazied the other people of the Coast.

This has none of the formal organization and classic beauty of the things we associate with the Northwest Coast, yet I find it extremely powerful, potent—in spite of the fact that nothing works properly here. For instance, the nose is a little, weak thing—it shouldn't fit with the other parts. The eyes are big, but not particularly well formed. It has lots of abalone giving off lots of glitter. But even with the abalone removed, it would still be a powerful piece.

Even removed from its function as a headdress, it has an immediate, direct, compelling impact. It must have been a spectacular thing to be seen worn and probably outshone the exquisite frontlets and headdresses of other people at the feasts or wherever it was displayed. It falls outside my sphere of appreciation altogether as far as Northwest Coast art is concerned, yet I find it a great thing.

HOLM: I agree with most of your comments. You like it better than I do. Probably that's because of my more single-minded interest in the formal aspects of this art. That colors my feelings of this so strongly that I have trouble in seeing beyond that. It's a strong piece—no question about that. But it's not refined; it doesn't follow what I regard as correct form. Although clearly intended as a frontlet, it's entirely different from any frontlet that ever was, as far as I know—in construction, in the way it's put together, in size, in just about everything.

The whole headdress is in one piece. Rather than having a constructed frame, with a fence of sea-lion whiskers attached, the whiskers were inserted in holes drilled in the wood. A baleen or wooden frame went around the head just enough to hold the frontlet. It probably had a trailer of ermine skins as well, since that was part and parcel of this sort of headdress, but attached directly to the frontlet itself rather than to the frame.

So, although it looks in general layout and shape like a frontlet, it's bigger than any other and has a different kind of construction. I think your comment about it outshining others may well be valid, primarily on its boldness and size.

REID: Look at it the other way: imagine somebody turning up at a feast or ceremony with that on and being laughed out of the company—having that ridiculous garment!

HOLM: Right. If that had been the case, we'd never have seen this thing. It would have been destroyed. Certainly it wouldn't show all the wear this shows. The inside has lots of good, old, forehead grease. The outside is also worn. It looks to me like it's been used quite a bit. I think he got by with it.

REID: On sheer nerve.

HOLM: Yeah. Maybe that was some of the courage you were talking about earlier.

74

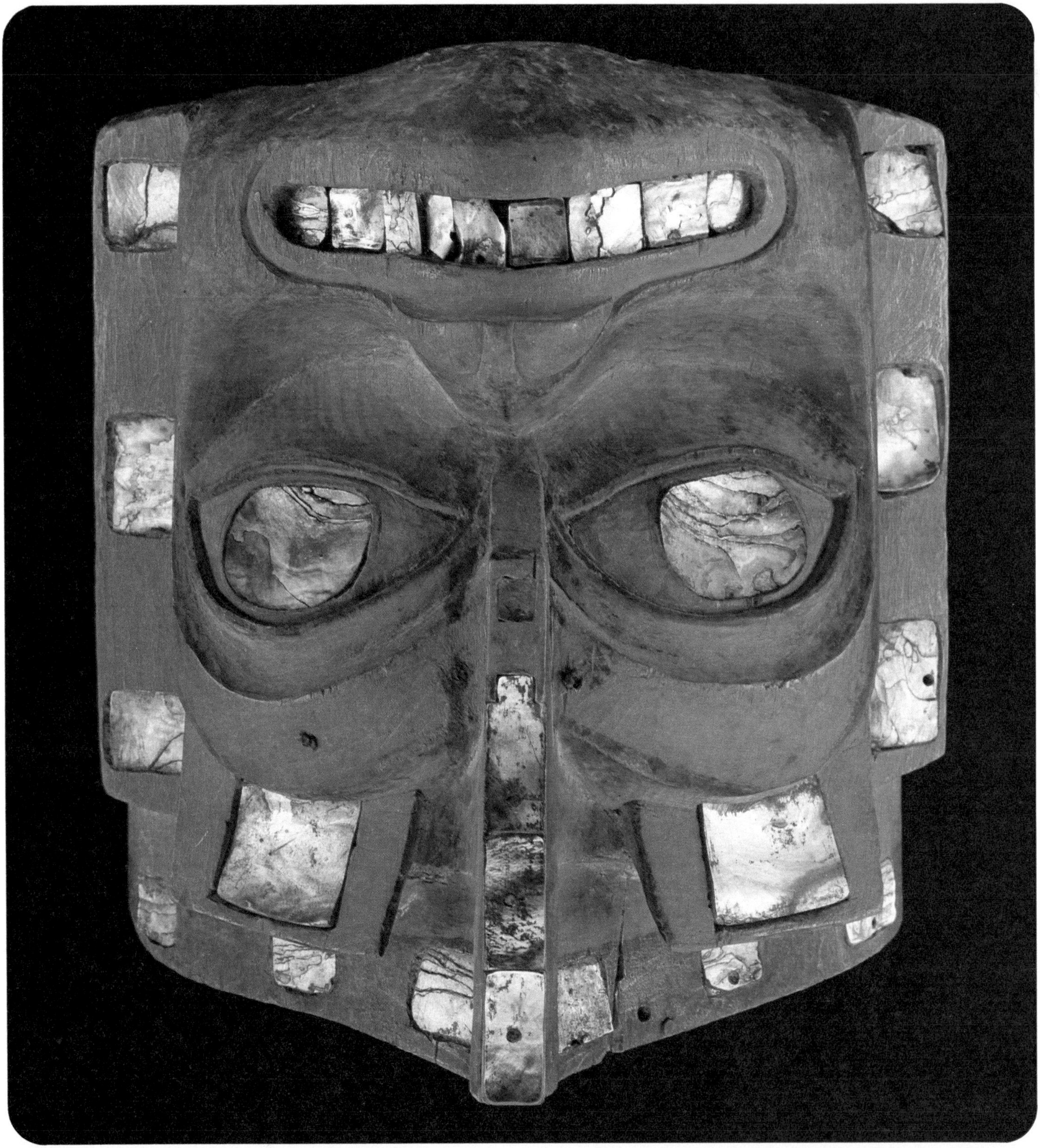

75

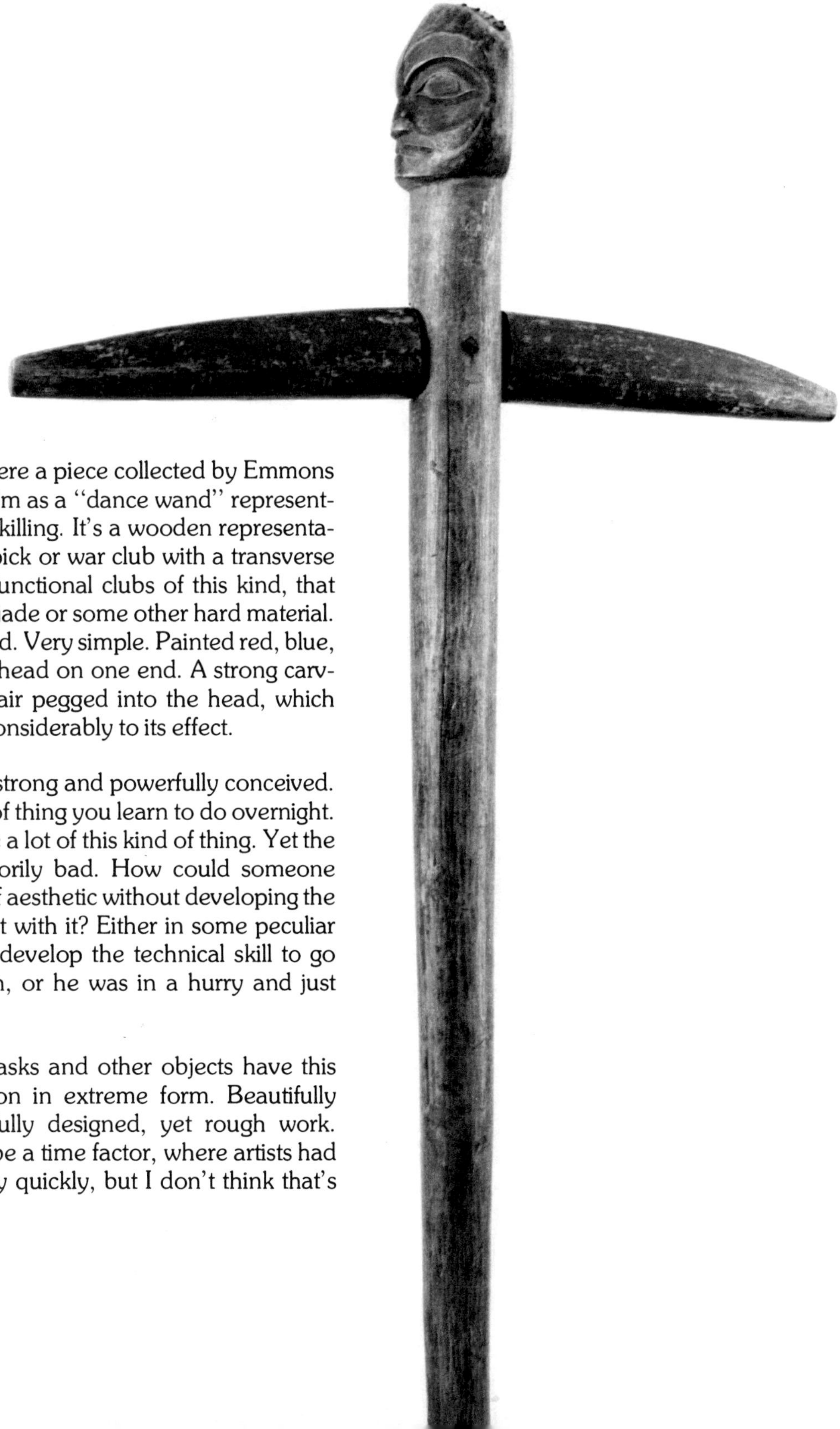

HOLM: We have here a piece collected by Emmons and described by him as a "dance wand" representing a pick for slave killing. It's a wooden representation of an old war pick or war club with a transverse blade. In the old, functional clubs of this kind, that blade was made of jade or some other hard material. In this case, it's wood. Very simple. Painted red, blue, and black. Carved head on one end. A strong carving. Had human hair pegged into the head, which must have added considerably to its effect.

REID: The head is strong and powerfully conceived. That's not the sort of thing you learn to do overnight. He must have done a lot of this kind of thing. Yet the carving is perfunctorily bad. How could someone develop that kind of aesthetic without developing the technique that went with it? Either in some peculiar way he just didn't develop the technical skill to go with his conception, or he was in a hurry and just dashed it off.

HOLM: Certain masks and other objects have this strange contradiction in extreme form. Beautifully conceived, powerfully designed, yet rough work. Some of that may be a time factor, where artists had to finish pieces very quickly, but I don't think that's the case here.

HOLM: A really beautiful rattle, apparently from the same period and the same region as #87. Listed as "Collected at Blunden Harbour," but surely from the west coast of Vancouver Island. In all features, it's exactly like late 18th-century rattles from that area, and like subsequent rattles from that area up to the present, though much more refined than many of them.

It's in the form of a bird with a small head, like a seagull. Nice blue trade beads serve as eyes, giving it a lot of expression. A very Northwest Coast eye—if there could be such a thing. Typical of rattles from the west coast of Vancouver Island, Southern rattles, globular or football in shape, with wings, and tail. The long neck and head are parts of this basic form, worked into that form so nicely the whole thing fits together.

A big, triangular space has been cut out of the neck. That's absolutely typical of Nootka rattles. It's analogous to the hole cut through the head of a Northern raven rattle. The only reasons I can imagine for doing this are to lighten the rattle and maybe increase its resonance by cutting away part of that sound-deadening area, the heavy neck, which would be difficult to hollow out from the inside. It's absolutely typical to have it cut through this way. It makes it look as if the neck had been constructed from two separate pieces. There's hardly any surface decoration except the fluting of the head and neck, which is terrifically elegant. It gives grace. Nicely shaped wings and tail extend on the back. Very simple little head, just eyes and mouth carved into it. Perfect example of pure Nootka sculpture. 188

REID: I think you've said it all. What's essential is its purity. Sculpturally it's superb. It's got an elegant combination of concave and convex curves, in some way perfect with the fluting on the head and neck. The sharp curves leading into the wings from the fluting on the neck show a master carver—a great artist.

It's another of those things about which you could safely say: this is one of the great pieces from any area, any time. In spite of its extreme simplicity, I find it superb. Everything about it is the way it ought to be.

HOLM: This kind of piece always gets me to wishing that I could have been there when it was carved—gotten into the artist's mind, known what he thought when he carved that plane that comes down the neck and into the wing, imagined how he might have related that plane to the other flutes in the head. I'm sorry I wasn't there.

REID: It's the complete antithesis of that first pipe which we discussed, where the artist pushed everything as far as he could. Here he carried it only as far as necessary, then left it. Both techniques are obviously the right ones to use at the right times.

76

HOLM: I wonder what that says about the Nootka and the Haida. I don't know, but maybe it says something.

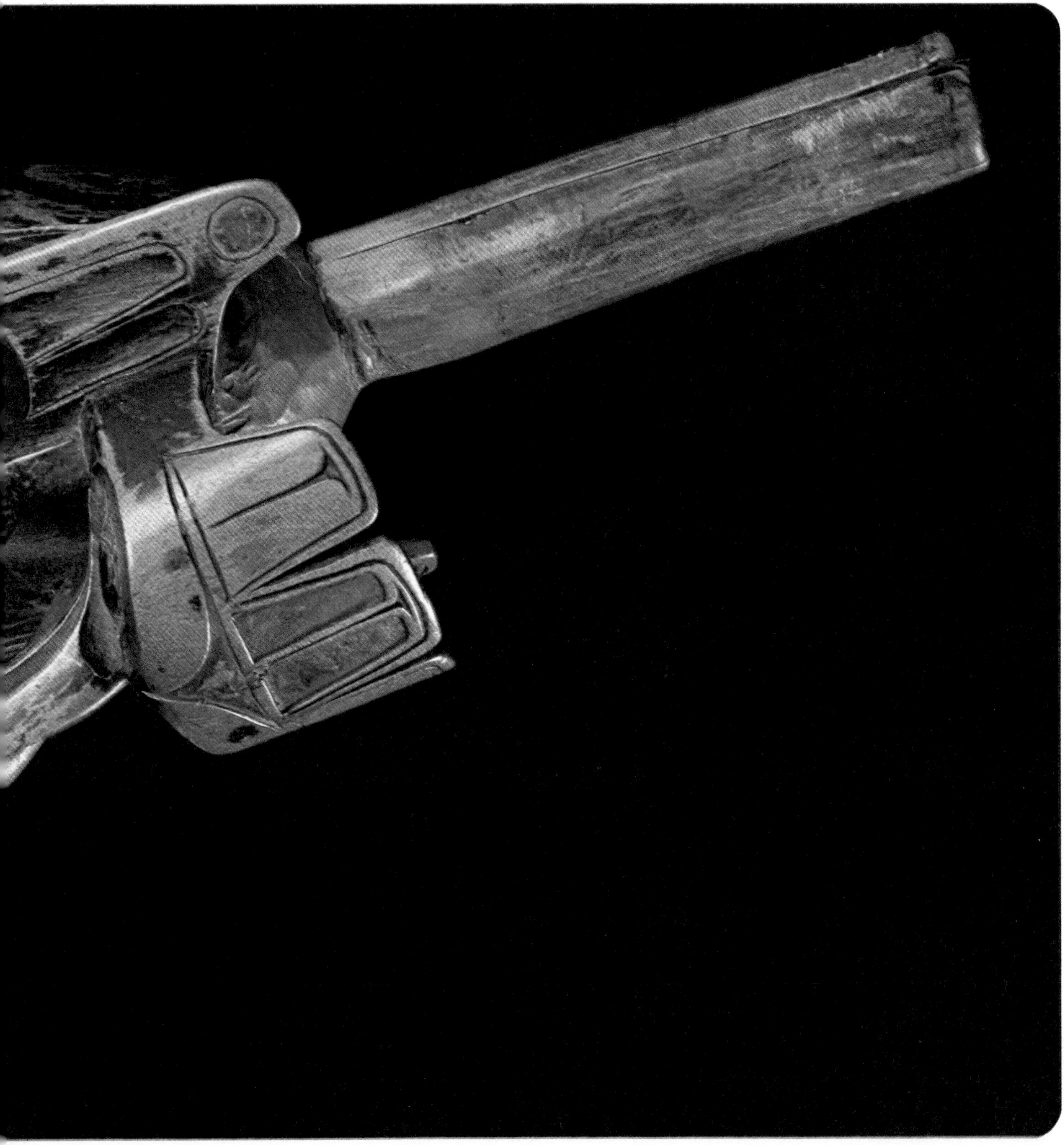

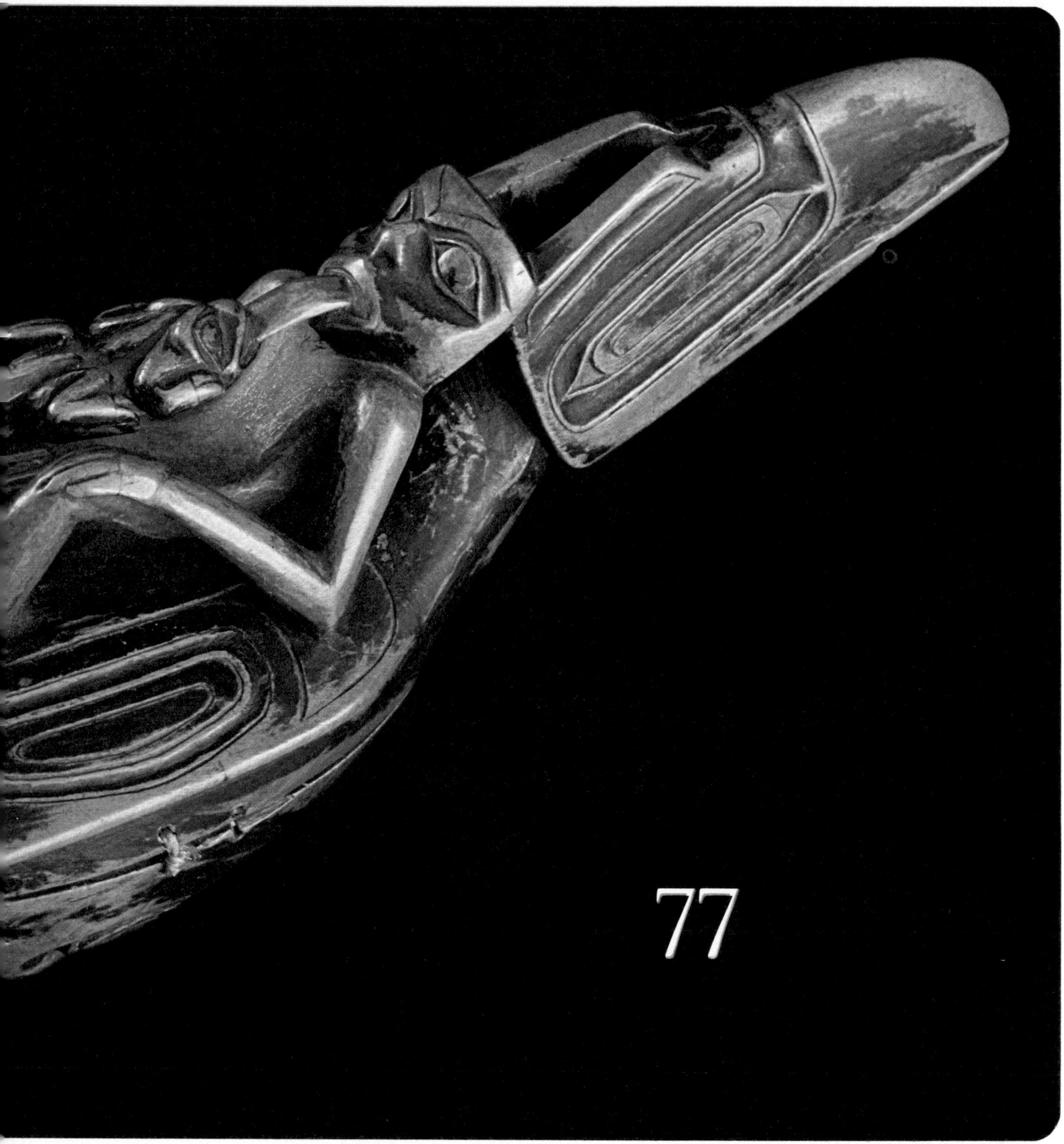

77

HOLM: At first glance this rattle appears to be a very conventional Northern "raven rattle." But when you examine it carefully, you discover features different from many raven rattles. Then it begins to resemble some I know, and others I know only as fragments—almost totally gone—that must be pre-19th century. So, I'm going to say right off: it's Tlingit and very old. I think it goes back to the early 19th century.

The features in common are: first, a rather straight configuration, with the raven's head coming out almost in line with the handle rather than sharply curved upwards. Then the little man lying on the back is flattened. The backs of the raven's wings are carved in a formline design. The kinds of shapes we see in that formline pattern are similar to the patterns on early dishes we have already described: massive formlines with some angularity.

So I think it's early and Northern, probably Tlingit. It has all the features we expect on a raven rattle: the very flat formline raven head divided right through vertically, like two panels coming back alongside the neck; the tail bird or the bird whose crest feathers represent the raven's tail feathers; the little frog who grasps the tongue of the reclining man; the creature with the

sharply curved beak on the breast of the raven; and wings spread out on the side. All these features are standard; these are practically required details for a raven rattle, but in style, different. It has a compactness, a massiveness, many raven rattles do not have.

REID: It's exquisite, in spite of the fact that it's chunkier and straighter than most raven rattles. It works as a form. The detail of the bird's head, forming the raven's tail, is absolutely exquisite with its finely drawn beak. The details of the raven's eyes are unusual, but beautifully carved.

HOLM: I keep coming back to the point I made earlier. Here's an object that follows a fixed arrangement. Its details, formline systems, and all that, are regularly handled, yet it differs from the next rattle we are going to look at and from many others as well. It continually amazes me how Northern artists from different periods and areas took a highly conventionalized system, with all sorts of strong rules and customs, and came up with individual pieces.

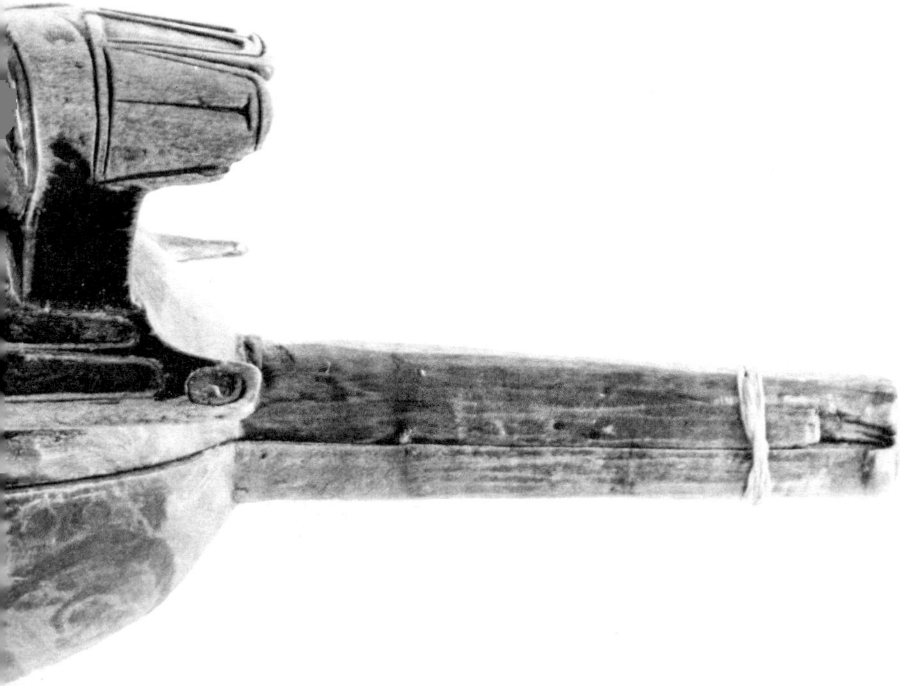

HOLM: Typical raven rattle. Our ideas about "good" and "not good" are so subjective, it's almost ridiculous even to say them, but this rattle, to me, is much greater than #77, yet nowhere as refined. It's more raven-like. It has the same figures, save the frog. The little man reclines on the back of a raven with swept-back wings. The raven's flat formline face divides right up through the middle of its head.

We usually call this bird on the breast a hawk or thunderbird. Its design, covering the whole belly or breast of the bird, is a straight, flat, formline pattern, painted and lightly engraved. It's just like the side of a big chest, with practically all of the same features, the same organization and detail, modified only enough to fit this shape.

Rules which might, to us, seem restricting, were twisted and turned and used in many different ways by Northwest Coast artists. This is a standard way of handling the breast of a rattle, yet it's also an individual expression of it. Aside from details, this rattle differs from #77 in marked ways. Much more curve. The curve of the raven's beak reverses in the neck, then extends on back through the body in a shallow, expressive S-form. The whole thing takes an S-shape. The wings sweep back, uncarved on the back. There was once a simple formline-like painting on them, but it's now obscure. The proportions of the body, in apposition to the size and curve of

78

the head, really satisfy me. It's a fine piece—cleanly carved, crisp, an expert piece. The modeling of the man's body is minimal. He's carved almost as a flat cut-out figure, with only slight modeling here and there, yet there's strength in that. It fits with the rest of the rattle—its precision, its crispness.

REID: I agree with you on many details. But the rattle doesn't appeal to me. It's more of an intellectual exercise than an intuitive one.

HOLM: Yeah, O.K. As we go along, it becomes apparent we have two points of view here. Call them "intellectual" and "intuitive." Maybe that's a good reason why we're both talking about these things.

REID: The carver was a pro. He could do a good rattle. I'm sure everyone was satisfied.

HOLM: I'm sure he was a pro. He probably made lots of rattles. We could probably even find others he did awfully close to this one. No question that he knew how to make a raven rattle, and probably quickly, as compared to a carver today.

79

HOLM: Absolutely classic raven rattle from the Northern Coast. Remarkable both in its fineness and size—it's one of the largest I've ever seen. Other than that, it's a straightforward, typical raven rattle. I know quite a few others clearly made by the same artist. He must have been a professional raven-rattle maker.

The workmanship is superb. Some of the carvings on the tertiary area of the breast show knife marks; it wasn't finished as perfectly as it might have been. There're other rattles that have a more perfect finish in the details. But it's absolutely fine work anyway.

Every feature of it is right down the middle of the road for a raven rattle and very successfully carried out. The figure of the man is blocky, which isn't unusual for this style rattle. The little frog sits upright and has a very human face—he's obviously not an ordinary frog at all. The bird's head forming the tail has been reversed from the others we've discussed; it faces astern and has a short, stubby little beak, rather than a long, kingfisher-type beak.

The rattle has an extreme S-curve so that the flat-sided head of the raven—typically pierced from top to bottom—is arched very much upward and curved in the beak.

And the wings themselves have a slight dip at the end, so the whole is an undulating form. It's a fine rattle.

REID: I think it's a great piece. I love the little frog—he doesn't really look like a frog at all—he looks like some supernatural gnome or troll-like creature.

The carving demonstrates extreme virtuosity. The reclining man on the raven's back is almost entirely separate from the raven itself—joined only here and there. The artist got inside all these forms and produced a perfect finish in areas almost impossible to get at with tools. Not only was he a good artist and designer, he was a master craftsman.

HOLM: He actually expended more time on the top than on the bottom, however. The tail feathers are crisp and precise. The lower part isn't as perfectly done. But I don't feel that detracts from it in any way.

REID: Again, we don't know why he spent less time on the bottom. He might have been in a hurry and it's not bad. The design of the belly is really good.

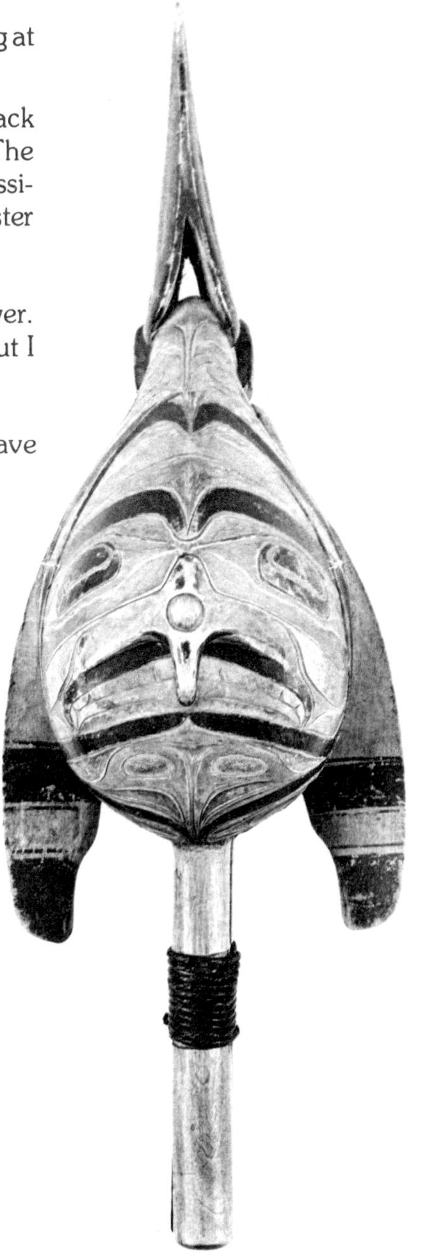

80

REID: Another raven rattle, more classic. The bird's head is in the right direction. The frog is altogether much more frog-like than the frog on #79. Classic raven-rattle form. Good workmanship; better carving on the belly than on #79, perhaps even a little better design. However, to me it's a slightly unpleasant affair. It's fine in detail, but misses in total concept because the gracefulness of the S-curve isn't there. It's a little chunkier. The man who made it was a good craftsman but not a sensitive artist.

HOLM: My reaction is similar. Maybe the carving on the bird's breast is a little better than on #79, but it's hard to tell—the whole design is more compact, and the hollowed-out areas are smaller. He didn't have that much room to leave knife marks, as the carver of #79 did. Certainly the arrangement of parts isn't as satisfying. Moreover, this one has strange things going on in the design. Nice workmanship but, from a design point of view, less satisfactory.

Not as good to hold, either. It's got a stubby tapered handle that I wouldn't want to hold onto in a dance—you've got lots to do when using a rattle, and this isn't a very secure grip. It may once have been larger and since repaired. It's very awkward to hold, whereas the others we've looked at had a good, solid feel to them.

All the masks and ceremonial things really have to be seen in use to understand how they were used and to get the feeling of them. The raven rattle, at least in recent years and according to most accounts I know, is the typical rattle used by a so-called chief dancer or headdress dancer. In that use, it has gone up and down the Coast. The Kwakiutl use it for this purpose, though it originated in the North.

There's a convention in their use fairly consistent over a good part of the Coast: they're held and shaken upside down, at least upside down in our view. Someone said that was because they sometimes came alive and flew off, if held the other way. I've seen them in use. Rather than shaking the rattle up in the air, keeping time, the dancer holds it down and to the side. He keeps vibrating it all the time.

When a rattle is in use, you really can't see it very well, but you know there's that rich little thing going on there. To me, part of the thrill of such a rattle is to know that it has all this stuff in it—details so small, so fine, you have to get within a few inches in order to see them. Yet there it all is, vibrating away in the half-light of the fire.

So, just another of those illogical, beautiful things that happen in these performances.

REID: Here's a little Haida clapper in the form of a raven. I suppose this was the sun . . .

HOLM: . . . I'm sure it was the sun disc on the back of the raven . . .

REID: . . . representing the light which the raven stole and scattered about the sky. It's vaguely in the form of the raven you find on traditional raven rattles—very good as far as the head is concerned, although the wings are treated differently and many other aspects aren't there.

It's a nice form, although not particularly well carved. But clappers aren't plentiful, so any are interesting to have. I don't think it's a very great piece, but it's a nice little raven.

HOLM: I agree: the carving isn't as expertly done as on some of the other pieces. But I think it's greater than you do. Not only is it a very nice shape on the whole, but its concept puts it a cut above so many other pieces. The raven with the sun disc is a surprising theme in some ways, even though we expect that familiar story to show up here and there. The disc coming up out of the back like that is

81

really unusual. It works very well. Notice how the wings come down and overlap the joints between the clappers. It gives a feeling of some kind of elegance. I like it very much. I think it's an excellent piece, not quite as well executed as some of the others, but very well conceived and carried through.

REID: Nice shape.

HOLM: Oh, it's very nice. The whole curve of the head and the body, with this break in the back and this rounded sun disc, takes it out of the ordinary.

REID: The shape of the wings goes well with the sun disc—the way they dip on the main part, then dip again, with the disc fitting into that upper curve. It's nicely done, but the proportion of the head to the body isn't quite as I like it. And the carving isn't all that good. But, you know . . .

HOLM: As you say, clappers aren't all that plentiful.

REID: It's silly to say this shaman's rattle has got to be one of the great pieces of Northwest Coast art.

HOLM: I don't think that's too silly, Bill. Go ahead and say it.

REID: But we could go on forever saying the same thing. It's not just great Northwest Coast art, what the hell, it's one of the greatest examples of human expression.

82

We have to see into the mind behind this piece. We don't know why it was necessary to make a rattle to represent a cockle. It's obviously a cockle because it has striations like a cockleshell has. Otherwise, it has two, presumably human, faces.

One of these is simply a face, whose significance I can't begin to guess. It may merely be the opposite side of the cockleshell. Surfaces which had no reason to be decorated were often decorated with human faces, because in Northwest Coast art that is the logical thing to do (a logic we're not going to get into at this point).

The human face on the other side has a tongue shaped like a cockle's foot. Instead of having teeth in its mouth, it has striated flesh, suggesting the interior anatomy of the cockle.

So this is a cockleshell.

That has nothing to do with the fact that it's a magnificent piece. I can think of nothing the artist could have done to make it better. It's just one of those things where an artist had the right idea and did everything right.

HOLM: I certainly can't explain that any better.

I probably differ with you in explanations of what is happening here, but I doubt if we'll ever know who is right. I see these faces as humanoid bears or some other kind of thing. I say "bears" because they come to mind, but we have to be careful not to oversimplify this iconography to a few ordinary critters who appear over and over. Lots of other things can happen. This could certainly be a cockle, or part of a cockle, just as easily as a bear with a cockle in its mouth. I see these little lines in the mouth as the rim of the shell, not as the interior of a cockle, because they have primary radiating striations, then concentric rims the other way. But that doesn't mean the whole rattle isn't the cockle. Perhaps we have an inside-out cockle. Maybe we could see it that way, with the attributes of a real cockle, just as they would be seen in nature: the teeth or mouth interior of the main face represented by the rim of the cockleshell, and the foot of the cockle—very naturalistic, looking just like a cockle foot—coming out of the mouth. Maybe the rest is a humanoid cockle, the man-like part of this stylized shell.

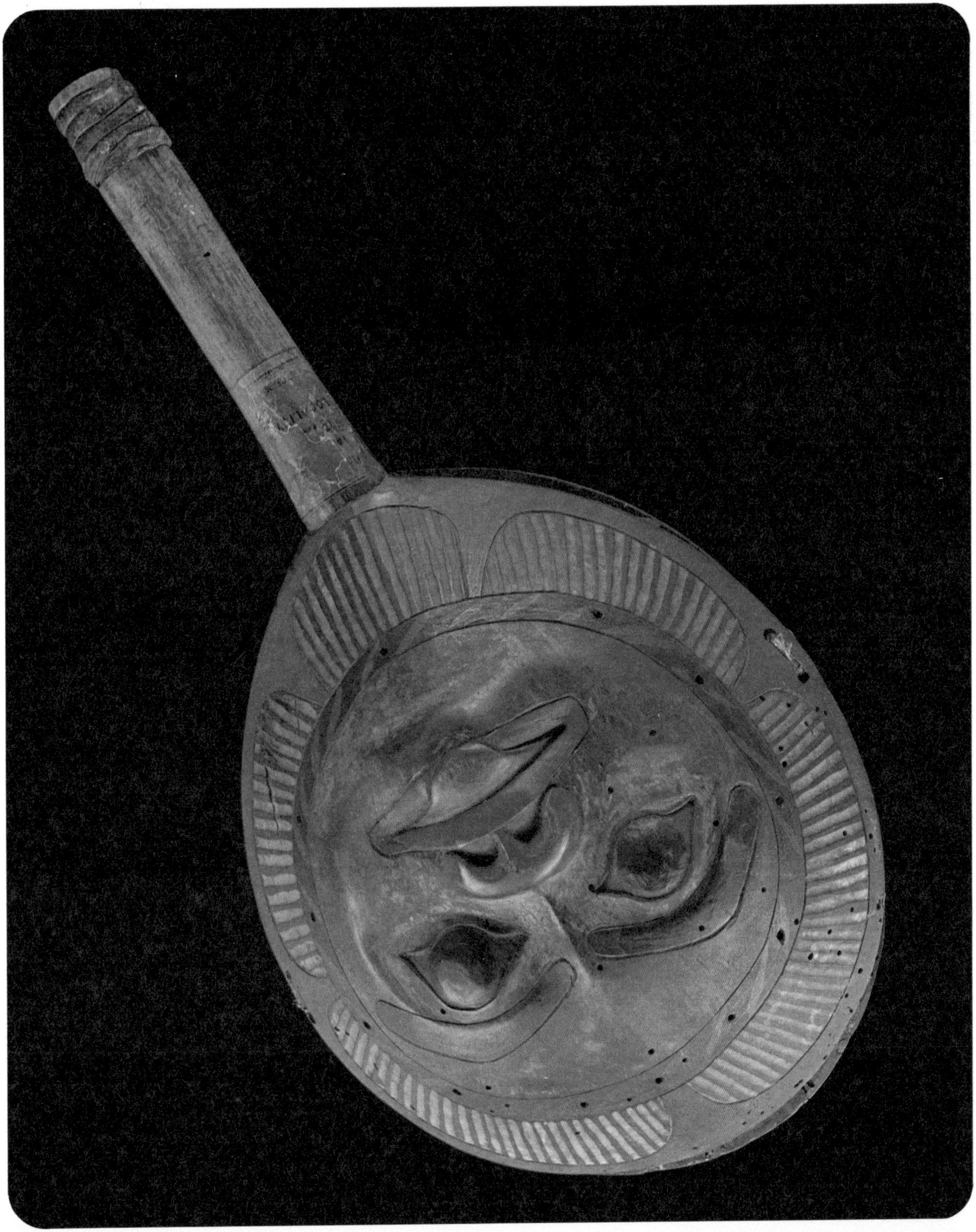

It would be completely unsafe to insist on this interpretation, though the tongue and mouth can only represent a cockle. What really is striking is how anybody could ever come up with that concept.

REID: That's really what I started out with—the fantastic imagination that went into this whole thing. Of course, there may be a legend concerning the cockle and this rattle may relate to that legend.

HOLM: It's so easy to go wrong on interpretation. Some things look obvious and we jump to conclusions. Others are so obscure we don't know what to say about them. If we really knew what was back of this particular piece, we might have a different story to tell. On the basis of ideas we do have and what we've learned over the years about the meaning of these things, we can guess, but that's all. Other than that, what can we say?

Maybe this is—I keep hoping we're not going to skip this part—but maybe this is the carving we were talking about when we began to describe what the artist must have felt, the great sense of satisfaction and joy that he must have had, in coming to this sort of solution.

REID: Yeah, he had a problem. He thought it through and obviously drew on all levels of his consciousness to bring this to fruition. He did it and it worked. He took it to the person who had commissioned it, and I suppose the joy of that whole creation eventually permeated the entire society; and now, if you want to get high-flown about it, it enhances the whole human experience by its existence. It's the other side of the human coin from the obvious, the trite.

HOLM: Yes, I'd say so. Certainly the other side from the obvious.

The artist who made this cockle rattle must have derived a lot of pleasure from struggling through this challenge and finally achieving this. He must have had great pride in his accomplishment. He had to feed on that pride to develop this sort of thing. And he must have enjoyed a great response from others. An artist needs, not complete satisfaction, but pride in what he does in order to go on. That pride derives partly from the response of others. That may not be the whole thing, but I accept what you said earlier about these things being appreciated as art. They have an impact as art objects and as solutions to art problems far beyond their importance as ceremonial or privilege objects.

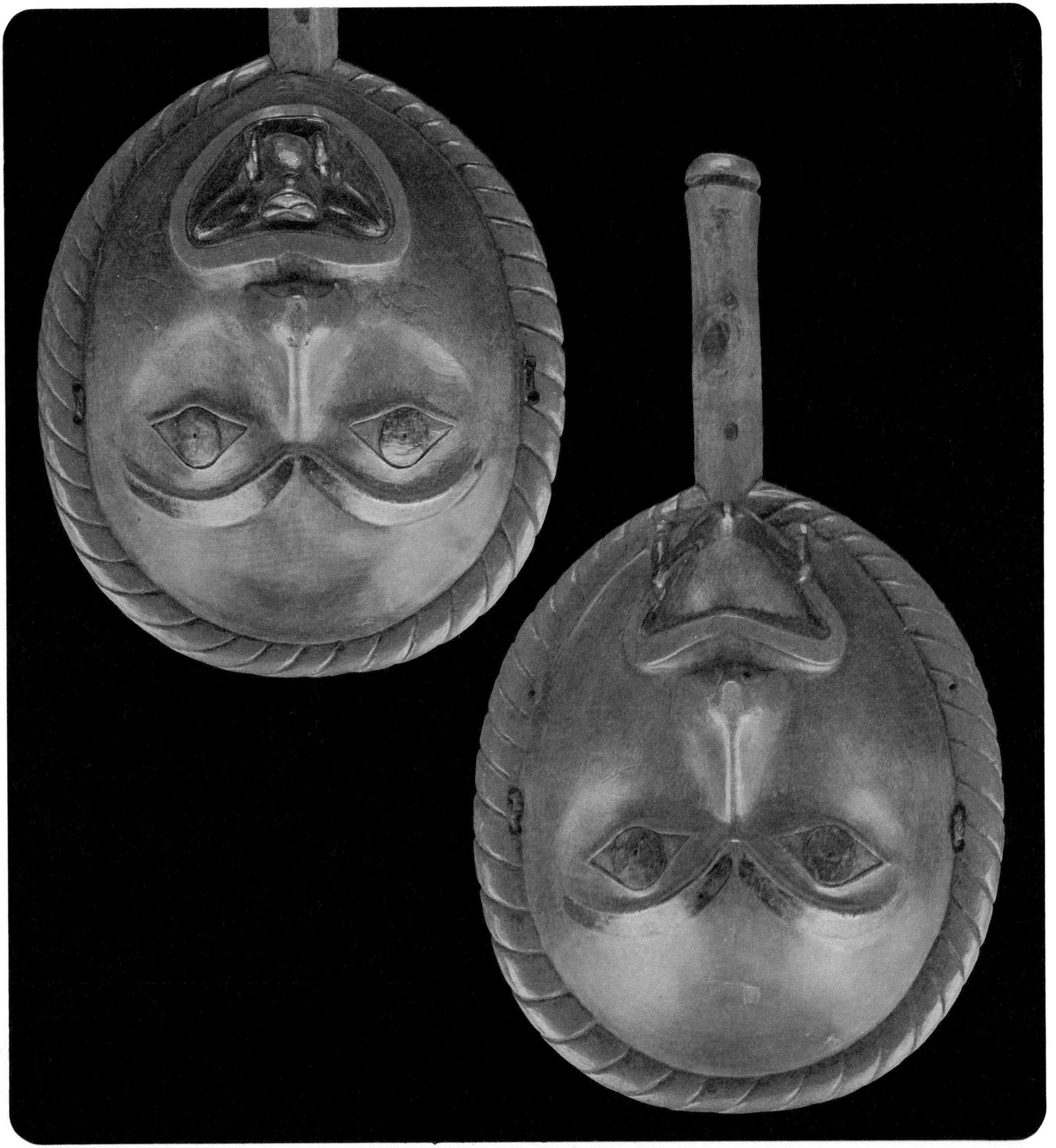

REID: Rattle with human face on either side, each containing a frog in a different position, apparently being held in the mouth. I have a theory that in all these Northwest Coast carvings nothing is happening: something has happened, something is about to happen, but at this moment, in this carving, nothing is going on. It's as though actors were waiting on stage for the curtain to go up. You can easily say the frog is climbing out of this man's mouth or the man is eating the frog, but I don't think that's happening.

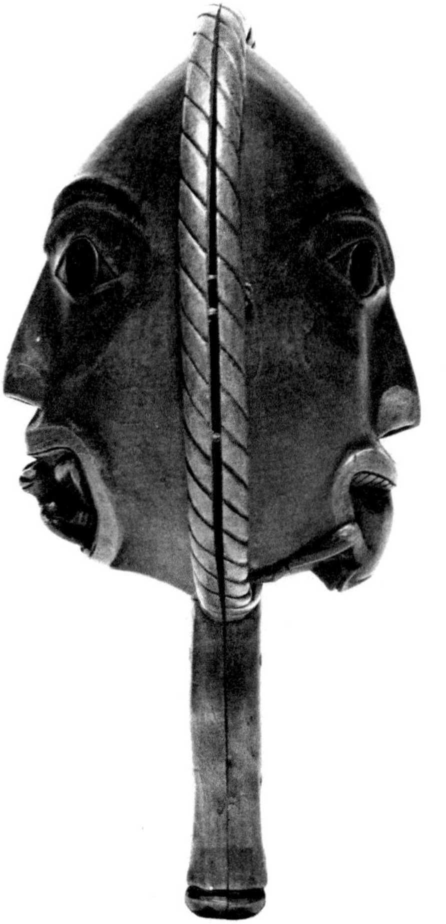

HOLM: I go along with your concept, though I can think of *one* case, not Northern, where something is happening right now. The one exception involves dynamic Kwakiutl portrait figures of a chief speaking, often holding a Copper, with knees bent, and a very stern expression, pointing one finger up in the air or directly towards the viewer. This posture captures the immediacy of the speech going on, right now! The chief's gesture underlines the words he's saying, and that very action is caught in the sculpture. That's very different from the complete timelessness of the rattle. It's a special thing, a real exception in Northwest Coast art. When I go through my slides and get to those figures, they seem to be doing something specific, at that very moment. The others don't. They have a different quality altogether.

REID: These are actors in a drama, not representations of real entities engaged in real activities. The frog on the other side is a most amusing little fellow—his arms behind his head, his feet propped up. He has to be seen to be believed.

Anyhow, this is a beautifully made piece, representing some mythological event we don't know. I don't feel I can say more.

HOLM: I believe it's Tlingit. It resembles certain pretty well-documented Tlingit rattles: fairly naturalistic treatment of the two faces; a red, rope-like rim, suggesting twisted cedar bark, around the round halves of the rattle.

According to information I've gathered, round rattles, especially with faces like this, belong to a class of doctor's rattles. Often they have faces which, if they don't resemble real skulls or corpse-like faces, have some bony structure giving them a death-like appearance. And often they have funny little objects, like frogs, in their mouths. What that means, I don't know, but it seems to fit into a traditional pattern. I think this is a doctor's rattle, not a festival-type rattle. It's very thin—its wood reduced to remarkable thinness—extremely hard maple. Its resonance is great, metallic in sound. It's a beautiful thing to hear the pebbles or beads inside striking against this thin hard shell. The handle is well worn from long use.

83

84

REID: Round doctor's rattle. Human face on either side. Around each face is a border of abstract, probably human faces. The principal faces on either side are related stylistically, but different in detail. They're typical; the same can be said of the borders. As I hold it in my hand now, what gives it its particular beauty is the superb patina, developed with age and by handling over the years, and ranging from a dark, honey color to rich brown. If it ever had paint, that's disappeared. At one time it had human hair where the two halves join, but this has largely disappeared.

But these are superficial things. If we saw this as it was the day it was made, before the patina had appeared, it would have a different beauty, but one equally potent and powerful because of its exquisite modeling, particularly of the human faces. They're done with a minimum amount of carving. In profile they're very flat, but the beauty of the planes and surfaces gives it its depth of emotional impact—something more powerful than mere richness of sculptural, physical carving. I don't know what to say about it . . . one just has to acknowledge its beauty, feel it rather than . . . I'll let you carry on with whatever technical comments you want to make.

HOLM: It seems like you're having trouble expressing our feelings about great pieces because there are just so many here.

I've known this rattle for a long time. I've always felt it was one of the greatest rattles and even among the greatest of all productions of Northwest Coast artists. These evaluations are subjective, but I've weighed it against a lot of other pieces and I don't know of any other way to express that.

It must be very old—it has every sign of great age. The color is almost unbelievable. In places deep, warm, almost translucent browns show through, set off by black encrustation. It's really a fine thing. Coupled with that great color is intricate, but still strong, formline detail around the heads.

The expressions on these faces are altogether different from those on the faces of the similarly arranged "cockleshell" rattle, #82. These are corpses or faces from the land of the dead. They're bony. The skeletal structures show in the rims of the eye sockets and cheeks. One face, with lips drawn back and teeth exposed, is skull-like. The eyes are half-closed, with an expression of death. I'm sure these faces relate to the doctor's own contact with the spirit world.

It's hard to interpret such faces. Every man in that practice had his own personal experiences and knew intimately what they were about. But the man who made this rattle understood that.

It seems to be maple—hard—with great resonance from the pebbles inside. The style is old Northern, but hard to pin down more specifically. The rattle has been variously attributed to the Tsimshian and the Tlingit; it could even be Haida. Whatever it is, it comes from long ago and is the highest expression of the work of those old artists, whoever they were. It's one of the greatest pieces I know.

REID: Both faces have a timeless, universal appeal that—I don't know . . . words are completely inadequate—but that transcends . . . I suppose that's the word . . . the normal problems and turmoils. They have something—some vision of some other humanity that the artist can see.

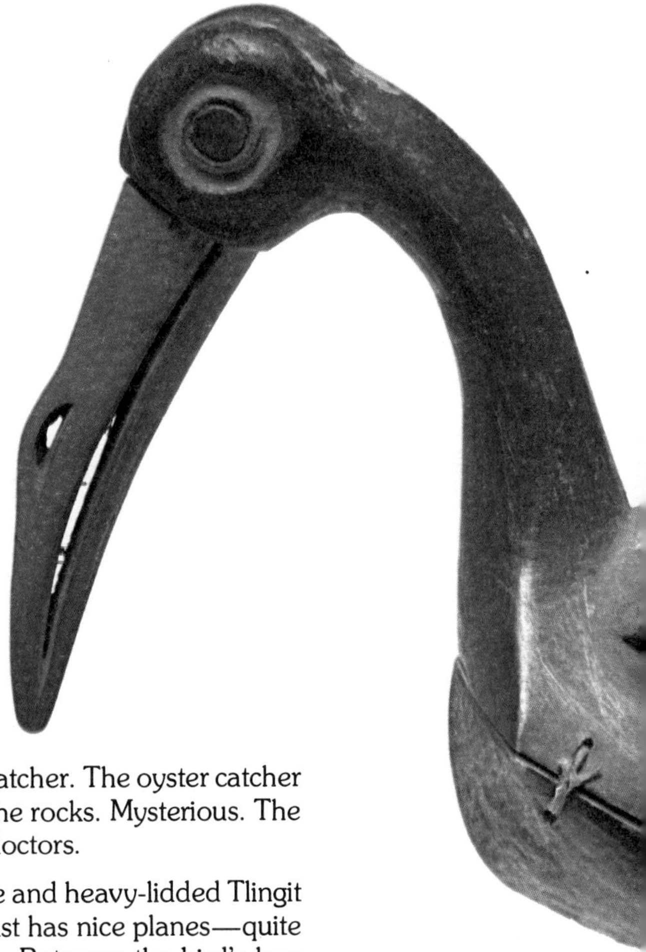

85

HOLM: Doctor's rattle shaped like a crane or oyster catcher. The oyster catcher is a crazy bird in nature, a peculiar one to watch on the rocks. Mysterious. The sort of bird I think would have something to do with doctors.

The head of some unknown animal, with long tongue and heavy-lidded Tlingit eyes, juts out at the rear of the body. The bird's breast has nice planes—quite bird-like. The design shows an exaggerated sternum. Between the bird's legs there's a little round disc—apparently the cloaca. Most oyster-catcher rattles have that. Some are pretty graphic. At least one, I know, has an inlay there.

Usual cluster of figures on the back. There're many variations to these figures. I don't know their significance, but since these rattles apparently were exclusively used by doctors in their practices, they tend to have mysterious things going on related to that work. Here two men squat on the back, grasping one another. Both have hollow heads. The head that rests against the ears of the animal was probably hollowed for lightness. But I don't know why there's a hole in the back of the other head. Possibly there was hair there.

REID: The angularity of flat planes and sharp corners gives the body a more interesting aspect than it would otherwise have. The carving of the head is excellent, and the little faces of the men, in spite of wear, seem to be excellent. The feet of each man either turn backwards on their ankles, which is unlikely, or project through the ankles of the other man, so that two forms occupy the same space.

HOLM: I think they're projecting through—another expression of that freedom and courage to do something when it needed to be done, whether or not it violated somebody's sense of logic.

HOLM: A little wooden head, Nootka I think. It looks Nootka in every way. It's not a mask but a solid head. Saying what it is would certainly be conjecture. There are holes drilled through the rim of the back—it looks like it was attached to something. Whether it was the head of a figure, or suspended from something, or represented a decapitated head, I don't know. It has the look of a corpse.

It's very striking. Not beautiful, at least not in my judgement, but powerful. There's painting on it—obscure—but what remains is effective and suggests a bloody face. I have a feeling this was intended to represent a decapitated head.

REID: It's one of those strange things that shouldn't work aesthetically. The abalone eyes are set in practically flush. There's little indication of features. The mouth is small and not well carved. The nose is elementary.

But something about the general form, particularly the treatment of the forehead and eyebrows, gives it forceful appeal. These slanted, flush-set eyes have a piercing quality that gives strength and vitality to the whole piece. The worn paint and beautiful patina of age enhance these qualities, in spite of the damage.

HOLM: All the characteristics you describe are good Nootka features: the eyes set flush on the cheek plane, rather than on separate orbs; the long sloping plane under the brow, rather than the bulge of the eye coming up close under the brow; the two planes of the face running backwards rather than being flat across the front; the long narrow nose, rather than a naturalistic one. All these are characteristics of Nootka sculpture. To me they don't reflect any inability on the carver's part to carry out his plan. I see, rather, a traditional form, beautifully carried through. It's quite Nootka.

I agree, it's powerful. If you get off from it a bit and turn it, you really can see that.

86

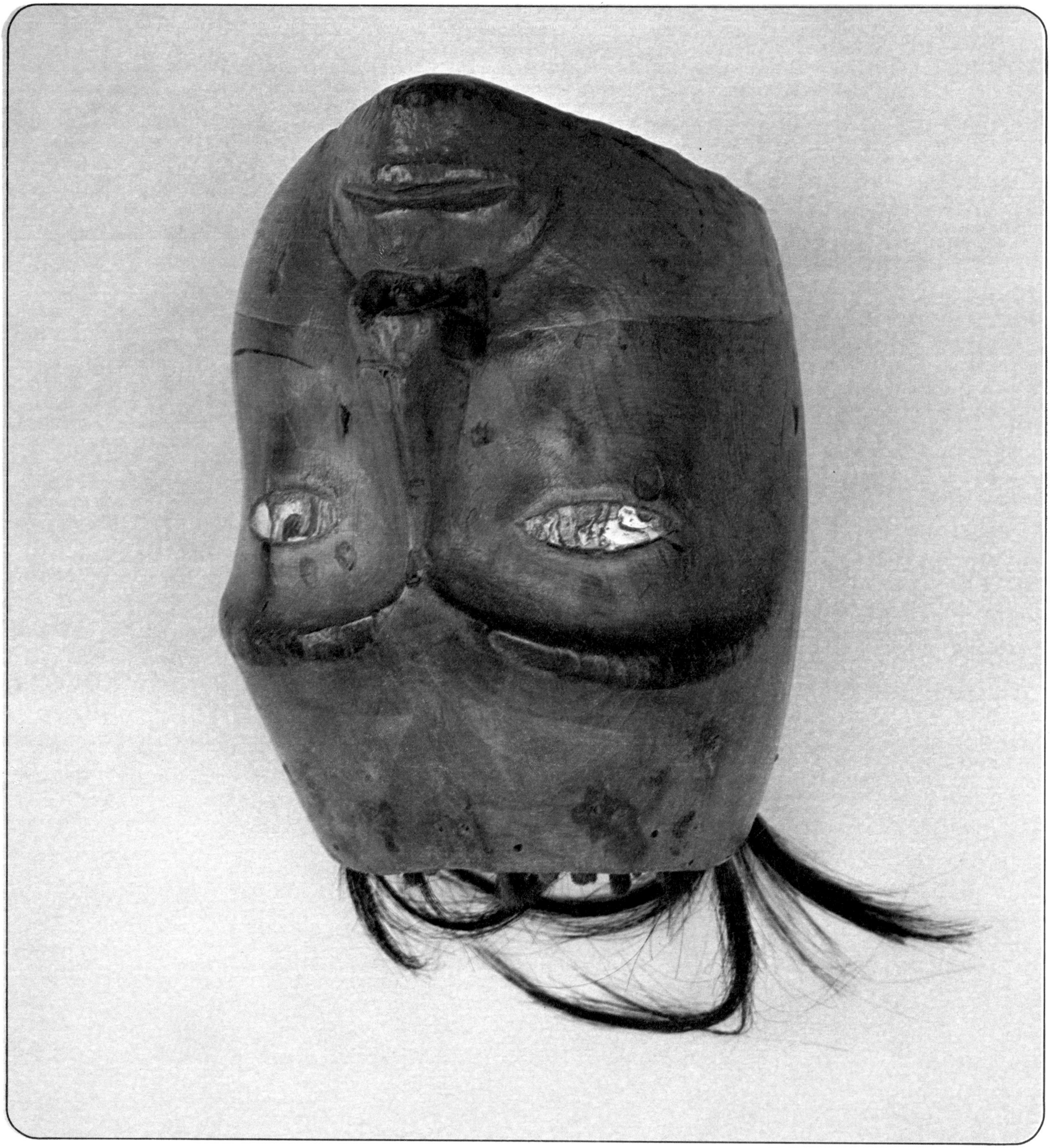

HOLM: This is a face-sized mask—it could be worn. It's said to be old Nootka, and I feel in perfect agreement with that attribution.

It's made of red cedar, carved quite thin. Related to the head we just discussed, #86. Has eyes with flattened orbs on the angle of the top of the cheek; a long sloping plane under the brow; and very narrow eyebrows along the upper rim of the eye socket. The eyebrows are cut in a bit, with pitch or something put in there. Quite a few Nootka pieces collected by the first Europeans in that region have this form of eyebrow—narrow grooves with pitch. This seems to have had hair around the rim of the top. Narrow nose, prominent nostrils, lots of good Nootka features.

The lips protrude and open in the form of the Kwakiutl "Tsonoqua" mask. I don't know if, in fact, it does represent that creature. But it's certainly handled much the same. There appears to be varnish or shellac over the surface, which I don't believe was there originally. At one time it had a loop of twisted fiber, maybe cedar, in line with the mouth in back: the wearer gripped this loop in his teeth.

Expressive face. Its wide-eyed effect comes, I think, from the Nootka convention of handling eyes. Maybe you can give us a subjective impression of it.

REID: Well, exactly—it's a very impressive mask. Beautifully modeled. That mouth is really calling. It's more than that. It's very simple, but human in every respect.

HOLM: This is what Cook and Vancouver were seeing when they visited Nootka Sound. If it's not from that period, it's just like ones seen in those days. It's the kind of mask that first came out of the Northwest Coast. All our later experience began with this type of thing.

87

88

REID: Face mask of a highborn lady with her labret. Attribution, I'm not too sure. Haida, Tlingit, or Tsimshian perhaps. Of considerable refinement, which is the kind of thing I like. She has a beautiful profile and a fine nose. When a carver can bring off a woman's face mask with its grotesque labret, and still produce a beautiful face, that gets through to me. The sensitivity of the mouth and cheeks, the soft curve of the whole face, are very appealing. She looks like a beautiful lady.

There's much aging, dirt, and paint, and some detail has been obscured. So it's hard to judge the workmanship. But it was probably not of the ultimate excellence. In this particular instance, however, it doesn't seem to make much difference. These strange, highly stylized ears don't look like ears, but that doesn't matter. The face painting is very nice—what you can see of it. I think she's just beautiful, that's all.

HOLM: I like this mask very much. There are a number of similar ones, if not by the same artist, by people working in the same tradition. The painting and some details on this mask are different from some of the others, but it resembles quite a number of them. I feel they are Haida. They are naturalistic and very beautiful. Compare this mask (A) with one collected by the Wilkes Expedition (B) and now in the U.S. National Museum [2,665], and another (C) in the Rotterdam Museum [34796].

What do you make of this surface? How can a mask get that way? I don't remember seeing many like this. It looks like the surface of a grease dish — inside and out. I can't understand that.

REID: Maybe we don't know enough about paint made with salmon eggs.

HOLM: We've seen dozens of pieces, maybe hundreds, nearly as old or even as old as this. They don't have this kind of surface. I'm familiar with several of those other masks which are so much like this one stylistically, and none have surfaces like this. It must have been soaked with something. I don't know how else it could get that way. Maybe that has something to do with its quality. It gives it a very interesting surface and color. But I don't think it was the artist's intent to make it look like that.

It has a strange, asymmetrical painting characteristic of this kind of mask. All the others I know are like that. Geometric in places, pure formline in other places. The painting on this mask is not as precise nor as perfect as on the other masks. I don't know what that means. Was the painter in a hurry or was it another painter? The concept, I suspect, is the same.

This little rounded chin is seen on all of them. In fact, there're a bunch of later portrait masks, made in the late 19th century apparently, of men and women with labrets and whatnot, and each has a similar little round chin. Whether that was a physical characteristic of the Haida, or just convention . . .

REID: . . . it gives her a strength which she wouldn't have otherwise.

HOLM: It sure does!

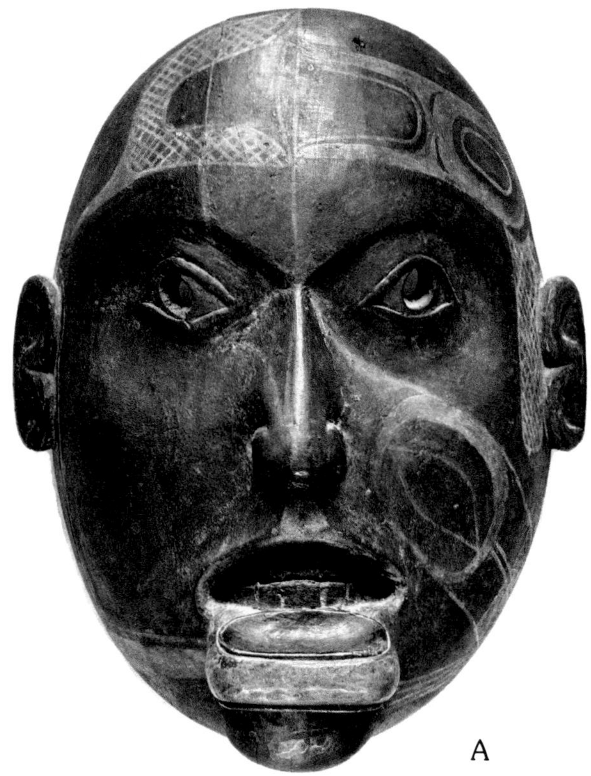

A

B

C

68

HOLM: It's a far cry from frontlet #74 to this mask, which is at the other end of the scale in refinement. Its power derives, not from deep carving, jutting brow, and glittery abalone, but from subtle modeling and a very stylized expression of an anatomical form, plus refined painting and carving.

It's a naturalistic mask of a male face once fitted with a glued-on hair mustache and hair goatee, both now missing. It also had human hair inserted in drilled holes along the rim. In its original state, it probably looked pretty real.

I feel it's Haida, though it could probably be seen in other ways. But it looks Haida and closely resembles other masks said to be Haida. Whether these attributions are good or not, I don't know.

Apparently it once had a lot of pale Northern blue paint on it. Most of that is gone. A great many pieces have that same characteristic—red paint in good shape, black paint in pretty good shape, and blue paint almost all off. I have a notion there's a chemical problem there, related to the reaction of the pigment to the binder. I hope somebody who knows chemistry can decide why.

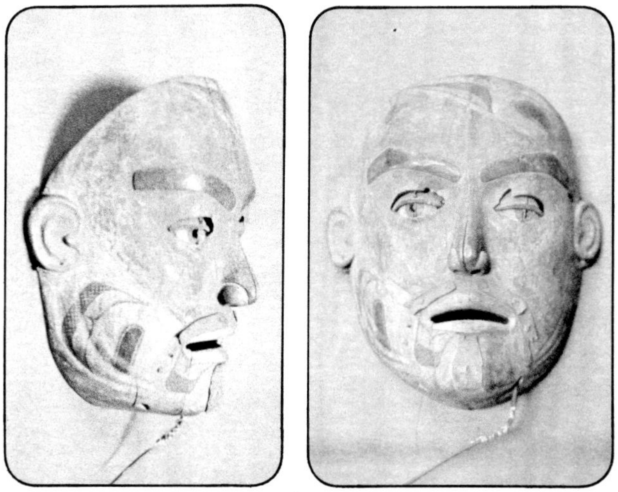

A

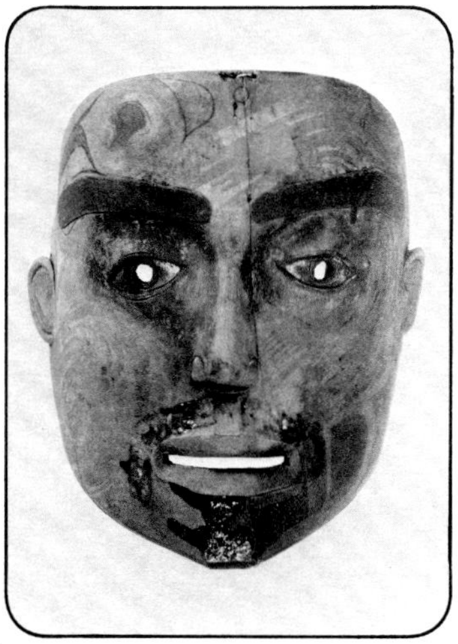

B

There're so many things happening on this mask which interest me: on the upper lid of the left eye the red paint looks worn off, perhaps *has* worn off, but I know of other masks, similar to this, with red paint in irregular blotches. In each, the painting looks deliberate, not just roughly streaked on by dragging a brush across the surface, but deliberately put on with irregular, draggy edges added to the edges of the painted spots. There's an awful lot about the painting of these things we don't know. Certain differences are so deliberate they must have some significance—exactly what, I don't know.

The fine formline painting is arranged asymmetrically. That seems characteristic of these early 19th-century naturalistic Haida masks. I don't know how they were used. I'm sure some were used by doctors in their practices and represented supernatural spirits or beings—familiars which the doctors contacted. Such spirits were brought into play by the wearing of masks. That's a possibility for this one. Or it may have been a festival mask used when people danced together, representing different characters.

Many of these masks are naturalistic, individualistic, expressive. Both the carving and painting are distinct enough for that. Here the wrinkles on the jaw accentuate the feeling of a real face, rather than just a stylized wooden mask. It has extremely subtle modeling of the orb of the eye. The little round ears are funny, but naturalistic.

REID: It's old, and obviously made by the same person who made a similar mask (A) now in the British Museum [1949AM22.62].

HOLM: It also looks like a mask (B) in the Smithsonian, supposedly from George Catlin's collection [73,332-B] although the records from that period apparently are mixed up. The carving style and painting detail are the same—not identical, but the same. The little ears are so close you could exchange one from each mask and not know the difference.

REID: The mask in the British Museum has the paint more or less intact. What interests me about these masks is the interplay of two disparate elements working together. In this case, face modeling and face painting are each separate entities. If the painting could be removed from the face and spread out, it would make a work of art in contemporary terms and leave behind a sculptural piece. Put them together and they make a unit, each enhancing the other and adding richness and interest to the whole. Of course, the painting is purely a representation of the actual face painting used by these people. Yet it's also an aesthetic design, existing on its own.

I saw a photograph of this mask before I saw the actual mask and it didn't come through to me as exceptional. Now that I actually see the mask, it appeals to me as one of the better things—very sensitive, extremely simple modeling around the mouth and nose, etc. The guy who made it approached the problem simply and directly and came up with—I don't like to use trite terms but I suppose we have to—a masterpiece of its form.

HOLM: Maybe this is another of those courageous things the artists were able to do. Essentially this kind of painting, as you say, represents the face painting these people actually used. But it takes boldness to strike out across this irregular shape with a painting and make it work. It's scary—I know, I've tried it. Once you get over the initial hurdle, it's not so bad. Still, to take shapes developed on flat surfaces, and plunge across hill and dale, takes courage.

90

HOLM: Another of those extremely powerful, highly stylized but naturalistic masks. Though the nostrils, eyebrows, and lips are all made with the conventional forms, it doesn't take much imagination to see this as a human face. But with an expression a little hard to interpret. It's said to have been collected by Emmons at Kitkatla and to be a Kwakiutl spirit borrowed from the Bella Bella by the Kitkatla Tsimshian. So, perhaps it's intended to be a doctor's mask representing a specific being. It has an expression of anguish or something . . .

REID: . . . it's been called "dying warrior."

HOLM: It has been and it could be seen that way.

The same things we said about the last mask, #89, could be repeated here, especially about the sensitivity of the modeling. But where #89 has a gentle, benign expression, this is much more emotion-filled. It has the same subtle, sensitive modeling and bold formline painting extending across the face and forehead. Many masks painted like this have blue painting where you expect black. I'm not sure what that means—why that should be a fairly consistent feature of painted masks.

REID: I think this is probably one of the greatest masks—at least of those I've seen—of any culture in the world and certainly of the Northwest Coast. You could analyze it centimeter by centimeter, if you wanted, to determine the reason for this. There's no need for that. But just look—the planes under those slitted eyes are almost flat, or so they appear at first; actually, they have subtle curves, giving a feeling of flatness which blends in with the forms of the cheeks. Everything has, within it, its own subtleties of form. Whoever made it probed to the very essence of whatever it was he was trying to express. I've seen this mask dozens of times—it's never lost its impact or appeal. I think it's one of the great masterpieces.

HOLM: These masks have the Northern structure, yet can be compared with the Nootka mask, #87, and the face carving, #86, we looked at earlier. You mentioned the subtle modeling of the space under the eye: these show that orb-like swelling representing the eyeball under the lids. It's one of the ways all Northern masks differ from Southern masks, where the eye tends to fall on the plane of the cheek, rather than on its own swelling orb. This mask shows modeling under the outer muscles and lids of the eye.

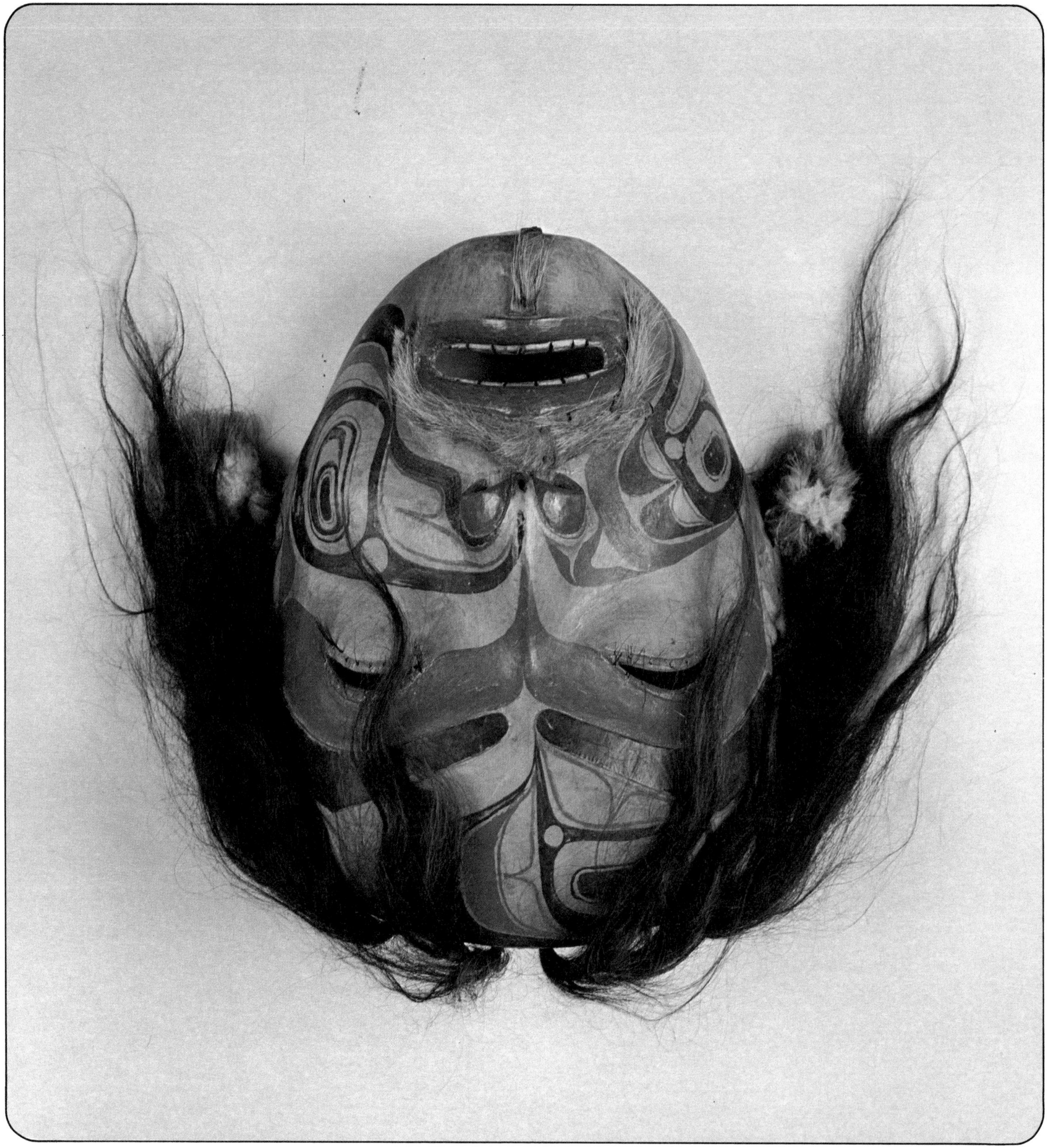

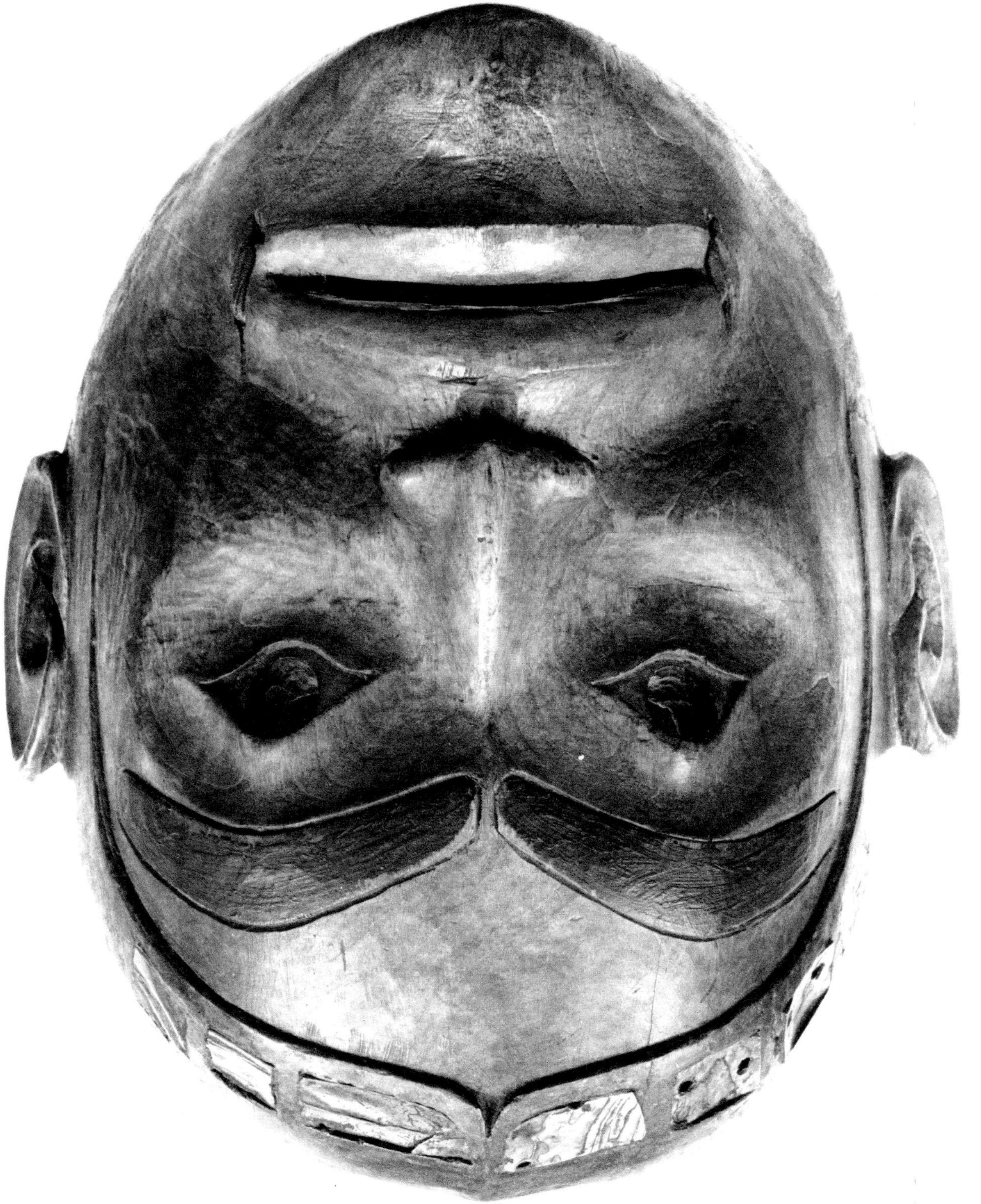

REID: This mask is very well done. A well-carved piece. Nice abalone inlays . . . all kinds of good things going for it . . . and it's pretty damned uninteresting. No, it's got nice ears and all that sort of thing. I think the guy had everything except whatever ought to be there.

HOLM: I go along with your analysis to a degree. This mask doesn't have the strength of #89 or #90, but it's interesting to me because I'm curious as to why certain masks look alike from one group to another.

In almost every way, it seems real Tsimshian. Typical Tsimshian eye. Small constricted lids. No border rim or eyelid line. Bony cheek structure. The aquiline nose is just as Tsimshian as can be, especially in profile. It dips at the bridge and then pushes back at the tip. The narrow lips run way back. Typical Tsimshian face. Expertly done. Has everything going for it as you say, yet I agree it's not as powerful as #90. But I wouldn't put it far down the line. It's a very good mask.

91

HOLM: Mask with Tsimshian look. Made of dense, heavy wood, possibly yew. The shiny surface doesn't look added but the result of wear and polish. It's Tsimshian in style, with one noticeable difference: the distinctly defined eyelid rims. In my experience, these aren't that frequent on Tsimshian masks. The typical Tsimshian eyelid just comes up into position and the eyeball begins with no line around it. But there're plenty of exceptions.

It's more stylized than some of the other masks we've discussed, but naturalistic, with good representation, in a formal way, of the bony structure at the cheek and the back of the eye socket. No special emotion to the expression—wide-eyed and calm. Mustache painted on. Asymmetrical painting, somewhat formline-like, with feather-like design. I don't know the significance of the design. Seems to be a style of face painting from the Northern Coast.

REID: It's a nicely modeled face. Minimal carving, obviously deliberate . . . not that he didn't want to carve more, but he did only as much as necessary to achieve the effect he wanted. Sensitive, particularly around the mouth, with that rather austere look you find on many totem-pole human faces. They seem to be contemplating things of some universality—something beyond the immediate, practical aspects of life. I'm probably saying too much about this mask, which isn't that exciting, but it has that calm, expressionless quality.

HOLM: Many of these pieces do have that timeless look, as if what we see isn't happening. Everything is there, but nothing is happening. You see that here.

92

93

REID: This, to me, represents a very pleasant person with a half smile. If you walked up to someone with this face, you'd feel at home, relaxed. Technically, it's well made. Nice modeling. Very expressive. God knows what it was used for. I think it shows these people enjoyed life and were satisfied with things as they were. I imagine its ceremonial function wasn't important—probably a secondary or subsidiary figure. The face painting goes from sharply angular to typical Northwest Coast subtle curves. The mask has developed a beautiful brown patina over the years. A thoroughly pleasant object. A nice thing to have around for a long time.

HOLM: I agree. I don't know where it's supposed to come from, but if I picked examples of typically Tlingit masks, this would be on my list, though that certainly wouldn't prove it was Tlingit. It has features just like Tlingit masks: wide-open eyelid lines without much constriction; small rounded nose; the long plane from under the orb right on out to the lips. The lips are flattened out and stand from end to end in a continuous band all the way around. The mouth is slightly open. The teeth show—that's a real Tlingit way of doing things.

The Tlingit don't shut their mouths when they talk. Maybe that's why mouths are always open in Tlingit masks. There're no sounds in the Tlingit language which require you to put your lips together. Maybe that's reflected in their masks. I don't really believe that, but it comes to mind. Anyway, that looks like a Tlingit mask to me.

I agree, he's very pleasant looking . . . enjoying life . . . things are going along fine . . . we would like to know him, etc. I think it's dangerous, though, to interpret expressions when we don't know what they originally meant. I remember a little flat design of a bear from a house screen or house front. It was reproduced in several books as a little round bear with a hole in its middle as an apartment entrance. That bear got to be called the "happy bear." Everybody thought he was jolly. The only reason he was thought to be happy was the style, the way the design spread out with a great upturned mouth. Yet I'm sure he wasn't intended to be a happy bear.

REID: There's a convention for doing bears. Bears always have upturned mouths, and in our way of thinking, upturned mouths are smiles. But in this particular person, it's not just the upturned mouth, the big grin. We find the face likable, which means we find it very human. What comes through is the wonderful human expressiveness of a good Northwest Coast mask. Masks #89–#91 aren't hacked-out pieces of wood. Through their makers, they've assumed lives of their own.

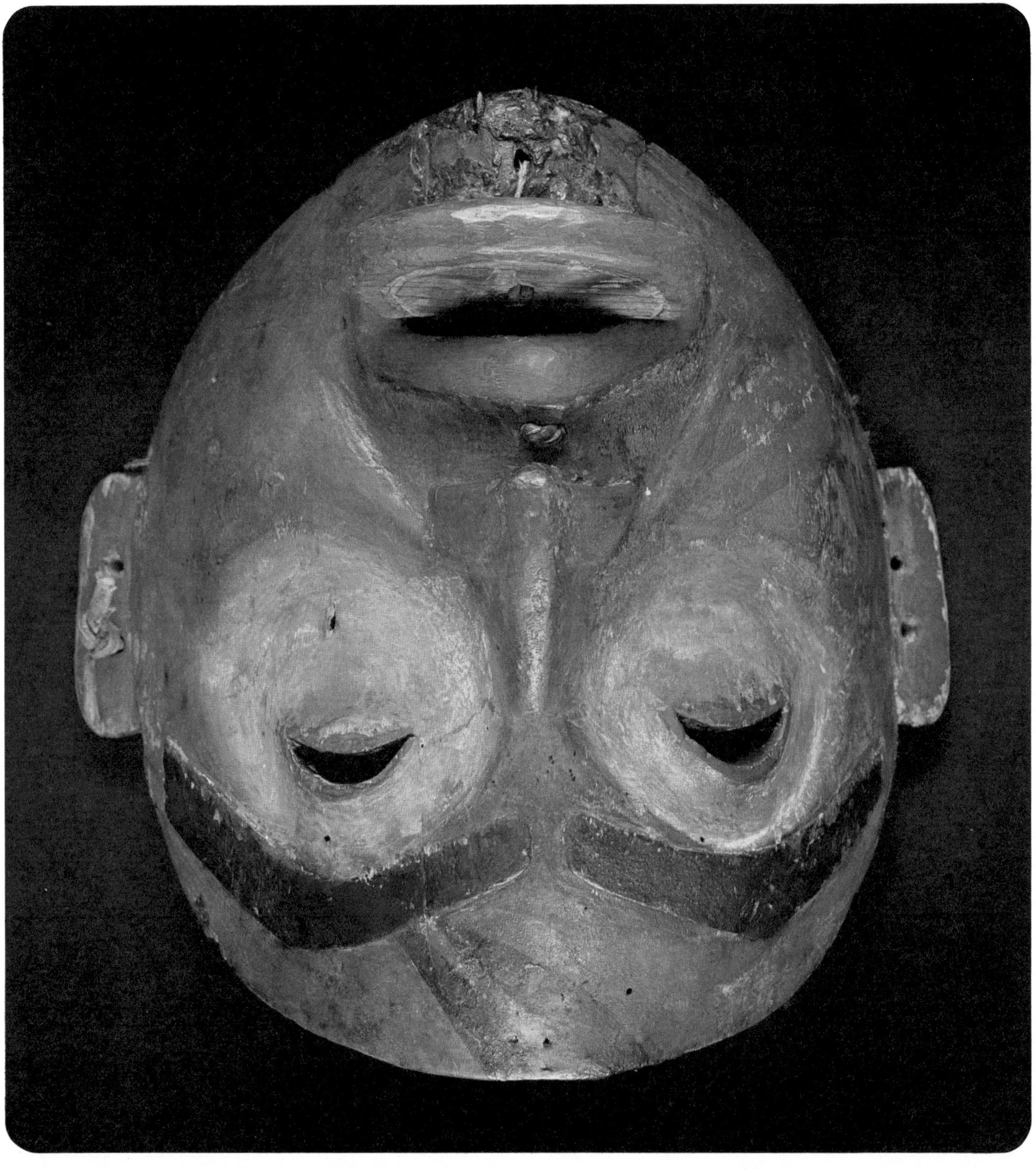

94

HOLM: Here's a lady with labret very different from #88. Big, mechanical labret that can be moved to express life or suggest speech or something. A little string operates it.

I want to make a wild guess as to where it comes from: Coast Tsimshian or Bella Bella, possibly Haida. Right in that little triangle you've got a tough job identifying pieces of this sort. Much less naturalistic than #88. More stylized in its features. A similar kind of asymmetrical painting but not so formline-like. This one has something on it that I hope someday I'll figure out—the weird painting on the side of the nose and over the side of the cheek. I've seen it on other masks, apparently Haida masks. And this strange band down here must have some significance. There is also a twisted-fiber mouth-plug for the wearer to grip.

The expression is very different from #88. That had a calm, benign look. This has an intense, almost pained expression, with arched eyes and flaring nostrils. Maybe it's evil. I don't quite see it as evil, although I guess you could certainly see it that way. It expresses almost pure anguish to me. It has a different kind of strength than #88. That has solidarity, strength of character. This one is pure emotion.

REID: This is not a beautiful lady, as was #88. Yes, "anguish" is as good an expression as one could find for it. A great theatrical piece. Not superb craftsmanship, but I don't think I'd go further than that. As a theatrical piece, it's magnificent. I'd give a great deal to have seen it in action.

HOLM: We don't know a thing about how these masks were used. There are a few very vague early descriptions. The rest is pure guesswork. These masks certainly can be dramatic. This one would be a real knockout. Especially the lip movement. Movable Northwest Coast masks really excite me. They're rigid wooden things with hinges, yet, when worn, they move. They don't look rigid. They look like the real thing happening. I don't know . . . I guess it's just an old mask . . . maybe the style . . . the light on it . . . I think it could come alive.

REID: I think it *is* alive. Discount the less than perfect carving, the inadequate painting, and everything else: it's a personality of considerable force—no, of *great* force.

HOLM: I think this mask is Haida or from the same central-northern coastal area. Movable jaw, movable eyes—a good theatrical mask. Formerly had a mustache and beard. Paint sloppily applied. Apparently a repaint job. Looks like traces of other, maybe better, paint under the surface.

REID: It's a good theatrical piece, but not as good as #94, that lady with the movable labret. If I were casting a Northwest Coast drama, I wouldn't give him an important part—maybe a spear carrier, something like that. It's a very funny thing because there are some nice parts about it. Very nicely modeled nose. But the whole thing doesn't add up to a great piece for me, either theatrically or aesthetically. As far as I'm concerned, I don't think we should bother with it too much. It's a good piece. (Afterthought: it looks a lot better in the photograph—like the defaced ruin of a darn good mask.)

95

96

HOLM: We really have seen a variety of Northern noblewomen with labrets. This one has an entirely different feel from the other two. She certainly doesn't have the calm detachment of #88, and she hasn't any of the anguish of #94. I'd say we're looking at a real aristocrat who knows exactly who she is and where she's been. I don't think I've ever seen a Northwest Coast mask which expressed humanity the way this one does. It's very stylized, not much more realistic than the other two, but something about the proportions of the features and the structure—the feeling of a fine skull under those muscles and skin—sets it apart. The eyes are really expressive. There are lots of masks with closing eyes like these, but none, that I can think of, come even close to the kind of reality these eyes express. The carving isn't as perfect in finish as some we've seen—there are lots of rough spots and irregularities—but that doesn't matter a bit. In fact, I think that the lack of perfect symmetry probably increases the realism. The painting is pretty rough too. It's one of those asymmetrical formline-like designs running diagonally right across the features that seem to be so favored by the artists who made these Northern naturalistic masks.

I think it's a Haida mask. Might be Tsimshian. A lot of details come together to give it that Haida feeling: the little semi-naturalistic ears, the arrangement of the hair, the very naturalistic modeling. No matter who made it, it's one of the very best. If it's a real portrait, that must have been a remarkable lady.

97

HOLM: It's more difficult to guess the origin of this mask than the origin of the others. My guess is the Bella Bella/Tsimshian region. It's a naturalistic mask, but nothing like the others. It's a much more stylized representation of a human face: the eye sockets are more designed; the cheeks outlined in a little carved rim; the lips more mask-like, at least more than in #89 and #90. The eyes are on a slight bulge, but not modeled in the sensitive way of the others. It's more of a design than an expression of a real human face. Across the brow there's an unusual asymmetrical painting—not formline, but almost geometric. A band of black across the top represents hair, with little lines coming down for sideburns in front of the ears. A bold painting over the face, in what appears to be dark blue. Very nice, but even as a designed mask, it lacks the power or sensitivity of #93.

REID: It has a fixed expression, as though depicting a reaction to some immediate situation. When that situation is over, the expression's usefulness and everything else is gone, whereas each of these other masks continues to have an inner light of its own—you can imagine many things going on behind the surface of each mask. But that's not to put this mask down in any way. As an object, as an abstract work, it contains many interesting things which make it a beautiful object, obviously an expression of a master carver.

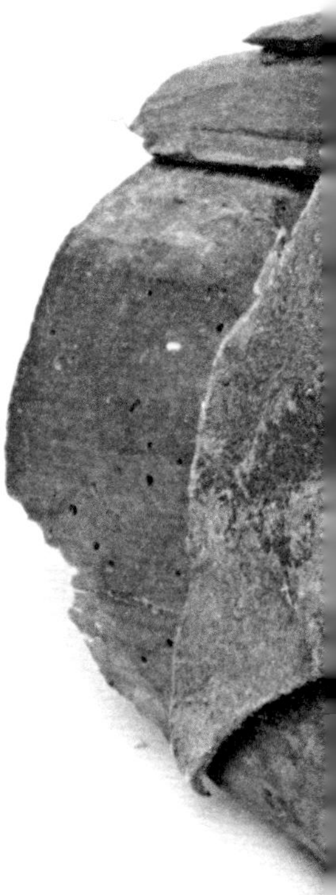

REID: A fish of some kind. Reasonably well made. Appears as though it should do a lot more than it does. I'd put it in the same category as #95.

HOLM: Like #95, seeing it at its best is seeing it in use with whatever else goes with it. It's clearly a front end of what could have been a larger costume decoration. Rough, direct modeling. Hard to appreciate by itself.

REID: It fitted into somebody's costume department. Probably made for one of those instant entrances—a fast run around a circle and a fast exit.

HOLM: In the dim light of the house and in the movement of dance, it would be hard to tell a piece like this from a detailed, refined one. A rough piece like this was all that was needed in many cases. It's a mystery to me why artists went to greater efforts, although personally I'd do the same. I wonder how to justify the time and effort put into some of the really refined masks.

REID: Because they served multiple purposes. The really fine ones were shown off as objects, as well as used.

HOLM: We don't know exactly how they were conceived or used or thought of in early times, but in modern times, masks aren't taken out at all, except for dances. They're not hung on walls to be seen all the time. I'm sure they might be occasionally brought out, displayed and admired, but their real use is in this half-light movement where detail is lost.

I've wondered about this. It seems strange. But perhaps we don't have to figure out a reason. As far as I'm concerned, the reason—my reason—is just satisfaction in making a refined mask, knowing what it's like to make it.

This is a really rough mask. You could turn one of these out pretty darn fast. In fact, you probably would. Might have been a last minute effort to have it ready for something going on. I don't know. I've thought about that sometimes, but . . .

86

HOLM: Killer-whale mask. In style, I think it's Tsimshian, although the face painting is almost Bella Bella/Bella Coola. Actually, in that area, the Bella Bella and Tsimshian are next-door neighbors. The Kitamac, whose village has a Tsimshian name, are North Kwakiutl-speaking people. There's a close relationship there and a chance for borrowing ideas.

I think it's supposed to be a humanoid killer-whale, though not knowing the Tsimshian story, it might be something else. The Tsimshian have more mythical beings!

It's missing part of the top—probably had the end of a fin. I can't imagine it being cut off square. The concept was really beautiful.

A hole for a cord went down through the "spines" of the fin, through the head and came out inside the nose. A strip of leather held the "spines" together. When the string was pulled, the fin stood upright; when the string was loose, it flopped down.

There's a whale-fin mask just like this in the Edward Curtis film, *In the Land of the War Canoes.*[39] At one point in the film, a curtain goes up and down. In the foreground, just right of center, there's a whale mask, maybe four or five feet long, on a person's head. The fin, with little radiating spines just like these, comes up and goes down. The Milwaukee Museum also has a whale mask with a fin that separates into little radiating spines [17297].[40]

A strip of baleen covered the leather. It's now brittle, but when it was fresh, it must have been very springy. There may have been a string attached to the back going down behind the head, so that when it was pulled, the spines of the fin fanned open. It would have worked beautifully. But I think the baleen was added later. Maybe the original works were getting worn and the baleen was added to stiffen the fin. Still later, strips of wood were added to both sides of the fin, thereby immobilizing it.

The dancer moved the jaw and eyes by means of strings attached to sticks. The eyes pivoted on sticks. The jaw has a hole through it, probably for a string. In some masks the jaw is fastened in a springy way. In the Curtis film,[41] when the grizzly-bear figure dances on the bow of the canoe, the bear's jaw isn't moved mechanically. It's just on a spring. As the bear moves, the jaw joggles up and down. It looks very realistic, just like animal movement.

Other masks were made so that the wearer held the jaw closed by keeping his mouth open slightly, and opened the jaw by closing his mouth. This mask doesn't seem to have worked that way. Maybe it had a string up over some eyelet or something so that it could be worked.

I don't know how this mask was used by the Tsimshian, but in the Kwakiutl dance, a man—a sea-being like *Goumouquay,* the undersea monster or undersea chief whose face is like a big human face, but with fins and things on it—moves very slowly around, as if walking under the sea, his mouth opening and shutting like a fish under water, not snapping. This mask may have been used something like that.

99

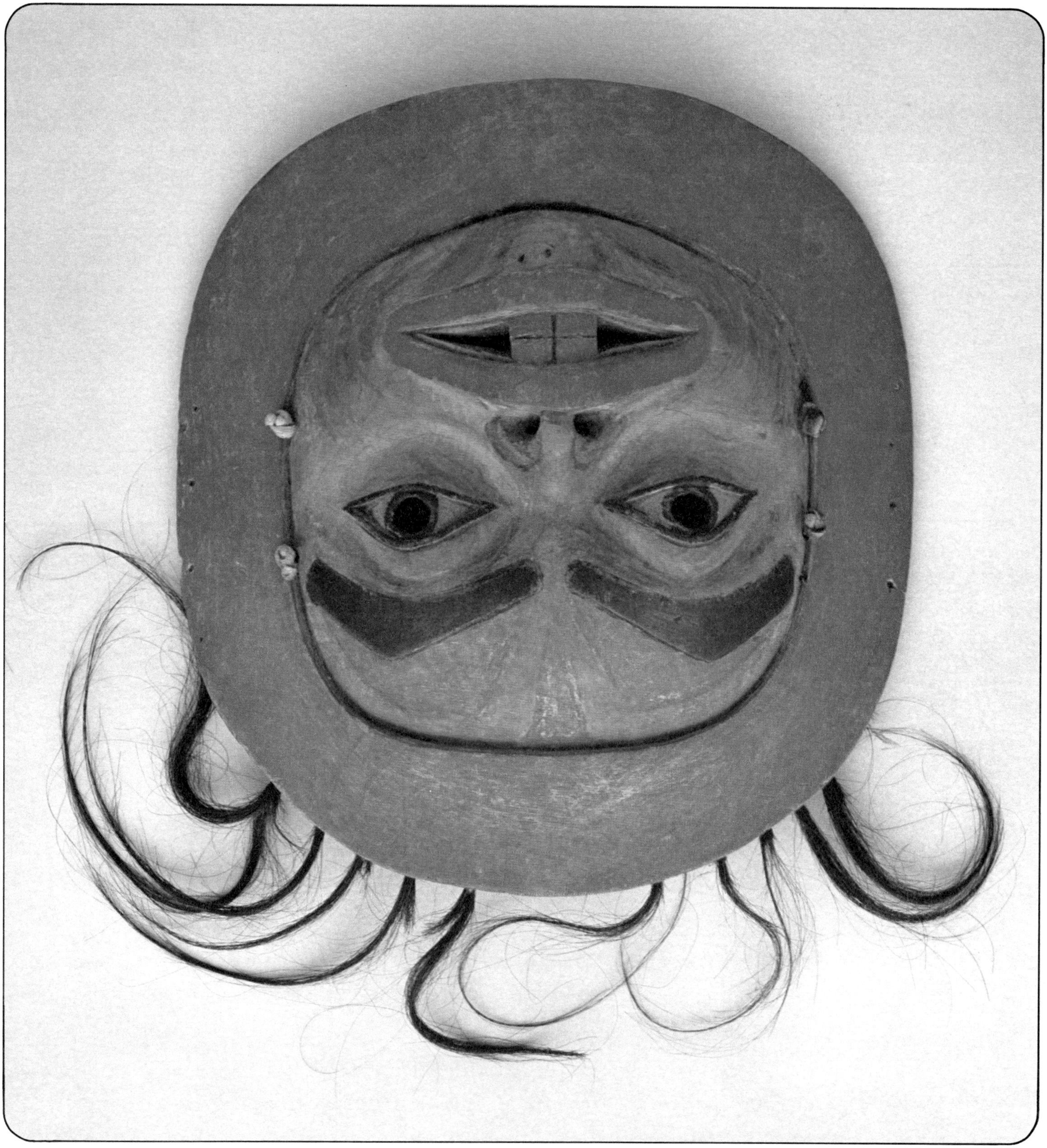

REID: One of those funny things. Adequately, but not superbly, carved. Lots of paint smeared over it. Probably been repainted. Very typical, flat Northwest Coast face. It has incisor teeth, which under some circumstances indicate a beaver, but probably not here. He's pretty human. Taken detail by detail, you wouldn't find much to classify it as a great masterpiece. As a dramatic piece, it's a fine mask. Probably it would work better in use than as a purely decorative piece. I certainly find it interesting and pleasing and wouldn't mind having it around.

HOLM: Certainly from the standpoint of craftsmanship it's not up to some of the other things we've seen. Its symmetry is faulty, if that's a fault! One cheek is more bulgy than the other, and so on.

But it's much closer to the masterpiece category, in my view. I believe it's a humanoid nonhuman creature, perhaps a beaver, handled as if it were a human face. It's clearly Tlingit, not that this makes any difference in its quality. It has a very, very characteristic Tlingit form, in every way, including the roundness, almost pudginess, of many Tlingit face masks or sculptured faces. The eye is fairly large, on a distinct orb, which is high at the upper lid and slopes back more deeply into the face below. This is characteristic of the Northern masks, but here the orb is very rounded. Then the eyelids are quite open. They don't constrict much on each side of the iris. They slant back almost to a triangular form. Quite long and open. Small, rounded nostril and rounded nose. The whole length of the lip extends outward, right from the edge to the middle. Most characteristic of all, the cheek plane extends from the bottom of the orb continuously out to the lip.

The whole thing, its roundness, everything, expresses an old-fashioned Tlingit style. I think it's very old, probably going well back into the last century. It has a good feel. My only reason for thinking it's not as great as some of the others is that its workmanship isn't as fine and precise. I don't know if that means anything or not. How it was used, I don't know. It resembles a frontlet, but it's larger than an ordinary frontlet. It has hair fringe at the top. Apparently it's just a mask, but I think a successful one.

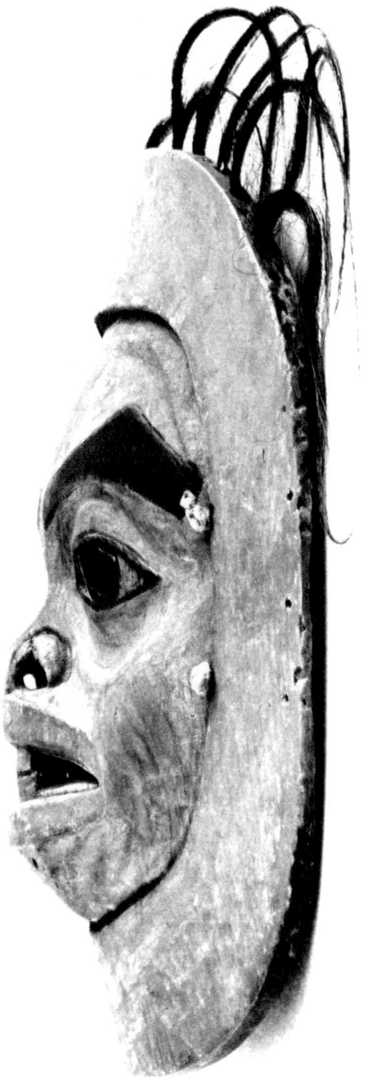

100

101

REID: One of the most enjoyable forms of Northwest Coast art is Nootka painting. For years I've loved those painted screens in the American Museum of Natural History—the ones you can almost see if you take your own flashlight. This curtain or screen isn't up to that standard, although that may have a lot to do with the material—trade fabric instead of adzed cedar—but it has the same joyous, exuberant quality.

I suppose it depicts the epic struggle between Thunderbird and Whale, but everybody seems to be having such a good time, it's difficult to take it too seriously. At the same time, it's a very powerful painting, as though all the animals represented great forces thrusting out in all directions. Just as a wall hanging, it's very impressive. As a backdrop for some great dance drama, it must have been pretty obvious.

Nice examples here of Northwest Coast symmetrical asymmetry: two little wolf figures, alike in concept but differing in detail; feathers differing in color arrangement.

HOLM: A really good Nootka curtain. The best. A wonderful thing. Its general arrangement and figures are fairly common in Nootka paintings, but the way these figures have been handled is unusual and spectacular. It's really a Nootka painting, yet there's a strong Northern formline feeling to it, almost as if a great Nootka artist had been impressed by some Northern design and decided to incorporate some of that super-organization, and even some Northern formline details, into his masterpiece. Look at this little red creature in the whale's mouth. At first view he looks like what we can expect of a little supplemental creature, in the secondary color, in a Haida or Tlingit screen painting. Some of the formline

U's—the red one in the whale's belly, for example—look perfectly Northern, even to the tapering turn at their junctures with other formlines. But he was a real Nootka and he didn't let those Northern rules hold him down. He hinted at them, and fooled us into thinking he followed them: then he just went full tilt into his free, startling Nootka style.

A nearly naturalistic whale encloses two wolf-like creatures, plus a pattern of massive formline-like figures. Above him is a great vermilion thunderbird with magnificent asymmetrical wings spread for flight. The black figures above must be Lightning Serpents compressed to fit into those triangular spaces. The artist showed his true Nootka colors in filling in the area above those creatures with free-flowing red elements which respond to the curves and angles of the figures, but then go off into decorative slits and curves of their own. Look at the little corner relief in the red design at the upper left—doesn't that look like a box kerf?

This curtain was probably never raised or lowered like the one in the Curtis film,[42] but stretched across the back of the house, as a partition, behind which dancers prepared and as a backdrop for their performance. Some Nootka screens hung like curtains and were drawn open like stage curtains. The Kwakiutl also hang this kind of curtain in a house, stretching it between beam and posts, thereby separating a room off from the main floor. It's a secret room, where only dancers and participants go.

The curtain was put up only at the time of the dance. In the old days, the Kwakiutl made these partitions from planks and painted them, working secretly at night, right before the dances. They took old roof boards, rubbed them down, smoothed and cleaned them, and painted like crazy all night. When they were putting them up, the dancers, especially the *Hamatsa,* were already in the house. The day after the *Hamatsa* had disappeared, leaving hemlock branches behind, they had lured him back into the house and kept him there until the people gathered the following day. All this time, the public was kept out. Only the initiates and the painters were permitted in there. Whenever the workmen got ready to do anything that could be heard from outside the house, they let the *Hamatsa* know and he began to shout, "HAP!" and blow whistles to represent his wildness. Then his attendants grabbed sticks and pounded like crazy, because he was supposed to be wild now, running around the house trying to bite somebody.

While all this was going on, the carpenters worked. Every time they got ready to do something that could be heard outside, they signaled the *Hamatsa,* who went wild again, making a great racket. When they were finished, the *Hamatsa* quieted down. I think everybody knew what was going on, but that was part of the whole game—to make it seem real.

Traditionally the old wooden curtains were burned once the ceremonies were finished. Few were collected. When canvas and muslin became readily available, backdrops were done on cloth and, after each ceremony, wrapped up and stored. Cloth curtains date from the turn of the century.

102

HOLM: This piece is just neat. It's an elaboration of the *dlooqwala* costumes. *Dlooqwala* means acquiring supernatural power. It's the name for the wolf dance. The Kwakiutl call this a wolf mask, but more often *kheesiwey* (teeth in forehead), because of the long row of teeth. The dance is still performed as a standard part of the winter ceremonial. It's an inherited dance and goes back to the days when wolves held the first winter dance at Karlukwees village. It's a nice dance . . . a wolf . . . [Holm dances] . . . YeeHeeeee, YeeHeeeee . . . right after the dancers come in, they run around, their thumbs up like this, the sign of the wolf . . . YeeHeeeee, YeeHeeeee [Holm runs around, barks] . . . it's great!

The dance is a privilege, like most Kwakiutl winter dances. The person who has that right is displaying his privilege. He may have a name that goes with that dance. A number of people often dance it together, but one person is usually being initiated and his or her family sponsors the dance. It's often done by a woman, or a group of women. If the others aren't initiated from another family, they're people with this wolf dance in their tradition. They go along with this new person to help him. They form a little pack of wolves and run around the house. The dance is supposed to come from the wolves. There are different versions of its origin and different songs, but the words say something like, "Your name is widely known among the wolves. You are honored by the wolves." Etc. The owner of the dance impersonates the wolf. But the wolf he impersonates comes from that never-never land where mythical wolves are human in one sentence and wolves in the next. That's why he runs upright, yet can squat and shout, "woof, woof."

This carving is an amazing thing—meant to be worn on the back of a dancer representing a wolf. It was made by Willie Seaweed, a famous Kwakiutl carver. I have an article on him in a monograph published by Louisiana State University.[43] I'm sorry I didn't have this piece to include in it. It can be dated pretty accurately by style, when compared with others by him. I have photographs and information on 85 to 90 pieces by him. His career is well known. We know enough to reconstruct the development of his style. He was over ninety when he died in 1967 and is well represented in different collections.

He was a Blunden Harbour chief and, I think, one of the all-time great Kwakiutl artists. Certainly his style was one of the most organized. It was very intellectual. Everything was thought through. Nothing was left to chance. His workmanship was always precise. You can recognize his masks from the inside as well as outside, because of the way he habitually finished them off. The shape of the hole in this mask is absolutely standard for this type of Kwakiutl mask, made to lighten it, but with Willie Seaweed masks, that hole is always smooth and always comes back like that. A perfect example of his style. Then you see these three little compass dots in a row: that's the way he made the eye. A lot of fine work and finishing went into this piece, compared to some Kwakiutl pieces. At ordinary speed he would have made the head in about a week, the body in another week. Everything about this piece dates it in the 1920s or maybe a little later, perhaps into the '30s. He made many wolf headdresses like this, each slightly different. I have pictures of seven or eight, but this is the first I've seen with a body. Probably the body was strapped on the dancer's back, over his shoulders, so that the end came up close behind. Then the wolf head went over the dancer's head. The whole costume didn't *cover* the dancer but sat on his head and back.

In the ordinary *dlooqwala,* there is only one moment when they crouch. But there are descriptions of this dance which lead me to believe that sometimes quite a bit of the dance was done crouching. The wolf's body would then be more horizontal, more wolf-like, its legs dangling over the hips and shoulders of the crouched dancer. In the upright parts of the dance, it would just be part of the wolf symbolism. But when the dancer crouched down like that, fists on the ground, it could begin to look like a real wolf.

This head, which is exactly like a *kheesiwey,* could have been used, may even have been made to be used, separately from the body. There's a slight difference between them in paint style, but I understand that the dealer who collected this piece removed some of the white paint in an effort to "age" it. It was a silly thing to do. It's clear, to anyone who knows anything about this subject, just when this piece was made and who

made it. When the white paint is replaced, the head and body will match perfectly! Both are red cedar, thin and light. Willie Seaweed wasn't really noted for that. Sometimes he sacrificed thinness for strength, to the disgust of the dancers. I have two big *hamatsa* masks, both heavier than need be because he liked solidity.

REID: It's a great theatrical piece. I'd love to have seen it in action. I share your opinion of Willie Seaweed. He was a great master Kwakiutl carver. This is one of his best pieces.

HOLM: He's my favorite guy. I knew him personally. Seaweed is a chief's name meaning "paddle owner" (the one who received paddling: that is, when everyone paddles up to big potlaches and feasts at this place, he is the honored recipient of that paddling).

His ceremonial name was *Hehlamas,* "making things right." His nickname, which everybody knew him by, was *Kwagitola,* "smoke on the top," like a volcano. And a lot of people called him "that old man." He was an old man—very likeable, well known, a really great actor, comedian, composer, song-leader, carver, painter—a great guy.

He probably started carving when he was young, around twenty, even earlier, in the 1880s, though the earliest piece we can identify for certain was made about 1910. It's fully developed, so he must have been carving long before that. I think he'd been carving for twenty or thirty years by the time he made a piece we know for sure was his. From that time on, he produced a continuous progression of pieces. These can be pretty well dated. The University of British Columbia has a pile of them. The Burke Museum has a few. They're all over. There are other pieces that I think are his, made before 1910. They look right stylistically, but I don't have any solid evidence for attribution. About this one, however, I have absolutely no doubt. It's his work in every way, the whole thing; one of the finest things he ever did—a strong piece.

All the details are characteristic of his style: the precise carving, the real thought, the relationship between positive forms and negative spaces. His style has some relationship to Northern style, but isn't Northern. It's a development of a northern Vancouver Island or southern Kwakiutl style. There were three or four carvers at Blunden Harbour and Smith Inlet who, if they didn't actually work together, at least influenced one another. Some of their work is a little hard to tell from Willie Seaweed's, but you can always tell. Even in this piece he did certain things that nobody else did as well or the same. Everything was very direct with him. If he made a straight line or a parallel-sided thing, that's exactly what it was. A little curve was deliberate—no wobbling. If the eyebrows were recurving, they came along, *wurrp*—like that. Some just swooped up. Yet, with all this precision, all this thought given to design and form, his work wasn't static in any way.

His son still carves and carves well. When he worked with his father, their work was almost indistinguishable. If Joe Seaweed made a piece, it was usually a mate to one his father made. The two worked side by side on a project—a pair of masks, say—using the same compass, straightedge, patterns, etc. When Willie put the compass down, Joe probably picked it up and made the same size circle. And they used the same paint can. Joe tried his best to make his mask the exact mate to his father's mask. So they look alike. They're really Willie Seaweed in content. Later, when Joe worked alone, his work was different. You can tell. But with a group, or a pair, you can't really tell—they look too much alike.

Postscript: By great good luck, following our discussion, I obtained direct information about this wolf costume. First I located a copy at the Riveredge Foundation, Calgary, Alberta. Then I got in touch with a Kwakiutl friend who is a good carver and singer and very knowledgeable about ceremonial details. When I showed him the picture, he matter-of-factly told me it had been his ex-wife's. It was made for her dance by Willie Seaweed about 1930 when she was a young girl in Kingcome Inlet. Her wolf dance came from the story of *Qawadiliqala.*[44] He made the copy himself and it matches the style of others of his known carvings. He sold the original to Bob Martineau, formerly of Echo Bay, Gilford Island, British Columbia, about 1960. This matches with a picture I have from a 16mm movie made in Alert Bay about 1960 which shows the head part worn in the June Sports Day parade. Someplace I have another picture of it from the "Pioneer Journal," the former Alert Bay paper, but I can't find it.

The mask never had fur on it—only a piece of dark cloth. It was worn and used much as a regular *kheesiwey.* The body part was worn on the back, as I suspected. The description I gave originally is O.K., but not so conjectural now.

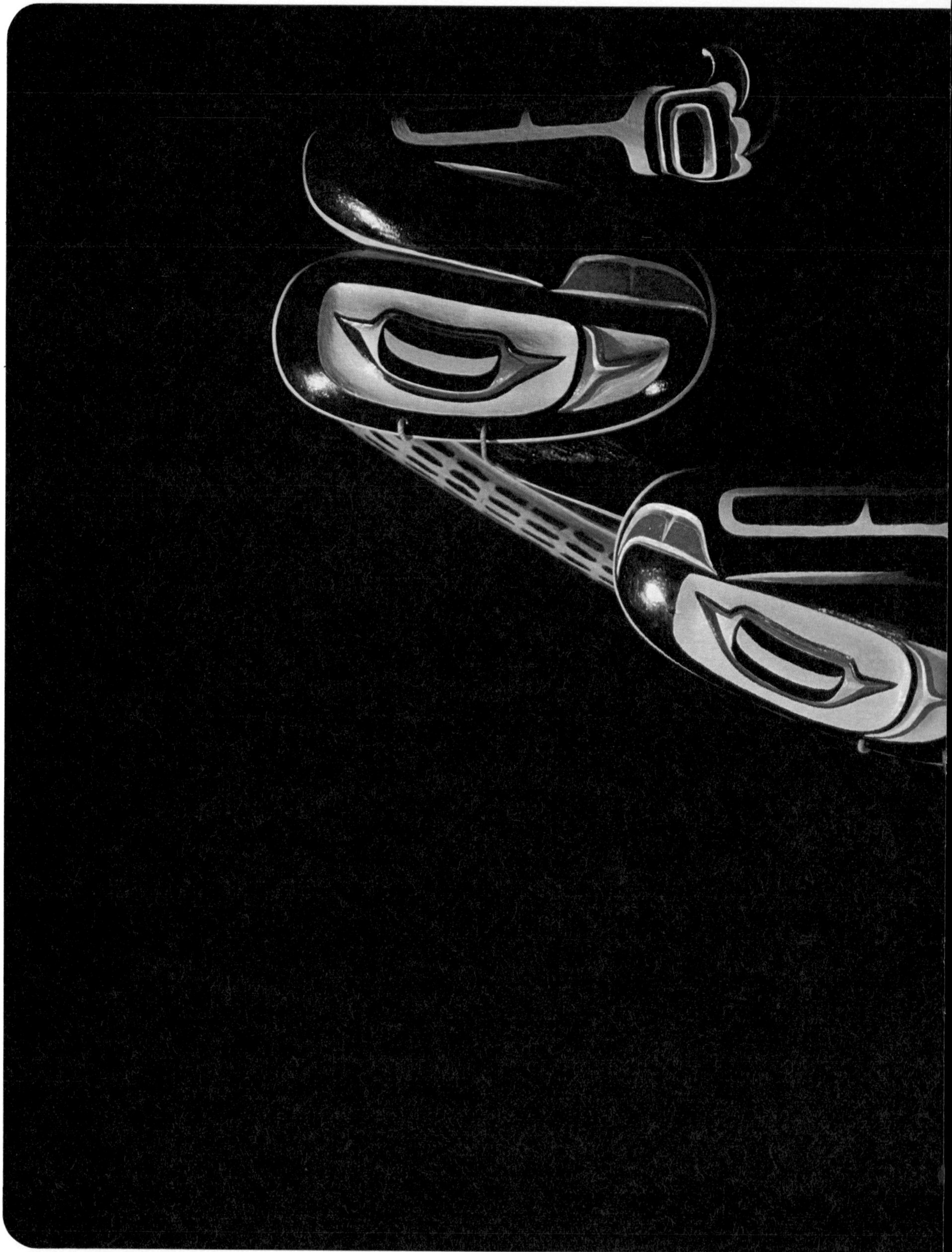

Notes

1. Personal communication, Max Ernst, 1955 and 1974.
2. Personal communication, Claude Lévi-Strauss, November 17, 1974.
3. Claude Lévi-Strauss, "The Art of the Northwest Coast at the American Museum of Natural History," *Gazette des Beaux-Arts* 24 (1943): 180.
4. Ibid, pp. 178, 180–81.
5. Ibid., p. 181.
6. Ibid., pp. 181–82.
7. Catalog of the exhibition *The Far North: 2000 Years of American Indian and Eskimo Art* (Washington, D.C.: National Gallery, 1973), pp. 237–38.
8. J. J. Klejman, a New York dealer, purchased both pieces at an auction from an English estate along with two Polynesian pieces: a Hawaiian image and a Hawaiian bowl with two human images. He also acquired three other Nootka pieces: a "slave killer" with human hair attached to the effigy of a human head (now in the collection of John Hauberg, Seattle), a wooden "slave killer" carved in the form of a human hand holding a ball, and a small wooden wolf mask or frontlet (the latter two remain in the collection of J. J. Klejman). The Hawaiian pieces, the human-hand "slave killer" certainly, and the wolf mask possibly, were sketched by Sarah Stone Smith in the Leverian Museum, London, in 1780. (Her sketches are reproduced in Roland Force and Maryanne Force's *Art and Artifacts of the Eighteenth Century* [Honolulu: Bishop Museum Press, 1968].) Dr. Adrienne Kaeppler of the Bishop Museum, who has researched Cook specimens exhaustively, wrote to me that there is no question, in her mind, that the entire lot came directly from the Lever Auction.
9. F. W. Holway, *The Ship Margaret: Her History and Historian,* Annual Report of the Hawaiian Historical Society, 1927 (Honolulu, 1927).
10. Warren L. Cook, *Flood Tide of Empire: Spain and the Pacific Northwest, 1543–1819* (New Haven: Yale University Press, 1973).
11. Urey Lisiansky, *A Voyage Round the World, in the Years 1803, 1804, 1805, and 1806* (1814, London: John Booth; reprint ed. Amsterdam: N. Israel, and New York: Da Capo Press, 1968).
12. The Museum of the American Indian has declined to make available for this publication either the catalog entries or field notes on these specimens. Perhaps some day the specimens and data can be reunited.
13. G. T. Emmons to J. A. Mason, April 1, 1942, University Museum Archives, University of Pennsylvania, Philadelphia.

14. Correspondence between Emmons and Boas, 1888–1911, American Philosophical Society Library, Philadelphia.

15. George T. Emmons, *The Chilkat Blanket,* with notes on the blanket designs by Franz Boas, Memoirs of the American Museum of Natural History, vol. 3, pt. 4 (New York, 1907), pp. 329–400.

16. Franz Boas, *Primitive Art* (Cambridge: Harvard University Press, 1927).

17. Edward G. Fast, *Catalogue of Antiquities and Curiosities Collected in the Territory of Alaska* (New York, 1871).

18. George M. Dawson, *Report on the Queen Charlotte Islands,* Geological Survey of Canada, Report of Progress for 1878–1879 (Ottawa, 1880).

19. Published principally in *Dyn, The Review of Modern Art,* ed. Wolfgang Paalen.

20. Extensive field notes and manuscripts by Louis Shotridge, University Museum Archives, University of Pennsylvania, Philadelphia.

21. Louis Shotridge, "My Northland Revisited," *The Museum Journal,* University of Pennsylvania 8 (June 1917): 105.

22. Louis Shotridge, "The Kaguanton Shark Helmet," *The Museum Journal,* University of Pennsylvania 20 (Sep–Dec 1929): 339–41.

23. Letter of Louis Shotridge, March 16, 1931, University Museum Archives, University of Pennsylvania, Philadelphia.

24. George T. Emmons, *The Whale House of the Chilkat,* Anthropological Papers of the American Museum of Natural History, vol. 19, pt. 1 (Cambridge, Massachusetts, 1916).

25. Shotridge to Gordon, January 27, 1923, University Museum Archives, University of Pennsylvania, Philadelphia.

26. Shotridge to Gordon, June 3, 1924, University Museum Archives, University of Pennsylvania, Philadelphia.

27. Gordon to Shotridge, June 30, 1924, University Museum Archives, University of Pennsylvania, Philadelphia.

28. Secretary of the University Museum to Shotridge, March 1, 1933, University Museum Archives, University of Pennsylvania, Philadelphia.

29. R. L. Wolfe, U.S. Indian Field Service, Sitka, to the University Museum, University Museum Archives, University of Pennsylvania, Philadelphia; Record of Death, August 31, 1937, and Certificate of Death, September 8, 1937, State Registrar, Juneau.

30. Louis Shotridge, "The Emblems of the Tlingit Culture," *The Museum Journal,* University of Pennsylvania 19 (December 1928): 350–77.

31. Bill Holm, *Northwest Coast Indian Art: An Analysis of Form* (Seattle: University of Washington Press, 1965), pp. 92–93.

32. John Dunn, *History of Oregon Territory and British North American Fur Trade* (London, 1846), p. 293.

33. John Witthoft and Frances Eyman, "Metallurgy of the Tlingit, Dene, and Eskimo," *Expedition* 11 (Spring 1969): 12–23.

34. George Thornton Emmons, *The Tahltan Indians,* University of Pennsylvania Anthropological Publications, vol. 4, no. 1 (Philadelphia, 1911), pl. 12.

35. Ibid., pl. 16.

36. *Far North,* p. 262.

37. Cataloged in 1947 by Dr. Marius Barbeau as "#209 box with lid, carved two sides—blanket inside—belonged to Shakes" and listed under "The Shakes Collection of Wrangell (consisting of specimens which belonged to the head chief of the Wrangell tribe)" when it was part of the Walter C. Waters Collection, Wrangell. It was acquired and later sold by the Regents of the University of Washington, Seattle.

38. Albert P. Niblack, *The Coast Indians of Southern Alaska and Northern British Columbia,* Report of the U.S. National Museum, Washington, D.C., 1888 (Washington, D.C.: Government Printing Office, 1890).

39. Film by Edward Curtis, *In the Land of the War Canoes: Kwakiutl Indian Life on the Northwest Coast,* 1914. Restored and sound added by Bill Holm, George I. Quimby and David Gerth, 1972.

40. Catalog of the exhibition *Masks of the Northwest Coast* (Milwaukee, Wisconsin: Milwaukee Public Museum, 1966), figure 45.

41. Curtis, *Land.*

42. Ibid.

43. Bill Holm, "The Art of Willie Seaweed: A Kwakiutl Master," in *The Human Mirror: Material and Spatial Images of Man,* ed. by Miles Richardson (Baton Rouge: Louisiana State University Press, 1974).

44. Franz Boas and George Hunt, *Kwakiutl Texts,* Memoirs of the American Museum of Natural History, vol. 5, pt. 1 (New York, 1902), p. 28, pl. 1.

Edmund Carpenter

Measurements

All measurements are given first in inches and then in centimeters parenthetically, and listed in the order of height, width, and depth if applicable. For round or conical objects, the maximum diameter is given in the place of height-width or width-depth.

1 3⅞, 1⅝, 9½ (9.8, 4.1, 24.1) **2** 3¾, 2⅛, 4⅞ (9.5, 5.4, 12.4) **3** 3¾, 3, 7½ (9.5, 7.6, 19.1) **4** 4¾, 3⅝, 6¾ (12.1, 9.2, 17.2) **5** 4¼, 2½, 4⅜ (10.8, 6.4, 11.1) **6** 4, 2¼, 4½ (10.2, 5.7, 11.4) **7** 3⅝, 1⅛, 1⅞ (9.2, 2.9, 4.8) **8** 18, 2⅜ (45.7, 6.0) **9** 18¾, 2⅝ (47.6, 6.7); sheath: 30½, 3½ (77.5, 8.9); head cover: 4, 3⅜ (10.2, 8.6) **10** 14⅜, 1¾ (36.5, 4.5) **11** 14¾, 3 (37.5, 7.6); sheath: 27, 3⅜ (68.6, 8.6) **12** 6⅞, 4¾ (17.5, 12.1) **13** 8⅝ diam. (21.9) **14** 13⅜, 1⅝ (34.0, 4.1) **15** 3, 1⅞, 25½ (7.6, 4.8, 64.8) **16** 9, 8¾, 54 (22.9, 22.2, 137.2) **17** 17¼, 4¾ (43.8, 12.1) **18** 17, 5½ (43.2, 14.0) **19** 15, 5 (38.1, 12.7) **20** 17, 4¾ (43.2, 12.1) **21** 13¼, 5 (33.7, 12.7) **22** 16½, 6¼ (41.9, 15.9) **23** 13⅝, 4 (34.6, 10.2) **24** 8⅛, 2⅝ (20.6, 6.7) **25** 9½, 2¼ (24.1, 5.7) **26** 9⅜, 2 (23.8, 5.1) **27** 10¼, 5⅛, 10⅜ (26.0, 13.0, 26.4) **28** 4, 4½, 8 (10.2, 11.4, 20.3) **29** 4⅜, 5¼, 9⅜ (11.1, 13.3, 23.8) **30** 3½, 5¾, 7⅝ (8.9, 14.6, 19.4) **31** 5¼, 6, 9¼ (13.3, 15.2, 23.5) **32** 7¼, 10¾, 12⅛ (18.4, 27.3, 30.8) **33** 6¾, 6, 9½ (17.1, 15.2, 24.1) **34** 3¾, 5¼, 5⅞ (9.5, 13.3, 14.9) **35** 7⅞, 16⅛, 20 (20.0, 41.0, 50.8) **36** 12, 20, 24⅜ (30.5, 50.8, 61.9) **37** 9½, 15¼, 18⅛ (24.1, 38.7, 46.0) **38** 8⅞, 14⅛ 15½ (22.5, 35.9, 39.4) **39** 7⅞, 15⅜, 17¼ (20.0, 39.1, 43.8) **40** 7⅝, 16¼, 20 (19.4, 41.3, 50.8) **41** 15½, 12¼, 12 (39.4, 31.1, 30.5) **42** 10¾, 19⅝, 14¾ (27.3, 49.8, 37.5) **43** 13¾, 19, 12½ (34.9, 48.3, 31.8) **44** 1½, 1⅜, 2¼ (3.8, 3.5, 5.7) **45** 18½, 18, 18 (47.0, 45.7, 45.7) **46** 31⅞, 22⅛, 19¼ (81.0, 56.2, 48.9) **47** 24¾, 21⅝, 19¾ (62.9, 54.9, 50.23) **48** 16⅞, 13½, 12 (42.9, 34.3, 30.5) **49** 23, 19⅛, 14⅝ (58.4, 48.6, 37.1) **50** 6¼, 7⅜ diam. (15.9, 18.7) **51** 12, 13¼ diam. (30.5, 33.7) **52** 7½, 9½ diam. (19.1, 24.1) **53** 3, 4¼ diam. (7.6, 10.8) **54** 4⅜, 3¼ diam. (11.1, 8.3) **55** 4⅞, 6½ diam. (12.4, 16.5) **56** 6, 6¾ diam. (15.2, 17.1) **57** 6¼, 7½ diam. (15.9, 19.1) **58** 53 with fringe, 64 (134.6, 162.6) **59** 53 with fringe, 69 (134.6, 175.3) **60** 48, 24½ (121.9, 62.2) **61** 43½, 59 with sleeves (110.5, 149.9) **62** 16½, 15 (41.9, 38.1) **63** 5¾, 2⅝ (14.6, 6.7) **64** 7, 15¼ diam. (17.8, 38.7) **65** 7, 7⅞, 12¼ (17.8, 20.0, 31.1) **66** 10⅝, 7⅝, 16⅛ (27.0, 19.4, 41.0) **67** 8, 8⅛, 12¼ (20.3, 20.6, 31.1) **68** 7⅛, 3⅞, 2¼ (18.1, 9.8, 5.7) **69** 7¼, 5⅜, 2 (18.4, 13.7, 5.1) **70** 6⅞, 5½, 2⅝ (17.5, 14.0, 6.7) **71** 9, 6⅛, 5¼ (22.9, 15.6, 13.3) **72** 9, 7, 5 (22.9, 17.8, 12.7) **73** 11, 8¾, 4¼ (27.9, 22.2, 10.8) **74** 9⅞, 9¼, 6¾ (25.1, 23.5, 17.1) **75** 23, 14½ (58.4, 36.8) **76** 6¼, 5, 16¼ (15.9, 12.7, 41.3) **77** 4⅝, 3⅝, 13 (11.7, 9.2, 33.0) **78** 4⅜, 4, 12⅛ (11.1, 10.2, 30.8) **79** 5¼, 5¼, 15 (13.3, 13.3, 38.1) **80** 4¼, 3⅝, 12 (10.8, 9.2, 30.5) **81** 2¾, 1¾, 10⅝ (7.0, 4.4, 27.0) **82** 12⅝, 6⅜, 6 (32.1, 16.2, 15.2) **83** 11¼, 6½, 5 (28.6, 16.5, 12.7) **84** 10½, 5¼, 4⅛ (26.7, 13.3, 10.5) **85** 5⅜, 3⅜, 15 (13.7, 8.6, 38.1) **86** 6¼, 4¾, 5⅜ (15.9, 12.1, 13.7) **87** 10¼, 7⅛, 5⅝ (26.0, 18.1, 14.3) **88** 9¼, 7½, 4⅞ (23.5, 19.1, 12.4) **89** 10¼, 9½, 5 (26.0, 24.1, 12.7) **90** 12, 9⅞, 5⅜ (30.5, 25.1, 13.7) **91** 9, 7⅞, 5¼ (22.9, 20.0, 13.3) **92** 9⅛, 7, 4⅛ (23.2, 17.8, 10.5) **93** 8¼, 6¾, 3⅞ (21.0, 17.1, 9.8) **94** 9¼, 9⅛, ⅛ (23.5, 23.2, 13.0) **95** 10¼, 9, 5 (26.0, 22.9, 12.7) **96** 8½, 7½, 4⅝ (21.6, 19.1, 11.7) **97** 8¼, 6, 4 (21.0, 15.2, 10.2) **98** 6⅞, 8¾, 16¼ (17.5, 22.2, 41.3) **99** 26¼, 8¾, 7⅝ (66.7, 22.2, 19.4) **100** 9¾, 9⅛, 2⅝ (24.8, 23.2, 6.7) **101** 81½, 247 (207.0, 627.4) **102** 13¾, 11¼, 46¼ (34.9, 28.6, 117.5).

Conservation Reports

72

Missing: side plaque on right side (facing), including part of bear's right hand (facing), forearm and paw; all but three of the bear's copper upper teeth; four "coppers" along the top of the frontlet; several inlays of abalone and mirror. *Replaced:* side plaque and forearm; all abalone pieces, except second from top, left side; all mirrors except those in the eyes of the smaller figures, the bear's left eye, and the first from the bottom, left side (facing); all upper teeth, except for left front and rear two; four coppers (two pieces each, bulged out to form a cavity, filled with glass "rattlers"); and the bear's right eye. New wood left untinted on back; new side plaque marked on back with my name and date.

Steven C. Brown — November, 1974

96

A surface coating, which had aged to dark brown and become almost insoluble, was removed without altering the original red pigment underneath. Aged, brittle paper labels on the forehead and back were removed intact, and saved, but no inscription could be read on either, directly or by infrared photography. Leather bindings that once permitted movement of the chin had deteriorated, and a linen strip had been affixed across the lower jaw, immobilizing it. This strip was removed without disrupting the design beneath. Using a reversible treatment, the chin was restored to mobility.

Jeanne L. Kostich — December, 1974

101

Damage: soiled; upper corners very creased from being twisted; small tears, upper right corner; tears and missing areas in upper left corner; long tear in lower right corner; several small, scattered holes; some puckers caused by paint; entire curtain wrinkled. *Conservation:* black cotton cord tied to upper right corner was removed and tacked to the upper right corner; curtain placed temporarily between sheets of nylon net, vacuumed and sponged; steam applied to one small area at a time; deep creases and wrinkles smoothed out by hand; treated area "squared up," pinned and left to dry; inlays of similar muslin used to fill in all missing parts; inlays held in place with sheer fabric coated with Beva 677; inlays painted where necessary to fill in missing areas of design; cotton fabric lining, sprayed with Beva 677, laminated to the curtain by applying low heat with an electric iron—using silicone paper as a "pressing cloth"; edges of the lining material stitched and an extra strip attached for hanging.

Kathryn Scott — January, 1975

102

Areas of original white pigment (collar, tail, and striped design down back) not treated. All recent in-painting has been separated from the original and is reversible. Black headcloth added, using old tack holes.

Jeanne L. Kostich — November, 1974

Explanatory Design Diagram

Two-dimensional surface decoration, on 19th-century objects from the northern Northwest Coast, conforms to a highly organized design system. This system can be shown to be based on a set of rules governing the kinds of shapes used, their relationships to one another, compositional arrangements and color use and placement. Among the best illustrations of the system are the designs on storage boxes.

The designs, although highly abstracted, are representational. The depicted creature is conceived as a flat design arranged to fill, or to relate to, the decorated field. The body parts and any necessary fillers and elaborations are shown as flat, conventionalized shapes constructed of elements called formlines. These are broad, line-like bands which outline and define the body parts, turning and joining to complete the composition. Primary formlines (a) delineate the design, forming an uninterrupted grid over the decorated area. They are usually black, but may be red (c.f. #16 and #40). The design is elaborated with secondary formline detail in red (b), or in black if the primary formlines are red. Some typical formline shapes are ovoids (c) and U's (d). Inner ovoids, sometimes simple (e) and sometimes elaborated into complex face-like designs (f), always float within formline ovoids. All other formlines are attached to one another. Junctures of formlines are relieved by tapering the joining formline (g) or by defining the joint with a crescent slit, a T-shaped slit (h) or a negative circle (i). Areas between formlines are often developed into tertiary shapes (j) by means of thin lines (k) outlining one or more edges of the space. If painted, these spaces are blue or blue-green. If the design is carved in relief the tertiary elements are hollowed or recessed. A variation in color and weight is achieved by crosshatching some secondary and subsecondary formlines in red or black (l). Pieces decorated in unpainted relief carving illustrate the same organizational system as do painted objects.

The most successful compositions are characterized by a rather even design-weight, without excessive variation in scale or elaboration, throughout the decorated area.

Bill Holm